LIGHT
AND
EMOTIONS

Exploring Lighting Cultures
Conversations with Lighting Designers

edited by Vincent Laganier & Jasmine van der Pol

powered by
PHILIPS

published by
Birkhäuser, Basel

Content

Preface

007 Rogier van der Heide

Publisher's note

009 Robert Steiger

Introduction

011 Vincent Laganier & Jasmine van der Pol

Lighting parameters to achieve emotion

015 Brightness
039 Contrast in brightness
059 Dynamics in brightness
067 Colour
093 Contrast in colour
105 Dynamics in colour
121 Direction

153 **Emotions**

197 **Conversations with Lighting Designers**
198 Nissar Allana | India
202 Peter Andres | Germany
206 Susanna Antico | Italy
210 Gustavo Avilés | Mexico
214 Francesca Bettridge & Stephen Bernstein | USA
218 Manav Bhargava | India
222 La-Orchai Boonpiti | Thailand
226 Ulrike Brandi | Germany
230 Howard Brandston | USA
234 Filippo Cannata | Italy
238 Jaspreet Chandhok & Vilas Prabhu | India
242 Ray Chen | Taiwan
246 Acharawan Chutarat | Thailand
250 Elias Cisneros Avila | Mexico
254 Cinzia Ferrara | Italy
258 Carlos Fortes | Brazil
262 Peter Gasper | Brazil
266 Paul Gregory | USA
270 Jürgen Hassler | Germany

274 Jonathon Hodges | UK

278 Barbara Horton | USA

282 Philippe Hutinet | France

286 Mee Jeong | South Korea

290 Yann Kersalé | France

294 Kiyoung Ko | South Korea

298 Heayun Lee | South Korea

302 Ta-Wei Lin | Taiwan

306 Mônica Lobo | Brazil

310 Luis Lozoya | Mexico

314 Martin Lupton | UK

320 Paul Marantz | USA

324 Kaoru Mende | Japan

328 Francois Migeon | France

332 Antonio Mingrone | Brazil

336 Roger Narboni | France

340 Enrique Peiniger & Jean Sundin | USA

344 Michel Pieroni | France

348 Vannapa Pimviriyakul | Thailand

352 Michael F. Rohde | Germany

356 Tapio Rosenius | UK

360 Andreas Schulz | Germany

364 Kevan Shaw | UK

368 Hiroyasu Shoji | Japan

372 Francesca Storaro | Italy

376 Satoshi Uchihara | Japan

380 Dolly & Anil Valia | India

386 Patrick Woodroffe | UK

Research Overview

392 Research Summary

394 Emotion is fundamental in lighting design

396 Context focused design

397 Personal profile

399 Inspiration sources

400 Honour original idea versus reinvention

403 Location index

407 Copyrights

413 Credits

Preface

The world of light and lighting is changing. In the first place, architectural lighting is experiencing an incredible revival, coming from a largely functional element in architecture, now gaining relevance again as a true spatial element, providing people with comfort, direction, inspiration and excitement. Secondly, the broad arrival of digital lighting or LED means that possibilities and ways to apply light change more rapidly than ever before.

If you would have studied architecture in the 19th century, a lot of your education would have been about light. How does light shape the space, set the scene, indicated function and creates performance of a building? These are the questions that you would have been answering as a student. Later, with the broad adoptation of electric light, the illuminance of architectural spaces became functionalised, focused on its own efficiency, and planned based on quantitative criteria.

I am excited to see now that light is being rejuvenated as an inspiring, authentic and intrinsic element of architecture. We're firmly moving to light that gives comfort, and sparks our imagination. New technologies, such as LED lighting, are accelerating this movement, and offer designers possibilities they did not have before. With the new, digital light, dreams are truly being realised.

This book celebrates the people who have these dreams: their thoughts and concepts, and their vision on our world. As lighting designers, they have a huge responsibility: 85% of our perception of the world around us is because of the way we see it. And at Philips, we aspire to help realising these dreams: with technology, with a holistic approach to lighting solutions, and by unlocking designers their freedom to create meaningful applications of light using our innovations.

With many of the designers portrayed in this book, Philips has created lighting solutions in a collaborative way. That is the future of light: solutions created together, that truly enhance our lives. I wish you lots of inspiration reading this book.

Rogier van der Heide
Vice President
Chief Design Officer
Philips Lighting

Publisher's Note

Dear Reader,
architects and lighting designers, landscape architects and urban planners, graphic artists
and product designers create buildings and interiors, gardens and squares, outdoor and urban
landscapes, objects for life and work. They are creative, designing everyday objects and
environments that are hopefully more than just useful: irresistible, conspicuous, desirable,
in short: beautiful.
Birkhäuser as a specialist publisher for architecture, lighting design, landscape architecture and
design publishes informative and inspiring handbooks and introductions, monographs and
dictionaries, collections of essays and textbooks for theory and practice. Our publications
convey practical knowledge but seek to be more than just useful: pleasing, attractive, exquisite,
in short: beautiful.

We are convinced that *Light and Emotions. Exploring Lighting Cultures. Conversations with
Lighting Designers* is such an intelligent and inspiring book that conveys not only a pleasure
to hold in the hand, but takes you a step further. The editors Vincent Laganier and Jasmine van
der Pol and their team have successfully managed to research and address a rich selection
of the most innovative and best lighting designers working today. Their individual answers
represent a fascinating realm of valid approaches to the challenging task of adding emotional
content and enhancing the unique sense of a place. It is a real pleasure to perceive the
richness of the Lighting Cultures emerging from the twelve countries and their specific
traditions from three continents.

Books have to be realized and financed. Professional project management by authors, editors,
translators, graphic designers, and publisher remain the expensive key to reaching the
envisaged quality level. Birkhäuser gratefully acknowledges the fact that Philips kindly agreed
to rework its first, non-commercial edition of this book. This Birkhäuser edition for the trade
performs with an optimized conceptual framework and with the congenial new layout by
one/one studio. Thanks to Philips' engagement it is possible to offer this book at a sales price
affordable for very young professionals, and even lighting design students.
Therefore this book could exceed the expectations placed in it through the intelligent and
truly international way it interprets its type as an inspiring book for established and up-and-
coming lighting designers in all countries.

Robert Steiger
Senior Editor
Architecture & Design
Birkhäuser

Introduction

The Light and Emotions research is the first global study on the work of independent lighting designers. Synovate was selected by Philips Lighting to conduct qualitative research. This study represents an attempt to go beyond the functional role of lighting and understand the aesthetic and emotional aspects of light through the eyes of professionals who are passionate about improving the quality of lighting. It attempts to understand the challenges they face, the trends they see and anticipate, and the meanings they associate with what is happening around them.

The methodology of the research as defined focuses on in-depth interviews with lighting designers in different parts of the world: Asia-Pacific, Europe and the Americas. The focus of the study was on architectural projects. With regard to emotions, little distinction was made between outdoor and indoor projects.

The research reveals certain trends, but the number of interviews conducted per country and continent is too small to support generic conclusions. The Synovate report focuses on the differences – and similarities – between lighting cultures. The results may be used to provide hypotheses for further research.

For this second edition of the book, it has been decided to make a clear distinction between the lighting parameters part and the interview part. In this way, you will get inspiration by browsing through the projects, and get deeper into detail by reading the interviews. The lighting parameters part has the basic structure of 'brightness', 'colour', 'direction' and 'emotion', illustrated by project pictures and quotes.

The interview part presents extracts of interviews. These extracts concentrate on the experiences of lighting designers in architectural lighting design projects. The conversations and the quotes extracted from them are based on the literal transcriptions of the face-to-face interview.

Small images refer to the projects in the lighting fundamentals part. Quotes from other lighting designers invite the reader to go to other interviews expressing similar or different views on the same subjects – like a dialog between lighting designers!

Lighting parameters to achieve emotion

Brightness

Brightness refers to subjective perception of two 'objective' physical characteristics: the intensity and the amount of light.

Brightness is often used to create a hierarchy and increase the understanding of a space. In outdoor, in general low light levels are preferred giving a cosy and friendly ambiance. On the other hand, in closed spaces e.g. underground, brightness could increase the perception of space and comfort people. Brightness is also used to guide the eye and focus on a specific object.

"We wanted to create a softer, friendlier, more welcoming environment. Everybody knows that picking up vertical surfaces will give you a sense of an illuminated place. If the walls are lit, the space will feel lit." *Tapio Rosenius*

"The New York Times lobby is meant to create an atmosphere of lightness and transparency. For the client, transparency implied a democratic process, suggesting there's very open

communication. We had to translate this into lighting terms. By using a hierarchy of light levels, we created a visual progression from the public lobby, through the garden courtyard, and into

Architect: Renzo Piano

"Due to the total absence of daylight, whatever was
not lit it wasn't going to be seen, remaining forever
in the dark. Lighting was going to definitely
define the perception and for this reason I felt
a big responsibility on my shoulders." *Cinzia Ferrara*

 → *Conversations, p. 380*

Architect: *Fariborz Sahba*

"The essential element is the architect or client's
brief – the lighting is just an add-on." *Anil Valia*

"Oscar Niemeyer is an architect, a sculptor. He is
someone who has influenced me because of his
behaviour, as a human being. He saw clearly that
light is an essential tool." *Peter Gasper*

Architect: Oscar Niemeyer

Architect: Tadao Ando | Artists: Gilberto Zorio, Mario Merz, etc.

"The idea was to think of pulling the spotlights out when they were needed and folding them back when they were not. This was something creative and backed up by reliable technology." *Cinzia Ferrara*

"This project is a jewel. I have had a wonderful
formal opportunity to work on how to reveal
the architecture through lighting." *Mônica Lobo*

 → *Conversations, p. 306*

Architect: Oscar Niemeyer

Contrast in brightness

According to many designers, lighting is composition: it has silence, bright and dark parts. Strong contrast makes a more dramatic scene. It can be used to accentuate specific features or to create rhythm by repetition. The discussion is about whether it is wanted in public spaces.

Artist: Mimmo Paladino

"Using varying levels of contrast, exaggerated texture,
a play of scale and luminaire locations, light was
used as a catalyst to try and create new metaphors
and have the audience in awe." *Manav Bhargava*

"Here we tried to do two things: lead you through
the park and show you the sculptures at night in
a theatrical or dramatic way." *Stephen Bernstein*

 → Conversations, p. 356

"The romantic route has a bit more shadow;
it is also more theatrical. We began by limiting
the light levels … The result is pools of light
and darkness. People like darkness because you
feel intimate." *Tapio Rosenius*

"We also used lots of contrast. It is very precise lighting. It offers a stunning visual perception, using both dim light and directional light, gold and Asian art. These elements together make the place look magical." *Vannapa Pimviriyakul*

   → Conversations, p. 352

"There's a big difference between light and
darkness. It's much stronger than in public
space.... dramatic or more talkative." *Michael F. Rohde*

"When the wall was lit it looked like an embroidery pattern, an entanglement of lines and textures. You saw the shadows of nails on the wall rather than seeing the nails in perspective. I wanted to create the illusion of embroidery, a lacework. The lacework didn't exist, it was generated by the shadows and empty spaces on the wall." *Carlos Fortes*

"You are never, in reality, lighting a space;
you are lighting what that space means."
Gustavo Avilés

Dynamics in brightness

Using light like music in variations of intensity and tempo is a metaphor that is frequently used; this is also relevant for colour and direction. Dynamic lighting can make a place breathe, representing the life inside.

Most lighting designers prefer subtle changes of light that have a calming effect on people. These dynamics are close to natural light. For memorials, a choice is often made to use no dynamic effects to ensure absolute silence.

"It was difficult to present illuminations to touch people's hearts by using the power of nature rather than artificially controlling it." *Satoshi Uchihara*

"There is the dynamic … that can provide breathing,
impulses, appearances, disappearances, orchestrated
in the way that you can." *Yann Kersalé*

Architect: Jean Nouvel

→ *Conversations, p. 324*

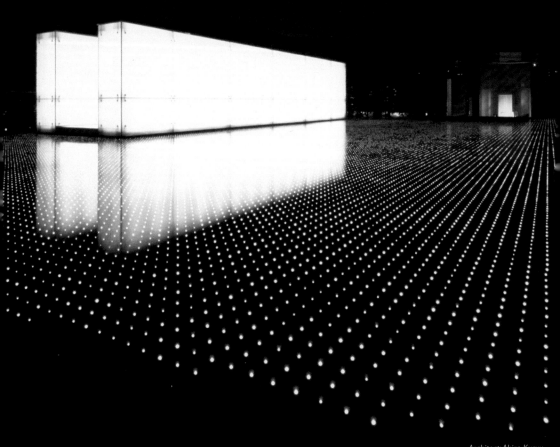

Architect: Akira Kuryu

''I need a very strong impact for the people to
know what the tiny light is, the difference for
the dead people. This is very mysterious these
70 thousand lights are moved by the wind.''
Kaoru Mende

065

Colour

Colour comprises two aspects: white light with its different shades from cool to warm, and coloured light with its different shades from saturated to pastel.

Lighting designers express their passion for colour close to natural light: nuances of white light, broken tints of colour and gradients. White is believed to make people feel better and healthy, warm white to make the place more comfortable and cosy. Colour is often used in a symbolic way. But the subject determines the colour of the light and the emotions created depends on the context.

Architect: Michelangelo

"Thus you find the four elements – fire, earth, air and water – symbolised in Michelangelo's concept. In my lighting, I used a combination of four colours – ochre for earth, red for fire, green for water and blue for air – with white in the centre." *Francesca Storaro*

→ *Conversations, p. 238*

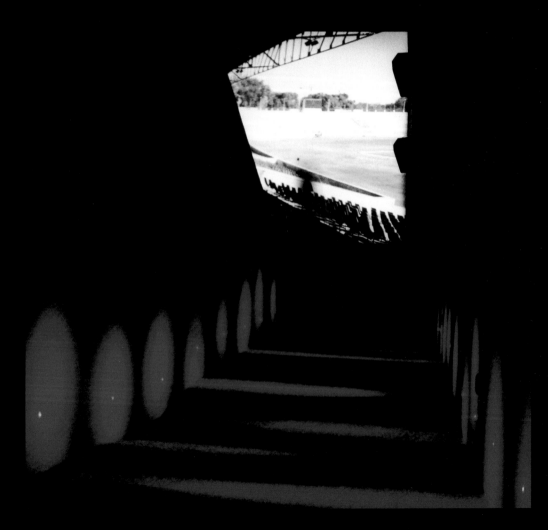

"The red carpet welcome was the architect's
concept so whatever we did was to enhance
that concept… a grandeur feeling… getting
closer to stardom and the film world."
Jaspreet Chandhok

→ *Conversations, p. 282*

Architect: Pierre Barillot

"And so we used red lighting, because this suggests
the lights of a truck. The building is pretty isolated
on an industrial site. From the national road, the
lighting turns it almost into a contemporary painting."
Philippe Hutinet

Architects: Henrich Böll Architectural Office, O.M.A.

 → *Conversations, p. 360*

"The whole building had a relation with two elements: one is fire and the other is steel. And steel is cold again. So we said, OK, if we're talking about light and the colour of light should be fire. And that's why we created this fire-coloured escalator… It reminds them of energy." *Andreas Schulz*

Architect: Rogers Stirk Harbour + Partners

→ Conversations, p. 274

"The colour we chose is sympathetic with the orange of the steelwork, which is such a striking feature of the building, and orange is an indicating, warning or signal colour; it grabs the attention."

Jonathon Hodges

"This is the region in Ipiranga where the declaration of Independence of Brazil took place. That's why we treated light with green and yellow colours… it was this strong appeal bound to a national symbol, which was the flag… here the visual impact is the idea of creating a real surprise." *Antonio Mingrone*

"Of course there are some people that don't like
the colour, but in general most do. One thing I
have noticed with colours is that you really have to
use just a little – and maybe make it temporary."
Susanna Antico

→ *Conversations, p. 328*

Architect: Thierry Van de Wyngaert

"We play with pearly, shifting colours. We have this volume of light that swells, that breathes with tides. The concrete part symbolises the volume of water in blue shades. The translucide parts are the shell lips. During low tides we started with a pearly colour, a mix of pink or yellow sheen. We based the design on this idea of an immense shell."

Francois Migeon

"It was really like the divine was seeping out of the tower. It was a risk, because I had been instructed not to use any colour. But this was really magical and the people actually liked it… For us, blue is the sky, paradise, and this is pretty much common in our western world." *Susanna Antico*

Architect: Jean Nouvel

"The principle is a real, very simple barometer…
There are three colours, three dominant ones, but
based on the three states of water: solid, liquid and
gaseous. In this way you create some meaning, you
tell a tale, there is a playfulness." *Yann Kersalé*

 → *Conversations, p. 290*

Architect: Harry Weese

"Inspired by O'Keeffe's painting technique, we drew from her careful blends of colour to recreate a painterly feeling with light." *Paul Gregory*

"It was clear that in this project there would be no colour. It would be just a very simple very reduced minimalistic approach, not only from the architecture but also from the lighting… colour would change the place dramatically." *Michael F. Rohde*

Contrast in colour

One colour contrast is particularly important for lighting designers: cool / warm light. It is linked to different meanings: the history, exterior / interior, cold / warm and inviting ambiance, dark / light.

Architect: Berdj Mikaëlian

"We would stretch a golden thread through blue needles, this symbol of elastic thread would maintain the gap and prevent the Peloponnese from moving away from the continent in a poetic way."
Roger Narboni

"It creates a haunting impression, as if the place has been deserted for years. Merely changing the blue to deep amber, immediately transforms the entire scene to signify a sunrise and metaphorically, a new beginning." *Manav Bhargava*

→ *Conversations, p. 298*

"I contract or expand the physical distance just with lighting. The principles of colour and intensity and many different principles which have to do with light either to bring something to the foreground or take it into the background; so I am constantly reorienting the physical distance with light…"

Nissar Allana

Dynamics in colour

Changing colour attracts people. It creates curiosity,
fantasy and fun. Most lighting designers prefer slow
colour change because it is more comfortable
for people and is more like natural light. Depending
on the colour it can change the mood of the people.
Dynamic lighting can make a place breathe and
come alive.

Architects: Archis Architecten + Ingenieure and Peter W. Schmidt Architect BDA | Artist: Yann Kersalé

"It's very important to have colour changes in a
much slower speed. Also I think it needs time to
interact with the bodies… It is always the question
of how much show time and how much 'stay in' is
the right proportion." *Michael F. Rohde*

"It's accented, with little highlights, adding to
the drama. And the lighting is interactive, with
dynamic colour-changing effects. Kids find it
a fun place to go…" *Barbara Horton*

"Each hour, the first 55 minutes bathes the tower in white light. The white colour represents the highest technology. The final 5 minutes is a lighting show. The concept is a flower, and we therefore made all the laser rays visible." *Mee Jeong*

"The content is graphic and amorphous and can produce everything from symmetrical lines and patterns to organic coloured ripples that pass across the lake. It's one of the most extraordinary things I've ever seen." *Patrick Woodroffe*

→ *Conversations, p. 386*

Architect: Freimüller Söllinger Architektur ZT GmbH

Direction

Direction refers to the angle of the rays of light.
It is closely related to the type of shadows that are
cast when light falls on objects from a given direction.

Several directions of light are used from the direct to indirect all with
different reasons behind the choice. The direction of light makes you
understand if light is natural or artificial.

Architect: Toyo Ito

"The concept allows the light to ooze through the interior of the architecture. For example, during the day, light oozes in through a wall inlayed with amorphous glass. At night, the glass on this wall glows, creating a feeling of excitement, anticipation on the path leading to the performing arts stage."
Hiroyasu Shoji

 → *Conversations, p. 234*

Architect: Nicola Fiorillo | Artist: Mimmo Paladino

"The light seems to allude to an underground
presence, another possible world that manifests
itself fracturing the soil." *Filippo Cannata*

"You see, natural light – and I come back to that
every time – comes from above. When it doesn't,
it's unusual and that brings visual challenge."
Kevan Shaw

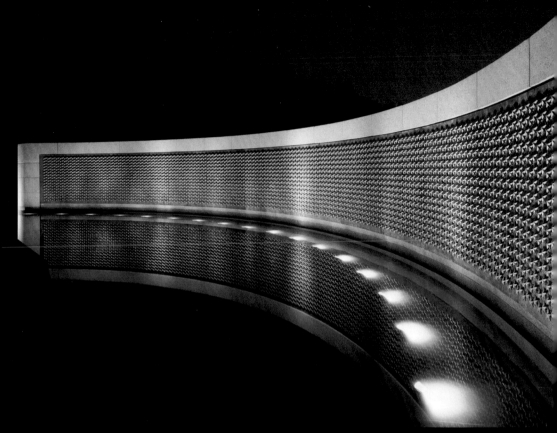

Architect: Friedrich St. Florian

''You can transform the space by bringing out
finishes, textures...'' *Barbara Horton*

"The light comes out from the openings so it becomes more welcoming, more inviting… the only thing we really did was light the walls. There were a few accent lights under the glass roof but basically, almost all the lighting is at the bottom… It glows."

Paul Marantz

 → *Conversations, p. 320*

Architect: Richard Meier & Partners

"For the lighting, we didn't want to concentrate on just the building; we gave consideration to the people and the functional needs. The container needs to breath. We tried to make the lighting come from the inside; it represents energy." *Ray Chen*

→ *Conversations, p. 242*

→ *Conversations, p. 202*

"For the Byodoin Temple in Kyoto, all of the lighting was achieved through perpetual, flowing reflections off of the adjacent body of water, expressing both the timelessness of this remarkable national treasure and the passing of the ages – the 950 years that it has existed." *Satoshi Uchihara*

"When people walk through the light, they don't want to feel as if the illumination is on them. As if they are suddenly in a spotlight. And so most of the lighting comes indirectly, from the side. It was important for my client that the whole thing should be as natural as possible." *Ray Chen*

"Sometimes it is very physical. If you continue with
the same rhythm of lamps in and out, it becomes all
one space. Don't let yourself be influenced by the
frontier of the door." *Gustavo Avilés*

"When it is illuminated it creates the impression
that the columns and all the elements of the
architecture are somehow merged into one."
Luis Lozoya

Architect: Stephen Williams

"We prefer different kinds of light depending on the time of day, luminance of the surrounding areas and objects, purpose of the room, the architectural concept and materials used and so on. All these aspects need to be considered when we want to achieve a lighting design atmosphere in which people feel at ease. A lighting design concept always has to be in context with the surrounding conditions." *Peter Andres*

Emotions

"Sunlight is happiness, don't you think?
When the darkness of night turns into day, there is
a big evolutionary association with positive change."
Martin Lupton

Artist: Frédéric Auguste Bartholdi

"The statue represents the dawn of opportunity. I made a quick note 'Needed: one lamp to imitate the morning sun, one light source to imitate the morning sky, one new luminaire that can throw the light a long way, perhaps not quite all the way to the sky, but a long way all the same."

Howard Brandston

"The idea was to create the feeling that you are
approaching a place with something precious inside,
and that you are happy to approach that place.
The trees are at the same time guarding the visitor
and welcoming him." *Kiyoung Ko*

"The warm light, in fact, it's rather a sensation, something that is engraved in ourselves, almost unconscious, of the incandescent lamp, because we use it at home, you are used to it, this cosy sensation, comfort." *Carlos Fortes*

161

Architects: Prof. Hascher + Jehle

People in the office of the Berlin Medical Society are able to choose their own colour. It is respecting the individualism of each person… that the people realized 'Ah, there's someone who's taking

me seriously as an individual'… If you're taken seriously, you will bring better results; if you feel happy, you will be a better employee."

Michael F. Rohde

''The idea of working with very tight light brushes,
little rising flames, playing on rhythm and repetition.
It gives a very classy side.'' *Philippe Hutinet*

"Shimmering effect at night… You feel as if
you were in an incredibly… it's not romantic,
but very magical sort of space in there.
They wanted something very special here."
Francesca Bettridge

→ *Conversations, p. 314*

"We buried some fibre optics in the ground and
stuffed them into apples, and they just glowed.
It was just like a fairytale – and I think people saw
it for the emotion that it had." *Martin Lupton*

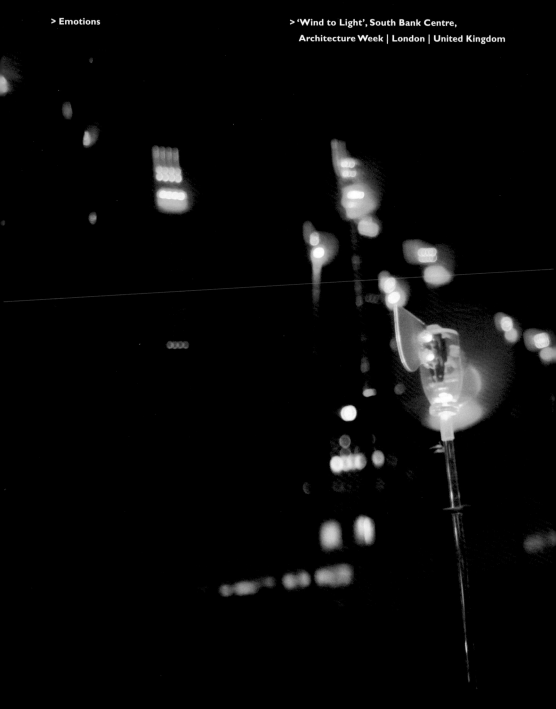

"We wanted to intrigue people. Make them
wonder what it does, what it is for… Could we
encourage people to think about energy saving
and new sources of energy?" *Jonathon Hodges*

 → *Conversations, p. 274*

"You also see that love of natural light at night. We love the moonlight. We even have festivals that were designed to take place at full moon such as Loy Kratong day and Visakabucha day. Moonlight provides enough brightness for public without artificial light. This has something to do with our climate: Thailand is hot and humid and we enjoy activities at night when it is cooler. Thais like mystery and refreshing light outdoors." *Acharawan Chutarat*

"The architect designed the bridge in silver. But from a lighting and Feng Shui point of view, we suggested painting it red. The bridge is part of a temple. So we used four patterns, meaning blessed characters. So I wanted to use these themes, such as dragon and cloud. But there is a Chinese meaning to it – go higher and higher at each step, calm weather, sufficient rain, excellent breeze. These transform into lighting patterns inside."
Ta-Wei Lin

"In the centre of the memorial, a quiet glow
of illumination emanates from the pavement,
creating an atmosphere of silence, contemplation,
and respect." *Jean Sundin*

Architect: James Ingo Freed

"There is no colour, it's all white. And nothing moves,
nothing changes. So it creates a very quiet, simple,
minimalist atmosphere." *Paul Marantz*

 → *Conversations, p. 320*

Architect: Masayuki Sono

"It is, paradoxically, slightly darker, because we wanted to create a feeling of intimacy by getting people closer to the action, so to speak. It's simply a matter of lighting the areas where you want people to come together and not lighting the other areas."

Kevan Shaw

"The building is meant to make people proud of
their heritage and feel part of it. The whole place is
semi-lit; there are light as well as dark areas. This
creates an inverted effect." *Acharawan Chutarat*

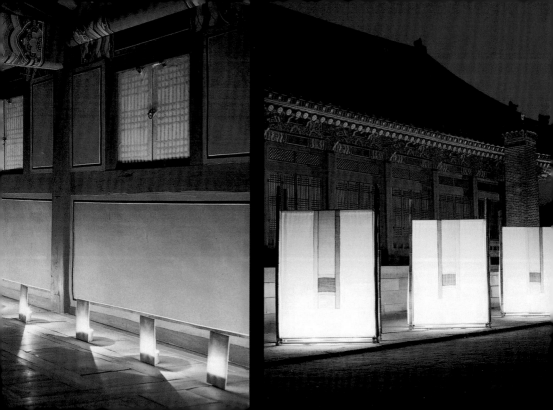

"For me, rule number one is to ask myself –
what kind of emotion can I put into the scene?"
Peter Gasper

    → *Conversations, p. 262*

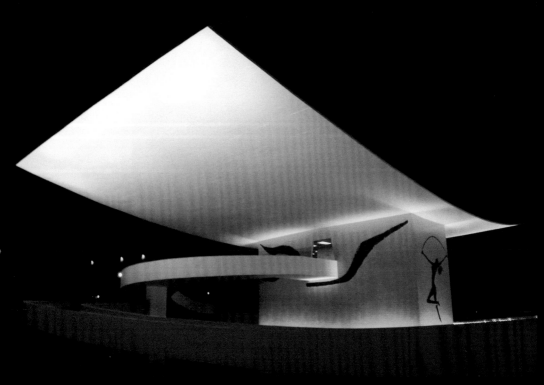

Architect: Oscar Niemeyer

"I want the people who come there to forget whatever is in their mind and to experience something new." *La-Orchai Boonpiti*

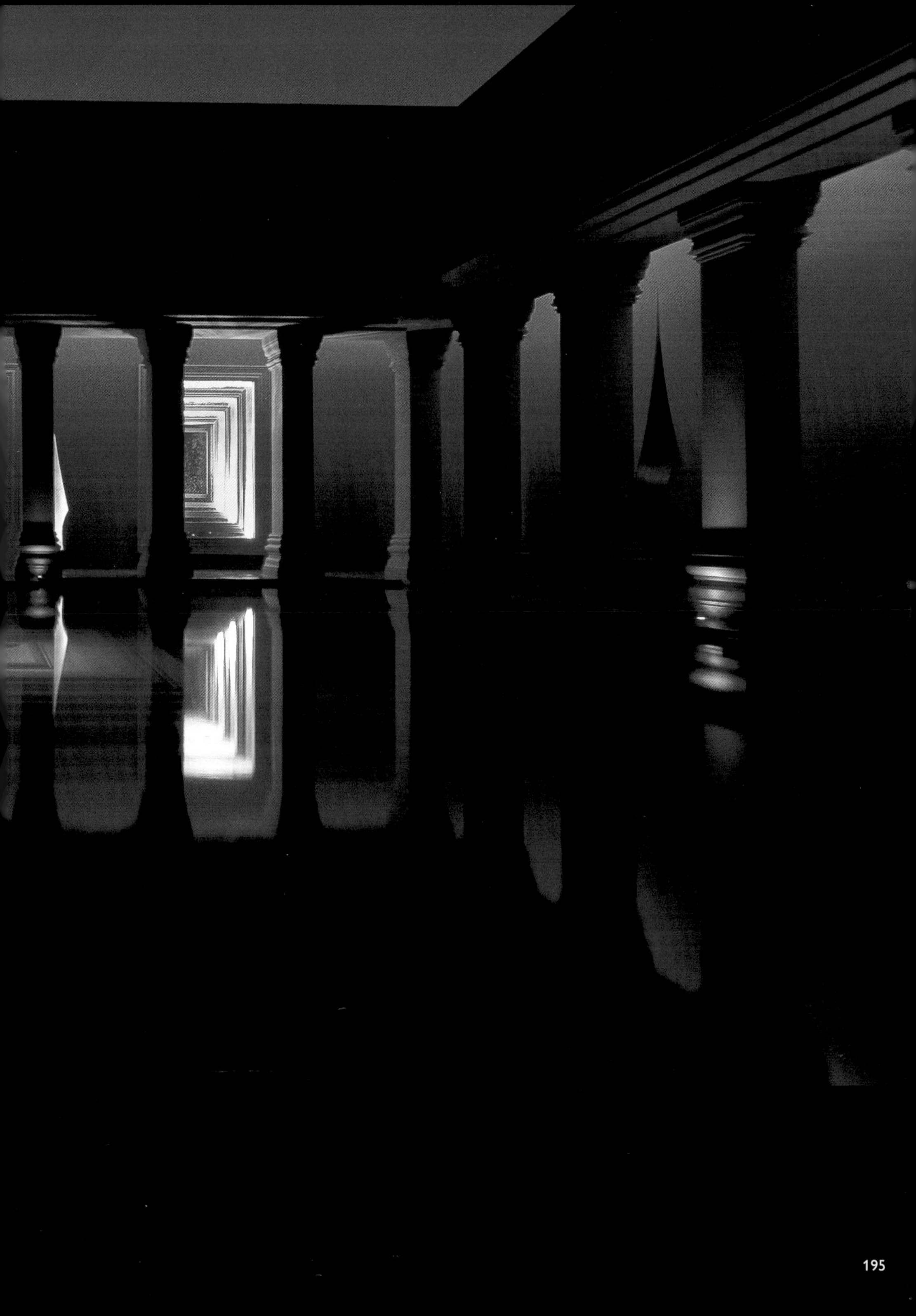

Conversations with lighting designers

Forty-seven highly experienced lighting designers were interviewed in twelve countries. The countries selected for the study are those where the profession of lighting designer has been established as an independent practice for at least ten to fifteen years – Brazil, France, Germany, India, Italy, Japan, Mexico, South Korea, Taiwan, Thailand, United Kingdom and United States of America.

The selected lighting designers are considered to be trendsetters and opinion leaders in different lighting fields: indoor, outdoor, art, stage and cinema. Most are active members of local or global lighting design associations, e.g. PLDA and IALD – the Professional Lighting Designers' Association and the International Association of Lighting Designers.

Nissar Allana

Even before graduating from medical school, in 1969 and again in 1970, I went to visit my fiancée who was working in Berlin (then in the GDR), as an apprentice theatre director in the Berliner Ensemble. In the productions of Beno Besson, Ruth Berghaus, and those that had been produced by Bertolt Brecht, that I saw in Berlin, I found lighting and set design fascinating; and because I didn't understand much German, I focused more on the image, and because I couldn't understand the text in detail, other senses took over. Back in Mumbai, in 1971, I then started working as a set and lighting designer, mostly for theater, and designed my first production, 'A Man's A Man' written by Bertolt Brecht. Later I became interested in lighting monuments and events. I founded the Dramatic Art and Design Academy in 2000 and we now teaching lighting there.

What aspect of lighting interested you?
When I first started, I was influenced by a more illustrative style of lighting, focusing on how to highlight people, and find a balance between the environment (set) and the character, how to emphasise and enhance the performance. When you shift the highlights between characters and the ambience, you change the spatial relationship between them and in doing so, the meaning of the sequence also undergoes a shift.

My lighting now has changed. I prefer to light characters and the environment separately and individually. In this way the spatial relationship between them becomes deconstructed and undefined. Action does not happen in its relationship to space, but becomes suspended in space. This is a new dynamic and creates a very fluid state.

What really interests me in Indian art is the use of iconic images, what they symbolise and how the aura that they create, can be translated into my language of space. I used to feel proud that my work had a western feel to it, but then I realised I had to find my own identity. This search led me to discover cyclical space. When I read Indian philosophy or the Indian Epics, like the Mahabharata, I interpret it as a document on the exploration of space, with the images being deconstructed from one meaning to another. I use physical elements on the stage, like

ramps and different shapes to extend the space. This physical state is
further explored with light, using it to contract or expand the physical
distance. The principles of colour and intensity, for example, can
bring performers or objects into the foreground or push them into
the background, so I am constantly using light to reorient the physical
distance. This creates a 'theatrical space' on the stage.

La Candida Erendira | Cartagena
→ *Contrast in colour, p.102*

In recent years I have tried to develop a style and theory of lighting
which relates more specifically to the concept of space and time in
Indian philosophy, art and performance. It's not about lighting, but about
being able to create the kind of spatial plasticity which can disorient.
This act of disorientation is very important because I do not want to
define things. The moment you define, you make it a 'visual language'.

By deconstructing definition you turn it into a spatial language and that
is much more interesting to me. The whole idea was to get away
from linearity. That was very difficult, but I did it through disorientation
of space. That led me to work in outdoor spaces that were created
not only for the performer but also for the audiences. We used a lot
of mirrors so the actors who were behind the audience were seen in
front of the real actor as reflected images. We juxtaposed images,
real and reflected, and put them together so we were literally playing
with spatial dimensions.

You intentionally used disorientation to avoid linearity?
Because I was disoriented, I disoriented the audience. After working
in existing environments outside the proscenium stage for 10 years,
I went back to the proscenium stage. Now I had to create a new
concept of space with lighting. That is when my way of lighting changed.
The physical space of the proscenium was limited and fixed. I needed
to constantly 'unfix' the spatial orientation. I lit the performance in such
a way that the lights on the actors never fell on the stage and the
lights on the stage never touched the actors. So they were actually
suspended in space rather than moving in a space, where there was
a direct and tangible relationship between the actor and the light.

What moods or emotions do you try to convey with lighting?
Mahesh Elkunchwar's play 'Sonata', is about how the characters walk
on thin lines of emotion, ready to crack at any moment, … how they
manage to sustain their characters and individuality. Interaction creates
friction, but only to the point where their lives are about to be broken.
To convey this effect, this thin line of emotion, I used glass to create a
sense of delicateness, and used black to bounce back and reflect, to

'Sonata' | Delhi

maintain the tension. The entire play is about the fragility of the experience of the environment. I interpret this partly by bouncing light off white, expanding the space. I darkened some areas, keeping them in very low amber light, to change the whole quality and made one side very bright to change the tonality, making the other side very powerful. It was changing all the time.

A situation can be constricting or liberating. For example, if you have a stone wall from one end of the stage to the other, and just have one character huddled in a corner, the wall is overpowering and oppressive, making the character appear as if in prison, If you change the context and create the sound of a riot on the other side of the wall, the wall becomes protective. There is no place for symbolism in lighting; what is symbolism? In symbolism once you've communicated the message, the set becomes redundant; it dies. It's the same in lighting. You can suspend the action and change the whole ambience by the way you use light and colour. Red is not anger and blue is not peace, they are not used in terms of meaning or emotions; emotion is indirect. If you put a person behind a wall and change the context, the same colour can change its meaning. You are expanding and contracting space. The emotion is created by contextualising and not by labelling. The whole concept of scenography is that the actors, the lighting and the sets interact with one another; it is the dynamics between them that keeps the play alive.

Responses to my work are not about it being good or bad. For me it's about developing a space and creating an experience. Life is full of complex experiences – four or five at the same time – so theatre should be the same. I don't try to achieve an effect, I just try to capture the sense of the moment, a scheme of dynamic change, so that within the space of ten minutes you have a whole set of changing schemes.

You moved on from material use of space to philosophical use of space; do these require different techniques?
Yes, the technique is different every time. Lighting depends on the material you use on stage. It is the material on which lights falls that creates meaning and emotion. In one project that I did, there was no 'physical' set. It was the lighting design that the performance was based on. It was very simple yet complex. There were four planes of light in the depth of the stage, with dark zones in between. Between each plane of light there were three segments of lights, which cut the actor into three segments, you could see the actor in three parts: you saw the legs, waist and torso, and head of three different people each in a different plane of light in the depth of the satge. The action was

Nissar Allana

created in a way that was vocal. Three different actors were cut and made into one body, so it seemed to the audience that one person was divided into three parts. If you light the person as a whole, the audience either looks at the face or the body, but if you light the body of different actors in segmants, they look at the details in each of the three segments. In this manner you can enhance the emotional impact of the moment. The head has one emotion, the torso another, and legs have a different one; so you can multiply it.

Has your approach changed over time?

Definitely, I have moved towards more philosophical ideas about space. We have better technical resources now and I like to do something different each time. These days I am interested in creating excitement, a sense of breathlessness in the audience.

What motivates you?

I don't need external stimuli, my motivation comes from within. I am exploring space; abstraction if you like. There's the image, the tangible visual language, and the architecture, the tangible physical language, and when you fuse the two you create a theatrical space. This has to go beyond, and encompass much more than the physical space or the image. Theatre is about perceived magic. An illusion! So if you have a fixed stage you have to create an illusion. The illusion I am interested in, relates to the physical nature of things, I want to suspend the actor. I use lighting to make it seem like the actor is there, and at the same time is not 'there', very much as if he is on water.

Lighting plays a crucial role in how the space comes alive.
It becomes dynamic and has a life throughout the play, rather than there just being four or five fixed images.

Education	Doctor of medicine, scenography
Design experience	38 years
Field of work	Theatre lighting, Son et Lumière, specialised events and art installations
Projects discussed	India 'Sonata', Premiered in Delhi | India (2001)
	'The Mahabharata project', Premiered in Prague | Czech Republic (2003)
	La Candida Erendira | Cartagena
	'Nati Binodini' (2006)
Agency	Theatre & Television Associates

Nissar Allana

Peter Andres

Why my fascination with light? That's difficult to explain, *says Peter Andres, founder of Berantende Ingenieure für Lichtplanung in Hamburg.* If you are walking around, you see daylight. If I go into a room, I first automatically check and feel the atmosphere in my inner brain, but then, within two seconds, I try to explain it: what materials are used, what kind of light, what causes the perception I have? And so I learn. I learn from morning to evening in every single room, in every situation. It never stops. I am constantly learning new things, new atmospheres, new perceptions.

Did you study lighting design?
I studied electro-technology in Innsbruck and my teacher there taught me about lighting technology, not design. I became involved in the lighting design for a church in New Zealand. I had the idea of illuminating the roof of the church – the shape was diametric, a very special form. This was the beginning of my interest in lighting design. That was back in 1974. My study was all about calculating lux, calculating the area of a street or street systems. I then worked with Christian Bartenbach for six years – incidentally, he had also studied with the same teacher as me in Innsbruck – and then I moved to a company producing special lighting fixtures. In January 1986, I started my own lighting practice. I think from then on it was largely self-instruction.

How would you describe your approach to lighting, your style?

Our lighting design is all about well-being. Creating the perception of well-being for each person. Regardless of the project. But our aim is always the same: to create an atmosphere which engenders well-being. We focus on four areas in our work: innovation, functionality, harmony and integration. And through this focus, to give people a sense of well-being. It is not our intention to make dramatic statements that can be seen 300 metres away. We are not artists, we are lighting designers. The techniques we use for bringing light into a room are different, but there is still that necessity for well-being. People need to feel this in a room as well. You know the typical Italian ice bar? It's very cool, and that is perfect at midday, but in the evening it's too cold. Or a restaurant, which has an intimate, romantic atmosphere during the evening, but is not inviting during the day, unless you can sit next to the window. Spectrum and correct lights are the basics for our work.

Can you explain that?

Let us take an example: we have been asked to redesign the lighting of the Phaeno in Wolfsburg. Originally the area was illuminated with blue fluorescent lamps and this, in combination with the concrete and asphalt made it impossible to create the right atmosphere.

Phaeno
Science Centre Museum | Wolfsburg
→ *Direction, p. 140*

We have created a new design, using the existing openings in the ceiling. We did a daylight investigation. We can see the daylight from the façade to the inner area. There you have only 10% daylight factor and in the centre even farther away less than 1%. Knowing this is important to get the right design for the artificial light compare to daylight. We have created a transition from very diffuse light, to slightly more direct light, to even more direct light, and finally to absolute direct light. If we are correct, I am thinking about sunshine and good weather; alternatively, I'm thinking about Germany and rainy days and clouds.

And how does this help create well-being?

We try to create an environment where people feel comfortable without thinking about why. It gives a better feeling. Light is not the most important thing that you see. The most important part is the people. If you see people in a diffused light, then they could look pale, even ill. But if you use the right mixture of direct light and diffuse light, people will look healthier, friendlier. Sunlight is our inspiration. And in the evening, we use a different, warmer light. More low level. I believe

Peter Andres

Pier Bar | Hamburg Airport
→ *Direction, p. 150*

that warm lights are better, more human in the evening, but during the day I prefer white light. We adopt the same approach in airports. In daylight you have a lot of light in airports, so if you need, for example, to get a good perception of say fruit in a restaurant, you need a lot of artificial light to counteract the light from outside. But in the evening, we can switch off the white light and switch on the warm, lower level light. It happens automatically. It's almost as if the sun is going down.

When you handle exterior projects, is well-being still your focus?

Certainly. But it is harder to design atmosphere to engender well-being outside. It's all about the temperature of the light, of not having glare from the light, the feeling of security, of not being afraid. I suppose it is… romantic.

Pfalzgrafenstein Kaub castle | Rhine river | Germany

We did the lighting for a small castle in the middle of the Rhine. We created a very warm and romantic light. It was my immediate reaction when I first saw the castle – that it needed that type of light. There is a curve in the street and then you see the castle, like a ship in the middle of the Rhine. It was very beautiful. And then I thought, if this building were a sensitive person, it would be wrong to use hard light. We built a model so that we could check our lighting design in simulation. The authorities stipulated that they did not wish the technical system to be visible. We use a beam system embedded in the rocks, and we can then adjust the distance to the surfaces being illuminated to create different types of light. The result highlights the difference between harder direct light and softer, cosier, more romantic reflected light from the stone surfaces and from the trees. It is romantic. And it creates, I am convinced, the feeling of well-being that is a signature of our style.

Education	**Engineer**
Design experience	**32 years**
Lighting association	**LITG, PLDA**
Field of work	**Indoor and outdoor projects**
Projects discussed	**Phaeno Science Centre Museum, Wolfsburg, Germany (2009)**
	Pier Bar, Hamburg airport, Germany (2008)
	Pfalzgrafenstein Kaub castle, Rhine river, Germany (2009)
Agency	**Beratende Ingenieure für Lichtplanung**

Susanna Antico

Acharawan Chutarat
*Back in the 80s, Thais liked
to mimic the West, but now
we are returning to our Asian
and Thai roots. Lighting is
culture.*

For me, culture and emotion are the most important factors in a
lighting design concept, *says Susanna Antico, the Milan-based lighting
designer.* These are the basis of every concept. Things may change, be
re-thought, become re-elaborated over the years, but there are still
different cultures and different heritages in concepts around the world.
I think that remembering history and underlining it and trying to work
within the heritage is decisive in every concept. Of course, this means
studying and looking for things, and falling in love with each little village
you are working on, each square, each building.

You know, in the past, if you went to the South of Italy, everything was
painted in light colours to stop the sun coming in, and if you went up
North, you had orange and blue and maybe deep purple colours, and
that was beautiful. Now, sometimes, if we are in the town centre we
don't know where we are, and I think this is really bad. In this sense, I
am against some kind of globalisation.

What is your background?
I have a degree in architecture and I'm specialised in lighting design. In
my office we do all kinds of projects, from private houses to temporary installations, for parties, parks, office and public lighting. Public light
has, for the last few years, been the field in which we have been working most. It is also the most visible. I am convinced that lighting must be
part of any project from the very start. Just recently I was discussing
with a colleague architect the role of lighting for a square he was
designing with a large group of people. He said that if the project is
good, light will make it marvellous. If the project is bad, light will make
it acceptable. It will save it. I think he underlined just how important
light is.

What do you consider when developing a lighting concept?
The most important factor for me is the people who are going to use the project. Then there is the place, the architecture. And then there is the social context. And last but not least, the latest available technology that a lighting designer always needs to use, I think. I build my design project on these four factors. And as I start to put this information together, it gives me the inspiration which results in the concept.

In my work, I also follow Gestalt psychology a lot, the rules of perception. It's actually what photographers, film actors and theatre actors do, and so there is a combination of these effects. Let me give you an example. When I was working on the lighting in Treviglio, one of the things I lit was a beautiful city tower. It is a Gothic Lombard building and there a lot of effects that we used for that, raising up-lighters to show the beautiful brickwork, soft projected light, and underlayered to define this imposing volume. And then at the end, inside the bell-tower, that was all dark, I put a cold electric-blue light – very small. And it was really like, you know, the divine was seeping out of the tower. It was a risk, because I had been instructed not to use any colour. But this was really magical and the people actually liked it. They are very devout Catholics, and the bell-tower is very important to them. The priest even came looking for me and he told me that he brought all the people and told them to look up and see how beautiful it is, you know, as though God is protecting us.

San Martino and Assunta Church |
Treviglio
→ Colour, p. 084

Why did you choose blue?
For us, blue is the sky, paradise, and this is pretty much common in our western world. Maybe in Japan we would have to use red!

How do Italians feel about colour?
They don't like it. They think on it as Disneyworld. We are not used to… I mean, in the last fifty or sixty years, we haven't noticed major changes in our cities. Things have been pretty slow. We don't have lots of big building sites or major development. if you think about what happened in Berlin… such a huge change. So, we like to keep our old buildings. We are very attached to that. So, if there is a big change with colour at night above an old building, this may be criticised a lot. Definitely if this is a permanent thing. For temporary lighting people accept that, but… if it is commercial it may be easier, or if it is a new construction. But let's say… the right quantity must be found.

Susanna Antico

207

Is the same also true of lighting levels?

I spent a long time working around Europe and looking exactly for that, how fixtures are fixed and how much glare there was and how things looked. And definitely in France and even in Belgium there are much higher levels of lighting compared to us.

I think that first of all it's a matter of money, and how much you believe in this tool. Unfortunately, ordinary people still think that glare is light. When I arrive, I take away everything. It looks like it's dark, as if you couldn't see anything. But because people's eyes are full of light, they think it's fine. So, it takes time for them to get used to it.

Are people becoming aware of glare?

Very slowly. They like it. In the beginning, they listen to you, but they don't really believe you. They insist on lots of light on the ground, but they don't understand that they don't walk with their nose on the ground. What they really do is look for places to look and to keep them moving.

And colour?

It's interesting because if you ask them they don't want it, and they don't like it. But these are just words. I was asked to do a project in Treviglio in 2003; they gave us a month and a half. I looked at ways of giving the people there some stimulus, something that wouldn't be a meaningless installation. I read the city guides and found out that centre of Treviglio has always been the same. There was a wall, there was a moat, and there were these four doors. They were torn down in 1800 or something like that. But those doors apparently mean something to the people. Each February, they celebrate a miracle that apparently took place 300 years ago. They go together to the centre of town and design some fake stemma (coat of arms), like heraldic signs. But they invented it! They give colours to these doors. So, in the discussion, we asked ourselves how we could highlight these doors.

City Doors | Treviglio
→ *Colour, p. 080*

I decided to light them in green. It was the colour that the citizens had chosen. It was not exactly the translation of what I wanted to do, but they were excited by it. The idea of having these doors lit up when they had their fair. And what has happened? Now they are leaving it on all the time…

Of course there are some people that don't like the colour, but in general most do. One thing I have noticed with colours is that you really have to use just a little – and maybe make it temporary.

Culture comes into this, too. And globalisation. I mean, there will be some mixing, because little by little as we take things from other cultures. We absorb them and we like to use them. But when it comes to blue, the western world will always think – in my opinion – about the divine. And for the Chinese, red is always going to mean fortune and luck. I mean, you can't take this away; there's no way.

Philippe Hutinet
I do like colour but if I apply it somewhere it has to have meaning. You shouldn't put colour in for colour's sake, because then it doesn't mean anything.

Education	Architect
Design experience	26 years
Lighting association	PLDA, APIL, AIDI
Field of work	Architectural lighting design, urban lighting, lighting master plan
Projects discussed	Lighting master plan of the downtown | Treviglio | Italy (2003-2008)
	San Martino and Assunta church | Treviglio | Italy (2003)
Agency	Susanna Antico Lighting Design

Susanna Antico

Gustavo Avilés

I am a light composer, *says Gustavo Avilés,* just like in music. When you compose music, you do not design notes; that has already been done. You use notes as the material to make a piece of music. This seems to me a more flexible approach: you do not design light, you compose, hide, remove, introduce it. For me, light is deeply related to music. I do not mean light as sound effects, but rather that the language is the same. You speak about speed, character, subject, intensity, colour, brightness. I think light is a binding force in itself and reverberates like sound. It is an invitation to see what is already there. We don't see people or things; we see how light is manifested and displayed on them.

The same is true of architecture. You have to know the light that architecture has by itself. Because it shows itself with its own light: in the corners, on the heights, on its materials. And then you know what it is. I have a theory that an architectural structure is simply a light structure that is rebuilt time and again. Light is constructive. But it can also be destructive. If a lamp is not positioned properly, you break everything. It is visual destruction. The information you get is all wrong, because it doesn't correspond to reality.

Why do you feel this?
I think light can inflict an illness on architecture. Only a few architects understand light. If used incorrectly, it destroys space. It doesn't shape space, but runs away from it and turns it into something it is not. Spherical becomes flat and flat becomes scratched; a lack of space interpretation can destroy the space. Lighting touches every part of architecture directly. It touches people, objects, all and everything. By illuminating something, by presenting it in light, you discover its nature, memory, present and future. You start seeing things and then it is impossible to become bored. Everything becomes unexpected: a stone, a puddle, a reflection, a shine, even the night itself. It is important that we react with the night, with a dark sky. It is the backdrop and support of everything we compose with light.

You are talking here very specifically about exterior lighting?
I don't believe in indoors and outdoors. For me that window and patio are indoors, because my sight allows me to go all the way from here to there. Sight does not respect indoors and outdoors. Because if I am outside and look in, then the inside is the outside from my perspective. It is as ambivalent as sight, which goes to the object and comes back to the eye.

Jonathon Hodges
We've learnt that architecture can exist beyond a building.

I refer to this as 'elongation of space' – expanding the interior into the exterior. Sometimes it is very physical. If you continue with the same rhythm of lamps in and out, it becomes all one space. Don't let yourself be influenced by the frontier of the door.

You are currently working on a major project in the city of San Luis Potosí.
Yes. I got a call from the San Luis Potosí Tourism Institute to illuminate the church of el Carmen. Just that. I replied that I would need to make the space around the church cohesive with an urban visual approach. We couldn't do just a selective fragmentation of the space. It would be like a lady only putting on half her make-up or just combing one side of her hair.

Lighting Master Plan | San Luis Potosi
→ *Contrast in brightness, p. 056*

The total space has its own logic – and that needed to be respected. They understood that, and the single project turned into a unique city lighting master plan. We have structured it into six lighting stages and will eventually illuminate the whole historic centre.

The first space we did was originally totally grey,dark. I transformed the place, restructured its use, and it has now become a clean, open space. Initially, only sodium yellow lamps had been used. It was too bright. You couldn't see anything because the light was directed at your eyes. The space was illegible. Our concept was like inverting the lighting. Before, everything was fixed to posts and it seemed as if the posts were providing the light. I turned the concept round and now it is the architecture that provides the light, not the posts. The light is reflected from the buildings onto the street. The architecture was inverted. The surroundings now give you the feeling that the light is being reflected onto the streets.

Do you prefer dynamic or static lighting?

When you are illuminating architecture, the concept of 'dynamic' might not be physical movement of the light itself. It can be the dynamics of contrasts, of light, half lights, shade, darkness. It is a dynamic process, but it is not moving. But neither is it static. I also use colour and the effects of colour changes. Any illumination is static in each single moment, but at the same time dynamic in the process of time.

When you talk of colour, do you mean different colours of light?

Yes. I have illuminated the domes using warmer colours at the bottom and a little colder at the top to create a balance and visual movement.

How?

It is a question of symmetry and asymmetry. During the day, in only one fragment of time at the zenith, natural light produces a certain symmetry. Just one instant later, by asymmetry, it produces visual tension, rhythm, movement, saturation. In lighting design you can start introducing asymmetrical principles that obey the fundamental principles of nature. This is also a matter of colour and contrast.

For me, geometry is always the foundation of what I do. From geometry comes the measurements, the proportions, the symmetry or asymmetry. An omni-directional balance is achieved, with visual highlights and compensations, which can help us understand and see the geometrical ideas of shape recognition. In an illuminated dome we have to be able to recognise its spherical nature.

What about emotion in your work?

Emotion is always there, but you have to release it. Lighting is always touching things that go beyond the mind. You are never, in reality, lighting a space; you are lighting what that space means. If you illuminate a modest dining room, you are in fact, lighting our most basic act of survival: eating. We are lighting the ritual of staying alive.

You have worked in both Europe and America. Do you feel there is any difference between them?

Certainly. When I worked in Finland, I got to understand the nature of horizontal light and the light of high hemispheres. I got to understand diffuse light and learned to capture light through architecture. Back here in Mexico, you have a light that cuts, tropical, particularly when you go to the southeast. It's a blinding light; there's so much light that you can hardly see it, but it is still there, an invisible element that you must then decipher. When I was young, I travelled through Europe, knocking on the doors of some of the great designers, my masters and friends. That trip opened the visual culture to me: the culture of open spaces, the culture of great cultural centres. That was very important for me, because it linked my love of architecture to my love of light.

I'm an architect light composer; my building material is light.

Education	Architect
Design experience	22 years
Lighting association	ACE, DIM, PLDA, IALD
Field of work	Commercial, corporate, historical, institutional, museums, residential, sculptural-artistic
Projects discussed	Lighting Master Plan | San Luis Potosi | Mexico (2005-2010) Casa Cubos | Mexico City | Mexico (2007)
Agency	Lighteam

Gustavo Avilés

Francesca Bettridge & Stephen Bernstein

My background is in history of art, *explains New York's Francesca Bettridge.* And then I went on to study design and architecture. I was lucky enough to meet Carroll Cline, one of the pioneers of lighting design, on a design jury and he asked me to come and work for him. In 1985 we formed Cline Bettridge Bernstein Lighting Design. I find it exciting working with different architects who have very different styles and types of building projects. We've never specialised: if you're a good designer you can take what you do into a high-end residence, a performing arts centre or anything.

How does architectural lighting influence moods and emotions?
Francesca: For me, it's all about the colour of light, and I'm not talking about red, blue or green. We're very sensitive to the balance of light… if I go into a space that is completely evenly lit, it immediately affects how I feel. Light can have a very positive influence, it's not just an emotional reaction, it's also about how people look in the space. That then evokes the emotion. It may seem a bit superficial, but whatever space you're working on, what it often comes down to is the way the lighting makes people look in that space.

When it comes to colour changing, there are certain colours that people react to strongly and like. So, if you put blue into a scene you'll find it changes people's perception. Even a 3000 K lamp will be much, much warmer. There are many architects or designers who, when they realise it is possible to change the colour of the light, immediately want to go into the blue range. This is the real danger of LEDs: it's like giving Dracula the keys to the blood bank! I suppose it's all a matter of taste.

For a long time our approach has been to use layers of light. You really need to have light coming from different places. A lot of the tools we have for adding layers of light, for example in offices, are being taken away from us now because the codes and conservation initiative programmes are limiting our watts and our design solutions. The idea of bouncing light off walls is fast becoming a luxury. Now we're really simplifying design rather than building up layers, which would enrich our design.

Stephen, what are your thoughts on this?

You know, without realising it, we always come back to Kelly's Three Principles of Light – ambient luminescence, focal glow and play of brilliance. You have to manipulate these three things and find the correct balance for each project. It's very much about layering. We really use these three concepts or attitudes of light to compose.

Michael F. Rohde
Balance between colour and white, between direct and diffuse, between general and accentuated.

What emotions or moods do you want your lighting design to evoke in the end-user?

I don't think of it specifically as an emotional thing because we focus on the architecture and the people within that architecture. It's more something that supports the function of the space. I suppose it depends on what kind of space it is. If it's an office, I always try to make it as comfortable as possible. Francesca does a lot of theatre projects. That's almost like creating a living room on an enormous scale. These places are complete celebrations and very joyous. I don't think the emotion is something we consciously think about, and yet, guess it's always a part of our solution.

What mood or atmosphere do you want people to experience when they see your projects?

Francesca: 7 World Trade Center, for example, was a wonderful project, the first building to be put up at Ground Zero. The architect and James Carpenter wanted the complete block to have the same shimmering effect at night that it has during the day. We used a combination of white and blue LEDs in a custom fixture for the lighting around the podium. The lobby was like the heart of the building. We lit it with white light during the day, changing to mauve at dusk. And then as night falls, the exterior is activated and the blue light inside goes on, first a light blue and then a deeper blue. The other sources around it turn to a saturated gold.

7 World Trade Centre | New York
→ *Emotions, p. 170*

You don't feel as if you're in a blue box, but in a very magical sort of space. So the serious daytime office lobby is transformed into a night-time New York experience.

Why not just leave it as an office lobby?

The building had to be something special, perhaps because it was the first to be built on the site of the World Trade Center, it had to have soul.

Stephen: It's both serene and exciting at the same time – very unusual. I don't know whether that's from the saturation with blue, but it's very much a singular space where you feel those two seemingly contradictory emotions.

Francesca: It's also reactive. When someone walks by, a blue band follows them down the street, as if the building is acknowledging their presence. If there are lots of people the effect is almost like a musical composition.

We also did the Estuarine Habitats Research Center in Lafayette, which has a wetlands area outside. The architecture is distinguished simply by using the colour of the light source. Blue dock lights create a sparkle. The lighting seems to enhance nature and at the same time draws you into the warm lobby. It also defines the other parts of building, with the warmth making this space feel more welcoming. The light reflects off the wood and brings out the natural materials, picking up on the warmth of the wood and enhancing the blue of the water. It's very simple, but it works well.

The light creates a mood and directs people to where they need to go. It tells them architecturally that there are different parts to this building experience.

Stephen: The blue is a bit theatrical, but it is architecturally sound and really makes the connection between the land, animals, water and what the lab is really about… it's a wetlands laboratory. It was just a little trick to underscore that connection.

Can you tell us about another project?

We did the New Orleans Museum of Art Sculpture Garden. At night, it really becomes this kind of magical journey.

There are glowing lantern structures as gateway elements, like land-marks guiding you around the garden. The glow of the lanterns is welcoming and inviting. In an exterior project it is critical that the foreground, middle ground and background are well defined so you can understand the space better and feel comfortable there – if the background isn't lit it just kind of falls off and is rather foreboding. Here we tried to do two things: lead you through the park and show you

New Orleans Museum
Art Sculpture Garden | New Orleans
→ Contrast in brightness, p. 046

Francesca Bettridge & Stephen Bernstein

the sculptures at night in a theatrical or dramatic way. We chose which sculptures to highlight in order to apply this notion of background and foreground so you get an 'a-ha' moment each time you turn a corner.

What does that do to the atmosphere?
It makes it absolutely magical. You just don't know where the light is coming from. It's a matter of having enough ambient light so you can see the person coming towards you, but the contrast on the art work means that this is really what you are looking at. Here again, there's a lot of layering.

Where do you find your inspiration?
Carroll Cline taught me to treat every project as something new. There are so many new sources and aesthetics. Each project is different, each has its own special need and it's our responsibility to fulfil that need.

Francesca echoes this sentiment: And not only did Carroll start by looking at everything new, with a fresh insight, he also quickly started calculating how much light we needed, bringing in the practical element of 'How are we going to achieve this, in a way that is different and innovative?' I find that truly inspiring.

Education	Francesca Bettridge: Art History, Interior Design
	Stephen Bernstein: Marketing, Accounting, Lighting Design
Design experience	Francesca Bettridge 34 years
	Stephen Bernstein 30 years
Lighting association	IALD, IESNA, DLF
Field of work	Interior, exterior, master planning
Projects discussed	7 World Trade Centre | New York | USA (2007)
	Estuarine Habitats Research Center | La Fayette | USA (1999)
	New Orleans Museum of Art Sculpture Garden |
	New Orleans | USA (2006)
Agency	Cline Bettridge Bernstein Lighting Design

Francesca Bettridge & Stephen Bernstein

Manav Bhargava

I trained as an architect and first became involved with lighting six years ago after seeing a sound and light show at Kurukshetra, *explains Manav Bhargava, a lighting designer based in Delhi, India.* The way light and sound were fused was simple yet so effective, it touched my heart; I still get goose bumps when I think about it. Now I work as a lighting designer and an architect and also teach architectural design at IP University Delhi. My current work is in interiors, architecture and urban redevelopment, and I've also done lighting for museums, residences, offices, showrooms, heritage monuments and the lighting master-plan for the Delhi heritage route network. I have been involved with a number of sound and light shows as well."

We adopt a multidisciplinary approach and use light, colour, texture, material, projections, and sound to create a setting that gives people a worthwhile experience. What's most important is the quality of the space, the emotion or feeling it evokes. I try to build an experience and engage the user with my creation – if I'm able to do that, I feel I've succeeded.

What kind of emotions do you create in your projects?
It depends on the project. It depends on how one interprets the space, the embodied meaning, and what one wants to project. In the king's private residence in the Amber fort palace there's a marble courtyard outside the Sheesh Mahal (Palace of Mirrors). This is in the Mughal style of architecture, based on the concept of Char-bagh (a paradise garden) which is about romance and poetry, so we wanted to create a fantasy-like feeling and not put lights here and there just to highlight the architecture. We proposed a moonlight-effect experience for visitors. The lights had to be concealed, so people wouldn't immediately know it was artificial. We also had warm coloured lights placed on the ground, along the Char-bagh layout pattern. They would flicker to imitate candle flames, and at the same time randomly twinkle like stars, fading in and out, creating a sense of mystery and timelessness.

When you enter the Sheesh Mahal the tourguide lights a match to reveal tiny mirrors on the ceiling which start to twinkle like stars. What we tried to do was to create a floormounted lamp that would work

Amber Palace | Jaipur
→ *Contrast in colour, p. 098*

like the oil wick they used in olden times. We wanted to recreate the space as it was, but also experience the nostalgia in our own way.

In Baradari, the harem courtyard in Amber, we wanted to create the perception of the pavilion as an object within an enclosure. While the pavilion was lit with white light, arches of the rooms surrounding it were lit in dim warm white. So, we were able to create a distinct object surrounded by a definite space. Another option was to render the pavilion as an object in limitless space. We achieved this by using soft light inside the structure, giving it a sense of intimacy, and using dim monochromatic light to blur its surroundings. That's how we can influence people's perception of space, merely through the creative use of light.

Let's talk about the Udaipur city palace project, a sound and light show.

A sound and light show is an architectural theatre. There are no live actors and no designed sets. A combination of sound and light helps the story unfold. Light simply adds direction. If the sound comes from the left and the light also appears at the same time, you know that's where all the action is happening Light, along with sound becomes the medium of story telling. Light could just be the tool for passing on information, or can be used for symbolic representation either literal or abstract. It becomes the actor; it can light up a bastion to symbolise the king, or create the setting for the act, the mood and, of course, provide the necessary drama. And at moments it can start interacting with you, and that is when magic is created. In the Udaipur City palace, we picked up certain architectural elements at the palace entrance to signify as the narrator who introduces the scene. So the central character of the story was represented through the most prominent part of architecture.

Udaipur City Palace | Udaipur
→ *Contrast in brightness, p. 042*

So how do you create the different kinds of emotion?

At the Udaipur City Palace, the script wanted to create an overwhelming interaction with the viewer and keep him engaged. The client's brief was not to use colour, just white or at most amber light, so I varied the intensity and the direction of light to play with the spatial character and the texture of the stone, jalis (trellises) and carvings. Texture helps draw attention to things – as soon as I see a lot of texture I see a lot of contrast. And high contrast draws the eye towards it. In the past I have also tried to use colour to create depth, and sometimes found that suddenly all the details were getting blurred. That's how one can manipulate where the viewers attention should go.

Manav Bhargava

Generally, one puts lights right in front of the building, aimed at the façade, so the light goes vertically upwards. As soon as I change the orientation of the light, to the left or right, shadows are cast on either side. This creates depth on the other side of the element, or may even blur the entire space. I have used this at Amber, in the sound and light show, where we have lit only the edge of the bastions with blue mono-chromatic light, which then casts eerie shadows. It creates a haunting impression, as if the place has been deserted for years. Merely chang-ing the blue to deep amber, immediately transforms the entire scene to signify a sunrise and metaphorically, a new beginning.

Are different colours associated with different moods?
Of course. There's definitely a connection between light and emotion – the way light changes throughout the day affects our mood. Some of these associations are generic, and sometimes there is a bias, like red means hot and danger, green is life or nature, blue is cold and distant, yellow is more neutral. These are cultural associations that have been passed on to us through generations. Movies, art and other images all affect our interpretation.
I tend to use red, amber, blue, deep amber and orange a lot and, depending on the material being lit, I love using lavender, but my favourite is halogen in warm white. It reveals the true nature of the material. I love the shadows you get with it. But the choice of colour always depends on the desired effect, mood or symbolic projection, along with the material properties of the surface.

How do you approach a lighting project?
The most important thing is to listen carefully and understand the client brief. I then think about it and – based on my intuition – give my advice.

The client may want colour to make it playful, and although I rarely think colour is necessary, I know people react to colour in different ways. But there are so many other variables you can use to create the desired effect. I always discuss the options and that is how the design evolves.

The interpretation of the brief is what defines my approach to the project. It is determined to an extent by our cultural background, our understanding of architecture, of space, whether we know the history, tradition and how the space is used. If I were to go and work in a different part of the world, I may not read the brief in the same way. There's a cultural association, I have a certain kind of cultural baggage – it helps me to interpret, reinterpret or find a meaning in my own way.

For example, in India, red signifies danger, but in China it is the most sacred colour. That's a cultural difference.

Vannapa Pimviriyakul
Like red light might make
people feel uncomfortable
while blue makes you feel
light hearted.

In the end, though, a project is not just about lighting: what's most important is to create an experience. Our multi-disciplinary exposure enables us to experiment and explore: What is the narration all about? What is the actor, who is he and how do we listen to him? We try to understand the psychology behind it, how people perceive things, how they react and how they are going to experience it. One could use any medium, but light is my medium.

Susanna Antico
And for the Chinese, red
is always going to mean
fortune and luck.

I like constantly to create an experience, because it is about living every moment – It could be as simple as finding pleasure in the moon and the stars. I want to move the audience, give them something to remember, even if it is only for a few moments. It doesn't matter if it is positive or negative. The experience begins when you enter the room and ends when you leave. It's about the emotion you feel when you are in there.

What are the key trends and changes you've seen in recent years?
The most significant change in the last five years is the use of LEDs. Though we still have a long way to go, LEDs are becoming a very useful tool for designers. And sustainability – its awareness has been growing and has recently gained great momentum. Integration of day-lighting and energy sensitive design has today become really important.

Talking specifically about India, finally the role of lighting and lighting designers is being acknowledged. Clients are starting to understand that good-quality lighting is not just a matter of positioning a source, it's more about the effect, ambience or mood the lighting creates and how it interacts with its users. It's no longer just about buying a nice looking luminaire; it's the quality of light that counts. And that's how it should be.

Education	Architecture
Design experience	8 years
Field of work	Sound and light shows, architectural & urban lighting, architecture
Projects discussed	Amber Palace | Jaipur | India (2008)
	Udaipur City Palace | Udaipur | India (2006)
	Chittorgarh Fort | Chittorgarh | India (2007)
Agency	Mandala

Manav Bhargava

221

La-Orchai Boonpiti

In the globalised world, there are new technologies every day, *says La-Orchai Boonpiti of Vision Design, Lincolne Scott in Bangkok,* but how to apply that technology to your art is a different question altogether. You build your own dream and vision. It is not about what trend there is out there. Right now there are a lot of light colour changes in Bangkok and it makes me wonder why people would spend so much money to do that. It will be outdated very soon. I have seen the trend in China and I know that it soon goes out of date. It's spectacular the first time you see the colourful lights but it gradually loses its charisma and is replaced by something else.

How did you become interested in lighting?
I came into this field by chance. I wasn't really looking at the field of lighting design. I studied industrial design and went on to New York for my further studies. I received my master's degree in interior architecture there. Then my sister came to New York to study and my parents wanted me to stay there to look after her. So I decided to apply for a second master's degree and entered a lighting design course at the Parson School of Design. During the first semester, one of my professors, a well-known lighting designer in New York asked me to work with him. I would work with him every day from 9 to 5.30 and then I would attend classes from 6 to 9. Our professors were all lighting professionals, so they could only lecture in the evenings. When I returned to Thailand, I joined my present company. I have been here for 12 years. So you see, everything happened by chance.

Have things changed in the course of your career?

Certainly. Fourteen years ago, when I told my father that I was going to study lighting design, he asked: 'And what are you going to do with that?' Back then, people didn't understand this field of study and its significance. It has changed a lot since then. Back then, we had to tell people why they needed a lighting designer for their building. We no longer have to explain why they need to hire us now.

Is there a Thai lighting style?

I think people like very high levels of lighting. In offices, people are used to a lot of daylight, so when you make lights in offices dim, people tend to work less or are not as efficient. I believe Thais are used to bright lights and therefore prefer them. For my projects, I like to make a mock-up to show the client. To help them understand. We show them what the effect will be, rather than use words. We show them colours and light effects on those mock ups. So they can see for themselves before they give approval. The use of colour also depends on culture. Some meanings are lost on some cultures if they relate to colours differently.

Where do you get the inspiration for your design?

When you talk to the architects and the rest of the project team, you get a rough idea about what can be done. I sometimes go to sleep and see the design in my head. The first thing I do then, is to write it down as soon as I wake up! I then discuss it with the design team for their opinion and only then do I come to any conclusion. There are a lot of influences. Every designer is unique. The next person you interview will be different from me.

Can you tell us about some projects you have done?

There is a famous rooftop restaurant here called Sirocco. It was a job we did about five years ago. The building is old and the interesting thing is that nobody thought it would be a successful restaurant. But the owner had a long vision and wanted to make the best of its beautiful view. It is now fully booked two weeks in advance. You first arrive on the 60th floor. It is a stage, a dining deck with a view of the Chaopjraya River. The challenging thing about this project is that everything is outdoors. There are no ceilings for lights. We had to use indirect light to provide the dining area with illumination. There are Spanish stairs and that is where all the lighting is integrated. The building has a dome of gold. We lit the gold and lit up all the columns. The gold dome seems far away from the dining deck, but it still reflects back the light into the dining area and that is wonderful. We wanted

Sirocco restaurant | Bangkok
→ *Emotions, p. 164*

to create something very romantic. The lighting brings out an excellent contrast between the old and the new. I think that is one of the reasons it is very successful.

What kind of experience do you want people to have through your lighting?

I think it also has something to do with an integrated design (architecture, interior, landscape and lighting design). For example, I did the lighting for a spa destination resort, called The Barai at Hyatt Hua Hin.

I want the people who come there to forget whatever is in their mind and to experience something new. You go into the space and you are fully submerged into its environment. Whether you like it or not. You will remember the experience. It becomes a memory.

How do you see the lighting trends in Thailand in the next five years?

I see two things. First, there is the awareness of energy conservation due to the green-house effect. This will affect lighting globally. This makes the task of designing very challenging, because while you want to achieve an aesthetic result, you also have to pay a great deal of attention to energy conservation. Second, people's perspective will change. People will give greater importance to lifestyle. Today, kids like to be by themselves, in their own world. They listen to iPods and mp3 players. They are gradually moving away from football and sports that involve coming into contact with other people. I believe that in 5-10 years, the lifestyle will change and so will lighting design. There will be a greater need for personal space. Everyone might live in a cocoon – in their own little world. Perhaps we may even return to using the candle for lighting...

The Barai | Hua Hin
→ *Emotions, p. 194*

Education	Industrial Design, Interior, Architecture, Lighting Design
Design experience	16 years
Lighting association	IALD
Field of work	Architectural lighting, indoor and outdoor, Hospitality, Malls, etc.
Projects discussed	Sirocco restaurant | Bangkok | Thailand (2002)
	Breeze restaurant | Bangkok | Thailand (2006)
	The Barai | Hua Hin | Thailand (2006)
Agency	Vision Design | EEC Lincolne Scott

Ulrike Brandi

Lighting is not just for the building, or for somebody's ego. It's not to make the building more commercial. It's a social task, *maintains Ulrike Brandi, founder of Ulrike Brandi Licht.* People who use a building should feel comfortable. I believe it is my job to help create a space that lets them feel like that. We live in a time where there are a lot of stress factors – it's part of the modern world. We have lots of visual influences, acoustical influences, information overload. We need places where we feel comfortable.

When I'm in the country, looking up at the sky, I feel myself. Being in the country can teach us to see what is essential for human beings. And much of this has to do with light. Here in Europe, we experience light differently than people living on the equator. I like dusk and dawn, which is very long and differentiated in the North and has nuances of white sky and the warmish, reddish orange sunset. But the steel blue of the sky can also be very beautiful. You don't get this at the equator: there it's light on, light off. Light gives me the feeling of being alive.

Did you train as a lighting designer?
I studied industrial design, and during my studies I had to develop a luminaire. I discovered I was much more interested in the light that came out of it than in the fixture itself. I was more interested in what the light did to the room around it than in how the object looked. I was offered a job with a lighting manufacturer, but I felt I needed the freedom to work on my own, so I started my own office. That was quite brave for somebody without any experience. I knew something about architecture, because my father was an architect; I knew some-

thing about light, because my mother is a photographer and I did light studies with her to help with her photos. But I knew nothing about the process of lighting design, nor about the whole planning process for buildings. I had to learn a lot. It was a very intense way to learn. Sometimes I had the feeling that I was inventing my profession myself. It was very empowering.

How would you describe your approach to lighting?
For me, comfort is the key thing.

Even in exterior lighting?
Most certainly. You know, in China and Russia you still have this idea of a building as a monument. A monument that should impress you, that makes people small. I don't want to make people feel small.
You can make a monument stand out by having much more subtle lighting, as well as dynamic changes in a very soft way.

I was faced with something like this when I was asked to light the town hall in Hamburg. The city started producing a lighting concept, and the idea was that the town hall would be the brightest building in the city. It's a public building, the centre of power, of democratic politics in the city, so it should stand out. Unfortunately, you can't legislate for that. And anyway, Hamburg could be a city that embraces energy saving, and embraces, in a way, subtle, smooth light. After all, we also have dark spaces that are beautiful. I try to make the contrasts between light and shadow not too strong. For that reason, for the town hall, I used a second layer of light. It can be highly effective to combine two different principles of light: to light up the whole building as well as to accentuate details. If you only were to have shadows it would look very dramatic. I don't think architecture is theatre.

Town Hall | Hamburg
→ *Contrast in brightness, p. 044*

Barbara Horton
Retailers want drama, theatre, or they want to be the brightest boy on the block.

But you also use theatrical effects in your lighting schemes?
I sometimes work with a light artist. That's not quite the same thing. I worked with Moniek Toebosch, who does installations of light and sound. We collaborated on the lighting for IJsei bus station of Stationseiland Amsterdam, designed by Benthem Crouwel Architects. It is a wonderful location, with lots of people coming to catch their trains. Monique's installation has birds or angels and they fade in and somehow change into something else — clouds for example. When you see them moving, there is only a tiny moment when they are in a really sharp silhouette, even though it can be soft with blurred edges. So it's really abstract. It is fantastic, poetic and sometimes even slightly irritating, but also very soft, with slow movements.

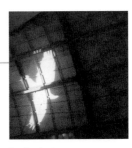

IJsei Bus Station
Central Station | Amsterdam

Ulrike Brandi

I think the whole place is a centre of movement. Lots of commuters come here, many of them stressed, in a rush to catch their train. Sometimes they also have to wait, perhaps they have missed their bus. They can be nervous, anxious to get home, and the gentle movement can relax them. It all has to do with movement again. Movement happens in nature, only slower. It can be fascinating and beautiful. Not everything has to have a function.

Where do you find your inspiration?
For Amsterdam, it was the sky and the daylight. The daylight in Amsterdam is very special, because you have a flat landscape. I took a photograph from the post office tower of the station. There was a very dramatic sky and the reflections on the water. And this really made me think of what is above the station – the dynamics of daylight and the changes of clouds. So my first idea was of clouds, and Monique added the birds and the angels.

But each project is in its own way unique. And so the inspiration is also unique. When we did the lighting for a wellness centre in Moscow, our inspiration was the woods. Outside, there is a forest of needle woods and birches. The birches have pale trunks, the needle wood is very dark green. So the contrast of light is already very beautiful. So we created an area inside with spots of light. We used controlled downlights with a very narrow angle, and they change, very softly and very slowly. It's like those spots of sunlight you see in the woods.

Wellness park Else Club | Moscow

The other area was all about water. Light and water – that works all the time and is also something that is dynamic and fascinating. But what makes this special is that we wanted to create a relationship to the outside. The reflections of the water back on the ceiling can be seen when you are in the outside area – in the forest. I'm glad we found that inspiration in the surroundings.

I think this sort of spa in Moscow should look different to a spa in London or Tokyo or wherever and has to relate to its surroundings. That was the idea.

How influenced are you by daylight?
I always relate my work to daylight, but daylight is not static. The sun moves and you have shadows from different sides. Candles also move. But with electricity, light became static. And that is, in a way, very unnatural. Today, we can change lighting situations. In offices, people sometimes say we don't need all this light – but regulations stipulate

Ulrike Brandi

what is required. I like to create the possibility of switching off the general light, so that people can sit in a little island of light: they find it comforting, relaxing. It may not be ergonomic for the day, but it gives people the opportunity to become, perhaps, more human. Because, ultimately, everything we design is for human beings.

Vannapa Pimviriyakul
I came to an understanding that light means peacefulness. People come in and they calm down.

Education	Industrial Design
Design experience	25 years
Lighting association	PLDA, IALD, DWB, LiTG
Field of work	Artificial light and daylight, lighting, master plan, luminaire design
Projects discussed	Town Hall	Hamburg	Germany (2005)
	Wellness park Else Club	Moscow	Russia (2007)
	IJsei Bus Station, Amsterdam Central Station	
	The Netherlands (design 2007)
Agency	Ulrike Brandi Licht

Howard Brandston

I grew up in the theatre, *says Howard Brandston*. I loved acting when I was young, and when I went to college to study theatrical illumination and philosophy I became involved with scene and stage lighting. I found it fascinating. People in the theatre are very creative, because there are no rules. In many cases rules are just a substitute for thinking. The crucial factor is creativity, but you also need to be open-minded, sceptical and curious.

What was it about lighting that fascinated you at that time?
I saw it as a medium that could be used to enhance the emotion in a scene. I knew I couldn't create the emotion, but I could enhance it. What really intrigued me were the subtle ways in which you can do this. Most people are not really aware of the impact lighting has. It is subliminal. They feel the effect, but are not aware of what is causing it or why exactly they respond to it in the way they do. I seem to have an awareness of this, a gift if you like, that enables me to see all kinds of lights. I once did the lighting for a fairly ordinary show, but I made sure it was different to anything that had gone before. There was no formula to it, everything was done very simply, but it was effective.

So when did you start working on architecture, monuments and structures?
I got a job with Stanley McCandless. He was an architect who worked in the field of lighting and taught lighting to architects at Yale. He was the head of the lighting part of the Theatre Department there. He noticed me when I used 102 beam projectors to create a single effect in a five-minute scene in a play! It was really spectacular! The play needed a bit of a spectacle and that's what I provided. Most of the things I did were simple, extremely simple, even if they seemed complicated. You have to keep an open mind and just do what fits the situation. What is right in one place may not be right in another. It has to be right for the situation, for the culture. Cultures can be so different, and you have to consider every aspect of a culture if you want to do a good job. You have to understand the people, know where they are coming from, what their culture is like and how they came to have this fashion or custom.

You were intrigued by the idea of being able to enhance the mood and emotion in the theatre. How does emotion come into play for architectural lighting?

You may not realise it at first, but you feel some emotion the minute you visit a space. It changes over time, depending on how often you visit the space. If you go to the theatre, there is an event atmosphere, just as there is at a ball game. When you go to work there is a different atmosphere – a work atmosphere. If, as a lighting designer, you go to a library, a museum, a show, you will find there is something intrinsic that you need to reinforce. It's a matter of identifying the essence of the space and emphasising that with the lighting. You have to be able to see it. I just ask one question: What is it that you want to see? Once you know that, you'll know what to do.

To me, lighting is an extremely simple thing. The hard part is knowing what you want to see and then making it appropriate for whatever culture or problem you are dealing with. Once you get that sorted, lighting is simple. You just have to consider the source, distribution, location and sometimes appropriateness. I always do everything in the simplest possible way.

One thing you have to bear in mind though: it's important to work on every last detail, because if you get it right people will think it's great. For example, you need great lighting in restrooms, where people really look at themselves. People know if they look good because they see how everyone else in the place looks.

What emotion did you want to convey with your lighting design for the Getty Center?

I wanted people who entered this space to understand what it was like to live when these buildings were built, between the 1700s and 1800s. I wanted them to feel like a guest in this room. It is now a well-illuminated space and the various items are accented very discreetly. You can see all of the different shadows. It is very important to see shadows but you have to be careful how you control them. Without shadows the room would be grey, it would be lifeless. There is nothing exciting about walking around in fog.

Can you tell us a little about your work on the Statue of Liberty?

I had no clear sense of the Statue of Liberty – you know, liberty enlightening the world. One morning I was sitting at the edge of the dock, just gazing at the statue as I waited for the boat to come.

Statue of Liberty | New York
→ *Emotions, p. 156*

Howard Brandston

231

Suddenly I realised that it looked best in the early dawn light. That was it! The statue represents the dawn of opportunity. I made a quick note 'Needed: one lamp to imitate the morning sun, one light source to imitate the morning sky, one new luminaire that can throw the light a long way, perhaps not quite all the way to the sky, but a long way all the same'. I said to myself: 'They don't make light sources to flatter ladies with green skin, and green skin she has!' So we created two new light sources, one to mimic the morning light and a super-highintensity flashlight: 40 × 250-watt lamps in all.

I wanted the people who come here – perhaps arriving on a boat in search of freedom – to see this statue and feel it represents the dawn of new opportunities for them. I've also seen others – people living here or tourists – recognise for the first time the freedom they have through seeing the statue in a new light.

The Petronas Towers | Kuala Lumpur
Architects: Cesar Pelli & Associates

The Petronas Towers project in Kuala Lumpur, Malaysia, was another really emotional project. The towers are a symbol of pride to Malaysians, and justifiably so. Just look at the scale of them, their sheer size is awe-inspiring. There is a lot of Islamic symbolism in the towers that is revealed by the lighting. The lighting system itself is extremely simple. The lights are essentially buried in the skin of the building as it goes up. It is hard to light stainless steel – the lights illuminate the building opposite, so what you get is a mirror image of the light from the other side. The lighting serves to delineate the building in a very simple way, to define each segment of the structure. The brightest part is actually the top. This emphasises the verticality, it draws your eye to the highest part. You come into town over a mountain and see these twin towers – they are literally awe-inspiring.

I've seen them so many times and yet each time I still feel a sense of wonder. When we did the lighting design for the Memorial for Women in Military Service I wanted to have very clear spaces, to make this a celebratory place where people could think about and honour these women, these heroines. It had to be done simply to allow all the emotion to flow freely. I wanted people to arrive here and to know they've arrived. I think the simple elegance allows the necessary emotional freedom. If you look at the memorial you see true emotion. It's emotion born out of respect.

So how do you use lighting to engender that feeling of respect?

It's not just about the lighting, it's the space, the people, and what's happening. It is when you put all of the various components together that the emotion is created.

What inspires you?

My biggest inspiration is trying to come up with something that will be of most benefit to the people who are going to use the space. It's not the space, it's the people who will be using that space. Or to put it in the terms of the theatre – which brings us back to where I started out – it's not about lighting the scenery, it's about lighting the actors.

Manav Bhargava
The experience begins when you enter the room and ends when you leave. It's about the emotion you feel when you are in there.

Education	Theatre
Design experience	37 years
Lighting association	IALD, IESNA, PLDA, SLL, CIBSE
Field of work	Architectural lighting, interior and outdoor
Projects discussed	Statue of Liberty | New York | USA
	Petronas Towers | Kuala Lumpur | Malaysia
Agency	Brandston Partnership Inc. (BPI)

Howard Brandston

Filippo Cannata

When you talk about light, there are so many aspects to take into account, *says Filippo Cannata of Cannata & Partners Lighting Design Communication in Italy.* There are the problems of restoration, re-structuring and conservation. There is light seen as communication. Light as an architectural element, and therefore as energy – a giver of energy! It is as if whatever you light comes alive. It gives off energy, as if it were telling a story during the day together with sunlight and during the night by means of the moonlight supported by artificial light.

What do you mean by light as communication?

Paul Marantz
It's a question of how little do you have to do to tell the story!

Light perceived as communication is an extraordinarily important matter. In fact, I changed the name of my company four years ago by adding the word 'Communication'. I feel attracted by two very important elements: the first of these is sustainability and the second is communication, because light is a form of communication. I am convinced of this. And I also believe that if light does not have elements of simplicity, it won't be understood. It is not the experts but the ordinary people, the man in the street, who stop, observe and smile. This is the communication of light. Often, however, the architect and the lighting designer go for the 'wow!' effect. Why? Perhaps out of an obsession with self-promotion. All the instruments that are now available on the market, starting with colour, and which are useful techniques, should be used to allow a simple response from lighting. Yet we have reached the stage of extreme folly: just think of Dubai, Shanghai, Beijing. In the eyes of someone like me, from the Mediterranean, the concepts involved are unimaginable. Here we are used to squares, something enclosed and human. There, however, there is a complete lack of humanity. A city such as Dubai makes me afraid and anxious; I couldn't live there. It's a completely artificial world without points of reference. Man is not perceived as human. I can understand the concept of safety, but it ends up with our having a huge amount of light. And then we talk of energy savings! It's like information: we are now full of it, dominated by a myriad of communications. How can you get rid of this confusion that surrounds us and use light to make a leap, to soar? At the same time, we must take the aspect of energy into account. We need to understand how artificial light can enter the magic of architecture, by trying to eliminate the 'wow!' effect and instead, to restore to light the value of language and communication. I feel that these are the most important questions that someone like me can ask.

What have been the main influences in your career?
I've met so many very important people in my life who have given so much to me. At the very start of my career, I was fortunate enough to meet Mimmo Paladino. He was an artist, but also a companion, a friend. The meeting led to the birth of a kind of experimental laboratory. Hearing an artist talk is always fascinating. I consider what I do not as work, but as my life. The experience of the stage consists of pursuing an emotion, co-operating with the artist, moving the lights in order to tell a story, rather than just to provide light. Then, I was lucky enough to meet Jonathan Speirs, one of the most important lighting designers in Europe. Together with him, I lived through the experience of the design. The experience with Jonathan was very useful for understanding what paths I should follow. Later I met people such as Dino Gavina, the exponent of extraordinary design. Munari, Aldo Cibi, Matteo Thun – people with whom I have become friends, with whom I have had extraordinary experiences. And at the centre of the experiences there is always man and his emotions. A simple message with considerable emotional content. That's more or less the story of my professional life.

And what part does technology play in your work?
For me, technology has always been the new toy; I've always been fascinated by it. I've always followed technology and the potential behind it is fascinating. But on the other hand, I am still a bit wary, because the wisdom that comes with age leads you to tread carefully. Sometimes I use technology – as in the Vinci Square. I advised the mayor to install a system which reduced the level of light between 2 and 6 in the morning, so as to save energy. They are now saving kilowatts and in that case the technology was necessary. I did the lighting quite some time ago. Mimmo Paladino won a competition for the square, with a whole series of artists. It was an extraordinary job, because it was carried out by interdisciplinary professionals, who converged on a single project.

Piazza Conti Guidi | Vinci
→ *Direction, p. 128*

This approach doesn't happen very often?

No. What generally happens is that the architect finishes his architecture and brings it to you. I think that everybody should work on things from the beginning. Unfortunately, that rarely happens. It is only the great people in architecture who understand the value of these things and are the first to involve you from the outset. Sometimes you meet up with them again after three months or a year, and you see part of yourself in the project, a bit of your own work. But you also see the work of the people who were responsible for the acoustics, materials, and other elements involved, and this results in a genuine design… this is real harmony, all working together for a single purpose!

Is there a specific project which marks a transition in your career?

Hortus Conclusus | Benevento
→ *Contrast in brightness, p. 040*

I did the Hortus Conclusus in Benevento, which constituted the most important moments of my life as an architect. There was the work carried out in a small square right in the centre of Benevento, where Mimmo Paladino was called in to restructure the square. We were working on two tracks constituted by art and architecture. Since we knew one another, and it was the first time that he too had done work of this type, it was good to meet up on the site in the evening when the workmen had gone away, in order to be able to understand what would happen when the work was completed. On the one hand I was enjoying myself, but on the other I understood the importance of the project. In the evening we met not so much to discuss the layout or the light, but to think about the people who would subsequently use it, what they would think and how they would feel. We also talked about it with friends from the most varied backgrounds. For me it was a training ground of professional life which helped me to understand how important travelling with fantasy is, rather than professional automatism.

Which emotions did you want to evoke with Hortus Conclusus?

The Hortus Conclusus is not a conventional public space: rather it is a work of art in the open air, something to experience and consume with the soul. Every single element has a symbolic value and transcends to suggestions that reach the soul of whoever runs this extraordinary place. At night I had the opportunity to complete the work of the artist with the definition of a night atmosphere that reveals tensions and energy that were impossible to see in daylight. I tried as much as possible to make the lighting fixtures invisible, because I wanted to give the feeling that light was born from the space itself, as if the architectural elements and sculptures had an energy power visible only at night.

How does it differ from the Vinci Square?

The main difference between these two spaces is that the Hortus Conclusus is a place that has an important historical stratification, a project that has been compared with the theme of memory and the influence that the past can have on the present and on the future, a metaphysical place for meditation. The square of Vinci is a reflection of a great artist on the genius of Leonardo da Vinci, an open space, a tribute to knowledge, an invitation to walk towards the knowledge. In both projects we have seen light as a material that enhances aspects most directly related to the emotional plane.

Education	Architect, Lighting Designer
Design experience	17 years
Lighting association	PLDA, AIDI, APIL, IES, CIBSE
Field of work	Architectural lighting design, indoor and outdoor
Projects discussed	Hortus Conclusus | Benevento | Italy (1992)
	Piazza dei Contio Guidi | Vinci | Italy (2006)
Agency	Cannata & Partners Lighting Design Communication

Jaspreet Chandhok & Vilas Prabhu

I've been working in the lighting industry for 20 years now, *explains Vilas Prabhu, who is based in Mumbai, India.* I started as a salesman, but when the company took a new direction I seized the opportunity to work on the design and technical aspects as well. Like a tiger tasting blood, I threw myself into photometrics, optics and lighting measurements. I've since moved on, but my basic grounding was at Crompton Greaves.

Vilas' colleague Jaspreet Chandhok joins the discussion: I trained as an architect, and right from my first year in college I loved researching into lighting design, and when we started integrating daylight and climatology in my second year, I knew that this was the field for me. I designed all my architectural assignments integrating light as a design element.

What exactly is your role now?
Vilas: We design lighting solutions. For us, it's about getting the basics right. Our job is to enhance or bring out the architect's and client's joint vision.

What would be your ideal project?
Vilas: A car showroom. For me buying a car should be a bit like going to buy jewellery. In a jewellery shop you are made to feel special, as if the product has been made for you. You may feel differently once you get home, but whilst you are in the shop it seems like you deserve it. I think you should get the same feeling when you buy a car; a sense of belonging or ownership.

What difference would you make with your lighting design?
Jaspreet: Conventional showrooms have basic functional lighting, sometimes with punctuation of the aesthetics, so you see the entire store and you see the car. We would like the customer's attention to be drawn to the car, because it is the car that is meant to take their breath away, not the showroom. People principally buy with their eyes… so it makes sense to accentuate the product on sale.

If you are lighting a building in India, how do you generally do this?

Vilas: For façade lighting, for example, we may create a design-based lighting solution, but the client might want floodlighting. Something subtle would not usually be considered. The client often doesn't just want individual features to be highlighted, he wants everything to be lit brightly, more brightly than the neighbouring property. In India, until very recently, lighting for a building façade generally meant floodlighting. We believe that sunlight does that job during the day. We try to keep things simple. So at night, we find it necessary to enhance the architectural details and forms. That's the most effective way to approach the project.

Mee Jeong
When you see the same building or environment during the day and at night, the night view brings more sensitivity. People become more sensitive at night.

Yann Kersalé
It raises a philosophical question: how can things be so different at night?

Tell me about some of the projects you've done and how you use light to create emotion.

Vilas: The first one that comes to mind is the one we did in Hyderabad, where we had something like four or five areas of water. We lit each one differently, so that each triggers a different emotion.

Jaspreet: The first thing we did was to establish a creative approach, moving away from the conventional and predictable. We wanted to create something fresh, like a painting, so that when you look at it you engage with it fully and temporarily forget everything else.

Vilas: In one we created the effect of molten lava, and another was based on a concept of floating lamps, derived from the scenes at the banks of the holy river Ganges. Most of these things are psychological. I know that if I like something, I can be sure that a major percentage of Indians will like it too, because we share a similar cultural background. If I were to do this project in some other country I would have to consider carefully whether it is appropriate for that particular culture.

'Anthem' Residential Township | Hyderabad

What is the general taste in lighting in India?

Jaspreet: Here in India we are used to having intense daylight, and yet when we go indoors we tend to have a lower lighting level than people in most European countries, where they are used to a lower level of daylight outside. This probably also varies from one region to another, depending on what people can afford.

Do you think we use too much bright light in India?

Jaspreet: For example, up to about a decade ago, a lot of homes in India had a refrigerator in the living room instead of the kitchen. It was a status symbol then. Similarly, some clients are of the opinion that if you are designing the lighting for a space, it is something that you need to show off with high levels of illuminance or colours. In our work we like to create lighting effects but we don't want the lighting to be too pronounced.

What kind of lighting do you have in your own office?

Jaspreet: One thing we were very clear about when we designed our own office was that we wanted a lot of daylight, not only for reasons of energy efficiency but because there is nothing nicer and more dynamic than daylight.

Nothing makes you feel so active as when you feel you are connected to the world outside. Eight hours of the time you spend at home is spent sleeping, so work is where you spend most of your waking hours. That's why this environment should make you feel good, it should help to reduce stress levels. I am not saying that good lighting alone can prevent stress completely, but it can help reduce fatigue. You need a pleasant environment, and if lighting can be used to create the right ambience this will boost efficiency and motivation.

Do you prefer to use specific colours for certain effects or situations?

Vilas: I like an intermediate lighting level of 4200 K. I would think carefully before using a coloured lamp indoors, but if I am using colour outside I like to use aqua blue and sunset shades.

Why aqua blue? What does it represent for you?

Vilas: I find it soothing, it's very easy on the eye.

Do you associate it with anything specific?

Jaspreet: It is a shade from the evening sky. We prefer the lighting not to be showy, although we do like the effect to stand out with a natural feel to it so it arouses curiosity about where the effect is coming from. Aqua blue or sunset red, when used sparingly, can give a reassuring touch to the illuminated environment.

What effect do you want your lighting design to have... calming, exciting...?

Jaspreet: As lighting designers, we work with a pallet of shadow and light. Whenever you design with light, you also work with shadow or darkness – that's how you make a flat effect into 3D and vice versa.
Vilas: If we choose only one colour, then we can use different degrees of contrast to vary the design from calming to exciting, depending on the use of space.

Ulrike Brandi
We have lots of visual influences, acoustical influences, information overload. We need places where we feel comfortable.

What kind of techniques do you use for dynamic lighting?

Jaspreet: Most of the time we would recommend a smooth wash with subtle colours. There's lighting and there's luminance, like a traffic signal, where the source itself is lit. Flashing lights are often inappropriate because the light then overpowers and dominates the architecture. In the majority of applications we prefer to re-create a surface, depth or gradient by proposing reflected colour change.

Vilas: If there has to be a change in light in an interior environment, it should be gradual like it is in nature and should be programmed in accordance with daylight. Colour changing attracts attention, it intrigues. Someone may see a blue light and after a while they may notice that the colour has changed. Colour changing therefore holds people's attention and creates a sense of anticipation about what's coming next.

Where do you get your inspiration from?

Vilas: The environment itself and creative architectural spaces are always inspiring. But also when I see a lighting job done shabbily, I immediately think of the simple things that could have been done a better way. I remember this so that when a project comes along and I have limited time and budget, I have the information stored away in my head and ready to use.

What is the first thing you play with, intensity perhaps?

Jaspreet: It is probably the desired mood – that is the starting point for a project. The application techniques, like intensity, are amongst the tools we use.

... mood or ?

Vilas: Mood or ambience and its intended impact on the users, it all starts from there.

Education	Jaspreet Chandhok: Architecture
	Vilas Prabhu: Engineering
Design experience	Jaspreet Chandhok: 9 years
	Vilas Prabhu: 23 years
Field of work	Architectural and technical lighting
Projects discussed	Adlabs Multiplex | Pune | India
	Sikh Temple-Sachkhand | Nanded | India
	Anthem' Residential Township | Hyderabad | India
Agency	Ethereal designs

Jaspreet Chandhok & Vilas Prabhu

Ray Chen

Lighting is a soft element, *says Ray Chen of Originator Lighting Design Consultants, in Taipei, Taiwan.* It is an emotional thing. Lighting and sound are the same to some extent. For example, when you listen to music, a higher volume doesn't necessarily guarantee good sound. This is the same with lighting. Asian culture prefers brighter settings, while in the west people prefer some level of dimness to add atmosphere. Initially, my clients tend to prefer brighter settings, which often ruin the atmosphere. I try to explain, in my proposals, that comfortable lighting can present different levels of mind. For example, there are red and green lighting, and the difference in colours brings a stimulus to the mind. I try to make them understand, sometimes by using music as well.

I need to educate my clients a lot. But lighting is an abstract object. Words don't help very much when it comes to helping clients understand. In addition to lighting simulations, we also do perhaps a mock-up or use an actual lighting setting. I usually take some lighting equipment with me to meetings and set it up to show the difference lighting can make. Seeing is believing. They can see what is good or bad, and this makes the message all the more convincing.

Has this something to do with the Taiwanese culture?
I think people often forget the root of their culture. People should not do lighting for the sake of doing it. It has to go back to your culture. Take Japan, for example. They place an emphasis on light and shadow. They care about the soft side. Look at their space design and material. They are quite sensitive about the relationship between materials and lighting. I am trying to figure out what that would be in Taiwan. In principle, comfort and softness is important. When people are in a comfortable environment they don't really notice the existence of light. They just assume that it is there naturally. It is just not something that is noticeable. But lighting should also be a business of conscience. When creating lighting, one cannot only have business considerations. There are also environmental issues and utility costs. People should have more environmental concerns about lighting.

Was there a particular event that triggered your interest in lighting?

When I went to study, I did not have much idea of what I was doing. But I was inspired by my teacher, Mr Chou. He told me I would have to get rid of everything I had learned in the past. I needed to forget things I had learned, because otherwise I would continue designing with the same inspiration. And you cannot use interior design logic to deal with lighting. I remember one very impressive class. It was my first class at Parsons. The teacher asked us to express the meaning of light. We could use anything – words or pictures – to show what light is. Some drew pictures, others wrote descriptions. And then suddenly a Korean girl in my class crumpled up a sheet of paper, flattened it out, then crumpled it again. She did this a couple of times then flattened the sheet of paper out on the table and said: This is light. The wrinkles in the paper showed reflections of light. The lighting was clear. That class inspired me. It was all about the way we look at light. It is a straight-forward object. We can see it with our eyes every single day. We shouldn't perceive it from what we are taught. It happens in front of you all the time. And you just neglect it. But it should be an inspiration. Do you want to have sunlight when you wake up in the morning? People only care about artificial light and neglect what natural lighting can do. And yet it is common sense. People become forgetful. People shouldn't forget about what is basic. People should think outside the box.

Can you tell us something about your projects?

We handled a unique project at the Villa 32 in Beitou, which is a boutique hotel. It was unique because the hotel has a hot spring and we were asked to do the landscaping. The hotel has areas dedicated to the hot spring and people move around there and they are either naked or wrapped in a towel. So when people walk through the light, they don't want to feel as if the illumination is on them. As if they are suddenly in a spotlight. And so most of the lighting comes indirectly, from the side. It was important for my client that the whole thing should be as natural as possible. The client engaged Mr. Chi Yun to do the decoration, and he made use of porcelain vases he bought in Ying Ge Town. At night, those vases simply turn into my lighting. The light comes out of the vases and the level of light does not cause any discomfort. Nor does it seem artificial; it blends in with the nature. We also decided to use halogen lighting. They consume more power, but they are ideal for a private place such as this. The colour is better and so, too, is the light. We tried to create a landscape. There is a

Villa 32 | Beitou
→ Direction, p. 144

Chen

Villa 32 | Beitou
→ *Direction, p. 144*

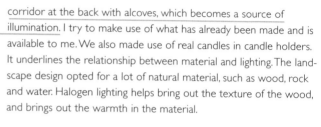

Zuo-Ying Station
High Speed Rail | Kaohsiung
→ *Direction, p. 136*

corridor at the back with alcoves, which becomes a source of illumination. I try to make use of what has already been made and is available to me. We also made use of real candles in candle holders. It underlines the relationship between material and lighting. The land-scape design opted for a lot of natural material, such as wood, rock and water. Halogen lighting helps bring out the texture of the wood, and brings out the warmth in the material.

A totally different project was the Zuo-Ying Station of the high-speed rail project. Here is was important to consider the architect's concept, because the lighting specialist is there to convey the features within the building. The base of the station is next to the Ban-Ping Shan Mountain and there is a lake at its side. The building blends in with the nature. The architect treats the station as a container which constantly gets bigger. It is a container filled with energy. The architect gave it a silhouette of an arc that would blend with the mountain and the water. Inside, he wanted to create a large interior space. But he didn't want it to look too stiff; he wanted to make it look like a shopping mall.

For the lighting, we didn't want to concentrate on just the building; we gave consideration to the people and the functional needs. The container needs to breath.

We tried to make the lighting come from the inside; it represents energy.
The overall illumination strategy is to light up the canopy. But in addition to the basic concept, I also had to take care of the basic needs. We created light racks, which mainly function to light upwards. Therefore the ceiling is bright. There is also wall illumination for those places that the racks fail to cover. The space is large, but I tried to make it as simple as possible and easy to maintain. The light poles are specially designed and give a balanced lighting, but also add a festive effect. We calculated the illumination by computer and that confirmed that the systems fit the functional needs. We also provided down lighting for the gate area. We actually combined direct and indirect lighting.

One final project – the Memory Cemetery. Here, lighting is used to express emotion. It is about the memory of the deceased. There is an arc of steel and a little statue representing the home town.

The light source is hidden, so you do not know where the light is coming from. As they move around, people feel embraced by the light.

It represents the spirit of the former law-maker, whose tomb this is. The light represents the influence the deceased would like to have on others. The materials used are mostly gray boards and concrete. There is a coldness to the material, but I wouldn't want to use cold lighting, which is generally chosen. I opted for warmer colours instead. That way it doesn't feel cold. I wanted to create the connection between the living and the dead.

For me, lighting is more about mental needs. Lighting should fit the psychological demand made on it by the user. People are emotional animals. They can be happy or sad; they need different moods in different spaces.

Education	Interior Design and Lighting Design
Design experience	18 years
Lighting association	IES
Field of work	Landscape, architecture and interior spaces
Projects discussed	Villa 32 | Beitou | Taiwan (2005)
	Zuo-Ying Station of High Speed Rail | Kaohsiung | Taiwan (2007)
	Sinyi Project Zone | Taipei | Taiwan (2007)
	Formosa Boulevard Station | Kaohsiung (2008)
	National Palace Museum | Taipei | Taiwan (2007)
Agency	Originator Lighting Design Consultants

Ray Chen

Acharawan Chutarat

I think people still prefer natural light, *says Bangkok-based Acharawan Chutarat.* They like to sit near the window. People in Thailand are very considerate. They will not pull down a blind at a window if they know somebody else wants the light. And if a manager is present, they will respect his or her space and not change the light to affect it. The way they control the light underlines the hierarchy – nobody will adjust the light, even if they do not like it, if they know their boss and majority people are happy with it.

You also see that love of natural light at night. We love the moonlight. We even have festivals that were designed to take place at full moon such as Loy Kratong day and Visakabucha day. Moonlight provides enough brightness for the public without artificial light. This has something to do with our climate: Thailand is hot and humid and we enjoy activities at night when it is cooler. Thais like mysterious and refreshing light outdoors.

Can you give us some examples of lighting and the emotion it stirs for a Thai person?
I think for gardens, Thais like moonlight. Lighting for a garden should not be bright and should flow with natural moonlight. For example, if there were bamboo trees, I would put light between the branches and let the light penetrate and come through the leaves and branches instead of playing light right at the very front. I would not have it at the back either. I want people to see the texture of the tree and the effect can only be obtained when light comes from amongst the trees. It is more natural and feels soft. We also have to look at the context and the material. You have lights at the very back when you do not want complete visibility. People then see a lot of black. It is good for columns. It brings a sense of mystery. I use that technique for temples and spas.

Do you light a lot of temples?
Yes. And in different ways. A very simple project involved a temple that belonged to a nun (Sathira-Dhammasathan Temple), with a beautiful garden. We recommended using candles to cut down the lighting cost

Sathira-Dhammasathan Temple | Bangkok

→ *Emotions, p. 178*

Acharawan Chutarat

while providing a quiet atmosphere. It suits the temple. People visiting can light candles for their loved ones. They create the lighting. At the other end of the scale is a new temple that has been built to celebrate the birthday of the King and also, of course, for the public. It will be the first temple to incorporate all the modern technologies of lighting to create the effect of serenity. It is located in China Town. A golden statue of Buddha will be housed on the topmost floor, while the rest of the building will be used for religious activities and a Chinese community museum presenting the history of Thai-Chinese people. The building is meant to make people proud of their heritage and feel part of it. The whole place is semi-lit; there are light as well as dark areas. This creates an inverted effect. We are still discussing the plan. There are two options: one is the traditional golden light and the other is more modern. What we must do is return to basics. We have to consider the feeling you want people to have when they come into a space. Since this building is meant to be an icon, I think we can employ both techniques.

Does the Thai culture prefer specific colours?
They might like colours during festivals, but not necessarily otherwise. Colour needs to be used appropriately. In Thailand, you also have to look at the materials used. It could be sparkling because of the use of coloured mirrors and a golden colour on roofs, columns, walls and entrance ways of temples and palaces. Thais appreciate the use of a gold colour for religious architecture since this material is used to create images of Buddha as an object of worship and as a means of spreading the Buddha's messages. Chedi or Stupa can be seen from a distance because of their golden colour. Most ruins at Chedi or Stupa are exposed red brick where a warmer colour or a yellowish light can provide its true colour. One time I was showing people around and when they saw a pagoda along the river, they were astonished at how white it was. But people do not necessarily incorporate the same in their houses. Houses are simple and made of simple materials. Religion, however, is of prime importance and therefore worth the investment.

How would you describe your approach to lighting?
I like anything challenging. Each project is different and therefore each lighting design solution and innovation is different. With the project's objectives and the philosophy of the owner or architect in mind, I try to produce a lighting scheme that can contribute to the success of the project in terms of atmosphere, energy consumption, environmentally friendly design, maintenance, and cost. And I am always concerned with both health and comfort.

Traimit Temple | Bangkok
→ Emotions, p. 188

Susanna Antico
For us, blue is the sky,
paradise, and this is pretty
much common in
our western world.

Acharawan Chutarat

247

Carlos Fortes

We created totally diffuse, homogeneous lighting with no shadows, just like Japanese architects do using rice paper, sometimes mounting it on a wooden framework. We placed a back-lit metal framework in front of a plain white wall, which reflected the light from this framework to produce indirect lighting. The reflection created the same sensation as diffuse lighting.

How would you define comfort?

It is of prime importance. And it has been influenced, I think, by the time I spent in the United States. Before I went to the United States, I was comfortable with the cool bright fluorescent lights. But in the States… I was there for about 10 years and during my second year I started to enjoy the kind of light people use there. It became associated with comfort. It was so cold in Pennsylvania and I started to enjoy warm colours. So my definition of comfort would depend on environment. In Thailand, people seem to enjoy direct light, but I don't enjoy it. I prefer indirect lights. I have also observed that most artists or designers prefer warmer colours, while people in manufacturing or typical office workers prefer cooler colours. Comfort is also about the way light is distributed in space. Indirect light provides less contrast and gives a softer look to the face and environment. Direct light gives harsh and strong contrasts which, to me, do not create a sensation of comfort. However, light that is too uniform may be dull.

Have you noticed a change now in Thailand?

Back in the 80s, Thais liked to mimic the West, but now we are returning to our Asian and Thai roots. Lighting is culture; it is related to who we are. The king can influence cultural thinking and ideology. His philosophy about looking at the Thai roots and preserving them has probably made us realise the important of cherishing what we possess as opposed to copying somebody else. Design is a cultural reflection.

And what about emotion? What emotions do you try to create through designs?

It depends on the context. In temples, for example, you need to create an impact. We think through the process of using light and slowly adapting it to create a contrast between the space people are leaving behind and the one they are entering. I use indirect light, maybe candles to get people to enter easily. I want to create a respectful environment and to quiet people down. I want them to focus. So perhaps I use bright lights and slowly draw them into darker light. It invites them to enter. If, however, the context is more playful, we use exposed lights or non-uniform lights. The materials used are exposed. Colours are used. The pattern of light. And perhaps it could move, instead of remaining static. When the colour changes, it attracts attention.

Traimit Temple | Bangkok
→ Emotions, p. 188

Acharawan Chutarat

And your approach to functional lighting, to lighting buildings?

We talked to architects about this and came to the conclusion that it depends on the purpose of each building. For example, we felt that embassies need accentuating. Government buildings for instance cannot look as if they are asleep like the rest of the city. They need lighting to seem alert, awake. It is cultural identity. If a building is associated with national identities, it needs to be treated differently.

Architects, however, are interested in lighting because it can make their work interesting and successful. It feels good to see beautiful buildings and to introduce lighting to the people. I enjoy lighting. And I try to exchange ideas and opinions about light with people as much as possible. At the same time, we try not to use too much light. Thais are used to simplicity. They do not, on average, prefer too much light.

Education	Architecture, Architectural Engineering in Illumination and Building Technology
Design experience	17 years
Lighting association	IESNA, IALD, PLDA, TIEA
Field of work	Architectural, daylight, interior and exterior/landscape, lighting master plan, energy-efficient
Projects discussed	Sathira-Dhammasathan Temple | Bangkok | Thailand (2007)
	Traimit Temple in China town | Bangkok | Thailand (2009)
Agency	BioArchitek

Acharawan Chutarat

Elias Cisneros Avila

I think we have a strong natural lighting culture, *says Elias Cisneros, one of Mexico's leading lighting designers.* For us, since the Mexicas and the Mayas, it has always been about sunlight.

You are the creative force behind your company?

Yes, I have a very creative job. And I also have an excellent team supporting my ideas and helping me to develop them. But this job also requires considerable discipline. People tend to think that creative people are free spirits, that we can do what we like. But the reality is that you need discipline if you are to achieve the results you have in your mind. I think a successful project depends on creativity, discipline and teamwork. Design also requires time – and that is sometimes difficult for investors to accept. They understandably want a return on their investment, but it's my job to ensure the quality of the final results.

How did you first become interested in lighting?

To be honest, I was diagnosed with a number of sight problems at an early age – astigmatism, myopia and Daltonism, that is the inability to distinguish certain colours, notably blue and green. I immediately wanted to become a doctor and find some cure for myself. I was very aware of light from a very early age, mainly because of those health problems and at elementary school I began studying optics and colours and combinations of colours. I also read a lot: I was very influenced by Albert Einstein and his theories of energy and light, and also by Thomas Alva Edison. Later, I studied architecture and the colour problem I had came out. So I decided to do collaborative work with other students. People knew I collected information about lighting, catalogues and so on, and they simply stuck me with doing the lighting. It wasn't because I was good at it, but because I had all this information about it. Each of us was responsible for a certain discipline. I think this laid the foundation for the way I work today – in a group, each member with his or her own special discipline. When I finished my major, I became a consultant and decided to study lighting further. I've been in the business now for 15 years.

You said that Mexico has its own culture in lighting.
It was strange, you know. I first had to travel and see how other cultures approach their natural and artificial lighting needs before I realised we had one of our own. I had always been interested in Asian philosophy – Zen, and some aspects of the Japanese and Chinese cultures. It makes you realise that you must look for balance. Nature does this all the time. And I believe the Mayans did as well. They made it a way of life. I think I try to create this balance in the projects we do. There are so many aspects that all have to be in harmony with each other. In Japan, I learned that there are many paths for achieving this balance, but that the result must still be the same. Today, I work with architects from both east and west. At the start, our cultural backgrounds often interfere with our understanding of each other, but gradually we learn each other's strengths, and I am convinced it is important to do that.

Satoshi Uchihara
So one way to look at architecture is as a receptor, a container for light.

How would you describe your approach to light?
For me, light creates a space within a space. The architect creates a space, then we create a new space within that given space. I consider myself a technician who achieves artistic results.

Mee Jeong
There is no boundary between lighting and space.

Technician?
Certainly. Nowadays one of the main aspects of any project – even if that is not explicitly stated by the client – is saving energy. I'm always looking for new ways to improve my work, so that it becomes useful. We like to consider the human aspect, the environment and the economy: if we can combine all three, we get a good outcome. But we also take into account the five senses, and the most important of those is sight. Do you know we only use somewhere between 10% and 18% of our brain's capacity; 80% is left unused. I do projects where people use their senses. Our design philosophy is based on this. It's like an artist who handles light and shade. Those are the raw material in the hand of the architect. And what we do is to manipulate the raw

material to communicate a feeling, an emotion. You can achieve wonderful things with light and shade. In fact, you know things better by the shade they cast. It helps you identify paths, and that's a very important thing for architecture.

Do you use this concept of paths in your work?

La Luz de los Itzaes | Edzna
→ *Dynamics in colour, p. 108*

Most certainly. There's a big project in Campeche, at Edzna. It is an archaeological site with pyramids, right in the Mayan jungle. And there is only one access route to the site. A path to the past. As people go along it, they feel like archaeologists. The lighting lets you identify new aspects of the trees, of the environment. And when they reach the site and the pyramid, the colours change. There is music, a characteristic smell and everything comes to life. You feel as if you discovered it. It is a complete experience for the senses.

You mention colour again.

We used colour to signify the Mayan culture. The Mayas had the north, south, east, west, supra-world and underworld and each of these has a colour and we used those. But there was also the chronology of time. The site took thousands of years to develop, and each new emperor added something new. So we also had colours to indicate time. For example, we had purple, but then an empress appeared and her construction period is lit in pink. Colours also have to do with contrasts. Blue suggests electricity, modernity. I like using blue LEDs.

Manav Bhargava
But the choice of colour always depends on the desired effect, mood or symbolic projection, along with the material properties of the surface.

But you also work monochromatically.

Of course, we do a lot of monochromatic lighting designs. It is, I think, an honest proposal, direct, with good lighting – natural sunlight and moonlight – and the building lit artificially. It is a way of representing the transition between night and day. I use a combination of lights to highlight the architecture with small details. The human mind is powerful and you have to guard against illuminating too much. The space has to be equal to the power of the light.

And where do you look for your inspiration?

Plazoleta de San Francisco | Campeche
→ *Brightness, p. 022*

To simple things, essentially: family, religion – these inspire me. They give me spiritual fulfilment. Another shelter for me is music, but also on the planes, walking in the forest, watching a sunrise/sunset, taking a vacation on the beach, watching colours in the water, in the sky. These all give me inspiration.

So what do you immediately think about when you hear the word light?

Space. Emotional space.

And lighting?

Then I think of technology. There's already a lot of technology, and it will only increase. Architecture allows you to discover new things – things which appear and disappear. And we enjoy creating the emotion.

Education	Architect, Lighting Designer, Renewable Energies, Art Curator
Design experience	17 years
Lighting association	IALD, IESNA, DIM, AIA, Tanteidan, CNEC.
Field of work	Urban and master plans, archaeologies world heritage sites, artistic and sculptor places, public building, commercial, hospitality, residential, theaters
Projects discussed	La Luz de los Itzaes | Edzna | México (2007) Plazoleta de San Francisco | Campeche | México (2007)
Agency	333 Luxes

Elias Cisneros Avila

Cinzia Ferrara

My aim is to achieve an elegance with light, *says Cinzia Ferrara of Ferrara Palladino e Associati, based in Milan.* This is not always easy today, because the trend is for over-exploitation of light, colours, for light as such. In general, the first thing is to make things visible – and that, incidentally, is the easiest part. The problem mainly involves the successful calibration of light and shadow and the control of it. In large scale projects, the relation between light and dark becomes more difficult. If these two levels are flattened and there is no longer any shadow, the light can lose its strength.

But it's not only a question of poetry and emotions; you need a strong technical background. I think we all have our own sensitivity, our own tastes, a certain ethical code, and we refer to these constantly. In my everyday activity I try to obtain something I would call an understatement of light, because light must mean so many things for us.

Could you tell us something about your background?
I obtained a degree in architecture, and then went on to do a Masters here in Milan. This was followed by a period of consultancy, during which I met my partner, an electrical engineer. We decided to form our own company soon after. Our aim was to create a combination of architect and engineer, each having competences that did not overlap, but that are strongly complementary to each other. We felt that in this way we could build a professional studio relating to light, which we

could offer to our colleagues. The combination of our two backgrounds allows us to go from the concept, the imaginary, to the more precise technical aspects and details. What I particularly like in my work is the cultural dialogue you get with people, either colleagues or clients. Therefore every project is a new experience.

Do you think light is a matter of fashion?
We have certainly found that our work moved in waves. We started with small projects, then there was a period in which we seemed to be handling offices, and then suddenly it was all churches. When that came to an end, we started to work on urban locations, and then museums. I think as years have gone by that there has been a change from a strictly technical approach, in which emphasis was largely placed on technology, to the present situation, in which light as such has become the issue.

Can you explain that?
This change is derived from the priority allocated to the project as a whole. Nowadays, on the one hand considerable importance is given to the concept, to imagination, the idea that is behind, but on the other, you have to know how to control the means of fulfilling that idea. There is a danger that the one is not supported by the other.

Can you tell us something about some of your past projects?
Several years ago, we undertook the lighting of the Necropolis, the Scavi in Vatican City. It is a catacomb, dating from the first century, and runs under the very foundations of St Peter's. It was a very interesting project because it is hypogeal – it is all underground. It is an important site, but the Vatican does little to encourage visitors. All visits have to be booked in advance and groups consist of just 10 to 12 people. It was discovered in the 20th century and this was its first restoration since then.

Necropoli Vaticane | Rome
→ *Brightness, p. 024*

The work was supervised by a special Commission, selected exclusively by the Vatican, and was very important and exacting. The incredible thing about this place is that there is no daylight, so there is no possible comparison between what you see during day-time or at night. This means that people can only see what you decided to show, to illuminate. For this reason in this project the personal responsibility was culturally very high. The aim was to define the perception of details as well as contribute to the general atmosphere.

Because of its very strong added cultural value, it means you are providing the work with a certain historical imprint, and that was scary but also very gratifying.

Do you consider that there are characteristics which are typical of Italy?

I think that the Italians (and in this case I am referring to designers) have incredible capacities, an outstanding way of dealing with matter which is not at all apparent. But here in Italy, everything is disputed, even the most banal things, too many people involved want to make comments, so that at the end no one recognises the final realisation, either a product or a project. In other words, it is hybrid work, and I don't like working like that.

Can you tell us about another project?

Perhaps the most important and significant project was at the Palazzo Grassi in Venice. The new owner, Mr Pinault told us that the lighting which existed at the time was not satisfactory – there was too much dazzle, and he didn't want that. Tadao Ando was the architect involved in the project and we got on very well; it has been a very stimulating experience. He immediately liked the solutions we came up with and this made everything simple. The design had to be expressed in a particular way, but with some ingenious flashes of inspiration.

The idea was to think of pulling the spotlights out when they were needed and folding them back when they were not. This was something creative and backed up by reliable technology. Everybody liked the idea right away and we went on constructing the prototype and then the lighting fixtures. It was a great experience to deal with highly qualified people and to have such a possibility to collaborate with Tadao Ando. I have always worked in a team and I often work with people with a certain presence. Confronting them and their capacity to see things is very challenging.

Did you think more about the interior lighting, the effect on the interior, or the effect of the light on the exterior?

The question makes me think of one detail of the Palazzo Grassi project on the Grand Canal. Like most of the palazzi on the Grand Canal, it has a piano nobile with decorated ceilings and once large chandeliers, highly visible from the water (this is the view when crossing the Canal in a boat, both now and in the 18th and 19th centuries). Nowadays it still happens for special occasions – Art Biennal for example – if you travel along the Grand Canal, you can

Palazzo Grassi | Venise
→ *Brightness, p. 034*

see all these magnificent halls highly illuminated. When lighting the Palazzo Grassi we highlighted the ceilings and the walls and also created dual lighting, one lot for the interior and one lot which could be seen from the exterior. It helps Venice relive the magnificence of its past.

Education	**Architect**
Design experience	**22 years**
Lighting association	**PLDA, APIL**
Field of work	**Architectural lighting design, lighting master plan**
Projects discussed	**Vatican Necropolis	Rome	Italy (1999)**
	**Palazzo Grassi	Venise	Italy (2006)**
Agency	**Ferrara Palladino e Associati**

Cinzia Ferrara

Carlos Fortes

After graduating in Architecture in 1986, *says Carlos Fortes of Franco & Fortes Lighting Design, São Paulo,* I moved here to work in lighting design with Esther Stiller and Gilberto Franco. Esther went on to open Brazil's first office specifically for lighting design, and Gilberto and I set up a partnership. I am very much self-taught and have learned a lot from other designers, from travelling, from exhibitions and seminars, etc. We work with four qualified architects, focusing on architecture and urbanism, although we also do scenic, theatre and event lighting. We don't specialise, so our projects vary in scope and nature, from apartments and retail outlets to airports, hotels and parks.

Paul Marantz

Light isn't an emotion. Architecture isn't an emotion. You have to ask yourself: 'What experience should the building give the viewer?'

Why did you choose to work in lighting design?

I originally wanted to work in movies, but when I started working for Esther Stiller and Gilberto Franco something just clicked, I felt inspired and wanted to explore this field further. Lighting design enables you to promote a sense of well-being, to create a specific ambience, although people are not always aware of this. You may not be able to determine what people feel, but you can enhance their mood, and that's very rewarding.

How do you like to use light?

We like to design artistic lighting for exhibitions, for example, where a more intuitive, emotional approach is required. When we were asked to light the 'Luzombra' ('luz' = light, 'sombra' = shadow) lamp show-room to demonstrate the kind of feelings, effects and atmospheres you can create with light, it was immediately clear to us that we would do this in an almost scenographic way using ambiguity, that paradoxical thing of light and shadow, full and empty, concave and convex, light and colours.

Luzombra
Showroom La Lampe | São Paulo

What concept did you use for this?

We worked in four different ambiences, each based on a different concept. The first was illusion. We tried to get away from the traditional living-room ambience by using hard, cold and plain black glass cube-shaped poufs with a curvy table made from a tree trunk. The concept was based on using opposites – organic versus geometric, nature versus industry – to show there is more than one way to light an object or surface and that light can create specific emotions.

Another concept involved the distortion of perception, using concave and convex surfaces and varying the lighting. Sometimes it was not possible to tell whether they were concave or convex.

Luzombra
Showroom La Lampe | São Paulo
→ *Contrast in brightness, p. 054*

We also used a wall of nails to show how you can distort perception and influence the way people perceive objects or ambiences. The nails not only had a design in perspective but were also positioned at varying depths in the wall – at the start they were almost completely buried and gradually they protruded more and more until at the end point they were almost sticking out of the wall entirely. What you see varies considerably depending on the light and whether there are any shadows. When the wall was lit it looked like an embroidery pattern, an entanglement of lines and textures. You saw the shadows of nails on the wall rather than seeing the nails in perspective. I wanted to create the illusion of embroidery, a lacework. The lacework didn't exist, it was generated by the shadows and empty spaces on the wall.

In a third room we worked with the reverse of the previous idea, an ambience without shadows. We created totally diffuse, homogeneous lighting with no shadows, just like Japanese architects do using rice paper, sometimes mounting it on a wooden framework. We placed a back-lit metal framework in front of a plain white wall, which reflected the light from this framework to produce indirect lighting. The reflection created the same sensation as diffuse lighting, and we used mirrors on the three other walls of the room to create multiple reflections. There was diffuse light from all sides and endless repetition of the images. We also fragmented one of the mirrored walls and then worked with both multi-reflection and fragmentation of the images. The idea was not to show the light sources.

Did you use colour in this project?
We played with colour and light using a white wall with acrylic pegs of different textures and shapes backlit by an RGB system. Depending on the composition and whether we used coloured lighting from behind the acrylic pegs or ambient lighting on the front, it seemed as if the pegs themselves were a light source or coloured object. If the ambience is very bright and the colour behind is not very saturated, what you actually see is small circles. You can't really tell if what you are seeing is light or coloured buttons on the wall. If you eliminate light from the ambience, however, and use completely saturated coloured lighting from behind the wall, you get a bright ambience that is lit by this colour. So, using the exact same light source and other resources we created the illusion of colour and light.

Carlos Fortes

259

Escape Pub | São Paulo
→ *Emotions, p. 160*

Do the feelings you want to convey vary according to the project?
Yes, definitely. A completely different atmosphere is required for a company canteen for 200 people than for a more sophisticated, romantic restaurant that serves 30. You need to feel you are in that place. It's not just about the food, it's about the conversation, the occasion, the ambience.

Tell us a little about your outdoor projects.
In 2007 we lit a small pub here in São Paulo called 'Escape'. There had to be a clear distinction between the street outside and the pub interior to create an 'escapist' ambience where people would feel at ease, as if they had left behind the hustle and bustle of every-day life. Through a garden, you enter a space with a very high ceiling and branches and tree trunks. There are mirrors on the ceiling and lights embedded in the floor shine upwards through the dry branches, like uplights, and the mirrors on the ceiling reflect the light back down, casting intense light on the trunks. Programmed coloured fluorescent lights change very slowly from violet to blue and we lit other ambiences with incandescent xenon lights in warm colours with low intensities. The lighting in the pub is diffuse, low-intensity and elsewhere it is localised.

We wanted people to feel they had left behind the hustle and bustle of everyday life and entered somewhere different with a cosy, entertaining ambience. We tried to create an ambience that was in such stark contrast to the one people had just come from that they would notice it the minute they entered the pub and instantly forget the world they had just left behind. I think we succeeded in creating an ambience where people will come to 'escape' after work for a drink with friends, as if entering a different dimension, a different state of mind.

What trends do you see in the market?
These days everyone is trying to work with sustainable sources, efficient, low-energy lighting solutions and considering the recycling possibilities.

What changes have you seen in the field of lighting design?
In terms of products and technologies, things are improving all the time. Ten years ago it would have been unheard of to use fluorescent lamps to create a cosy, friendly atmosphere with lowintensity lighting and good colour rendering. In terms of emotion, I think the minimalist approach people favoured in the 80s and 90s has been reversed and instead of wanting their homes to be white, clean, almost devoid of

emotion, with no shadows, defects or texture, people now want a home that is less perfect, more expressive, with more emotion – and the lighting to suit.

Do trends vary from one country to another?

The way you project and see light is determined by the kind of climate you live in. Here in South America, where the weather is sunny and the sky is blue for most of the year, our experience of natural light and light at night is different from that of people in Scandinavia, for example, where they have very few sunny days and months without any sunlight. Their experience of the environment is bound to be different from ours, and this will be reflected in their understanding of architecture and their approach to lighting design.

What inspires you now?

There are so many different things that inspire me – an art exhibition, cinema… The photography in a movie sometimes makes me want to see certain effects, to use light in certain ways.

Which projects are you proud of?

Estação da Luz in São Paulo is one of them. This is an old railway station, a listed building which was renovated and converted into the Museum of the Portuguese Language. We designed the lighting both for the exterior and interior. Our concept focused on the lighting for the exterior, which was based on homogeneous and subtle illumination washing across the entire façade. We used very soft lighting to bring out the volume, the original design of the building. It's not too dramatic, yet it still emphasises certain effects or parts of the English-style architecture. We also used the door and window openings to make it seem like the building has internal lighting, as if it is 'alive'. The lighting for the museum itself had to be adapted to suit this very contemporary interior space that incorporates electronic media and projections. This project received the Award of Merit from the International Association of Lighting Designers in 2007.

Estação da Luz | São Paulo

Education	**Architect**
Design experience	**22 years**
Lighting association	**PLDA, IALD, IES, ASBAI**
Field of work	**Interior and exterior lighting**
Projects discussed	**Luzombra, showroom La Lampe	São Paulo	Brazil (2007)**
	**Escape pub	São Paulo	Brazil (2007)**
	Museum of Portuguese language at the Estação da Luz |
	**São Paulo	Brazil (2007)**
Agency	**Franco & Fortes Lighting Design**

Carlos Fortes

Peter Gasper

I was born in East Germany, but my family came to Brazil in 1951, *explains light scenographer Peter Gasper*. I was 11 years old. Ten years later I started studying architecture here in Rio de Janeiro. But I had no money, I had to work. So I got a job at Tupi TV Broadcast in the scenography department. I was young and full of ideas. A year later, I got the call to go work in the movies and the theatre. At a certain point I started to see things clearly: it was light that was lacking! If I designed square scenery, the lighting guy designed a round light. If I made light scenery, he made a dark light!

I was happy sometimes, when I saw my scenery lit in a wonderful way – and at other times less so. I asked myself: 'Is it me who cannot make scenery for the light, or is it that the guy who makes the lights cannot make them for my scenery? I realised that if I could handle the lighting, I could guarantee my décor would be exactly as I wanted it.

In 1974 Brazilian TV started working in colour – at that time colour was brand new. The head of scenography at Tupi TV was invited by the German government to intern on German TV, to familiarise himself with colour TV. From the lighting department, no one went. So I said: 'I'll go!' I talked to the scenography director, who was my boss: 'You have to send someone to learn about light!' 'Yes, true, but who?' 'ME!' 'But you're a scenographer!' 'Yes, but I want to learn about light!' 'Why?' 'Because my scenery depends on light! If I throw in some blue light, my scenery becomes blue, right? If we turn off the light, there's no more scenery.

And you started to realise that light could be a tool to help you?
Yes. I studied at the German TV company Sender Freies Berlin, the Free Berlin Broadcasting Company, because at that time the wall was still there. So I spent one month there studying lighting.

What I learned most was colourimetry. It was like this – up until then I did colour subtraction; there, I learned to do colour addition. So colourimetry – more than light and dark, more than shadow, the domain of colour – became my life.

What does it add?

It adds the certainty of what you should use in terms of colour.
And colour is a very important piece of information, in all cultures.

When you use colour in your work, do you use it with any particular meaning?

Not necessarily. I use it like an emotion. What matters to me is that it transmits an emotion. For instance, red – a very red surface – shocks you, right? So, you'll make sure you don't use that red in your house, because you don't want to be shocked every night. Well, using colour is about emotion: like when you enter a room and go 'Oh!' … the light must be an emotion.

Museu do Paraná | Curitiba
→ *Emotions, p. 192*

Is that the intention, to capture an emotion?

In my case, yes, it is! Maybe not in the case of a lighting technician, whose main concern is to light up a soccer pitch, for example. He sees the emotion in the game, not in the scenery; he will do the lighting correctly, beautifully, but he is not concerned with the emotion. The engineer didn't study to bring about emotion. He studied to do an exact science. The architect is not concerned with exact science, he's concerned with emotions.

And how did you go from scenography in the arts to architecture?

I'm still a scenographer. That is my profession. I use light as a sceno-graphic element. Everything is scenery! And what defines its graphic form? It's not audio; it's light. Scene graphics are made with, for example, wood, fabric and light. Without the light, the wood and the fabrics are of no use. It's all worthless, because the eye will not see them.

Because I am a light scenographer, I use light as my scenographic tool. I don't have to build scenery, I have to light the scenery, and thus it bears my signature.

What aspect of light interests you most in scenography?

Light simplifies everything. If you know exactly what the eye will see, you build fewer things. Let's say you're building theatre scenery, and you want to suggest night-time in a forest: a big tree branch with blue lights will do! There is no way of not understanding that that is night in a forest. You don't need to make the forest, draw bunnies, grass, the whole nine yards. The light gives you the freedom to simplify your art. I feel like an artist. So I express myself artistically!

Peter Gasper

What has influenced you most in your career?

In terms of media feedback, it's Oscar Niemeyer. I love him deeply, he's a brilliant person. He's someone who has influenced me because of his behaviour, as a human being.

Ibirapuera Auditorium | São Paulo
→ *Brightness, p. 032*

He worked without a lighting person for many years. After the first job I did with him, he never called anyone else. I'm sure he saw clearly that light is an essential tool. Many architects are now becoming aware of that.

The Brazilian architect is extremely vain in his talent and creativity. So he pays attention, 95% of the time, to problems related to his profession. And he can only dedicate 5% to lighting, because he's so focused on getting his thing right. That's his worry. It's different from the engineer, who cannot make a mistake or the building will fall down. The architect cannot make a mistake for the sake of his name.

One other question about influences: which lighting culture do you identify with most strongly when it comes to design? European, American, Asian?

Kiyoung Ko

I try to find the sound in an area and then I visualise that sound into lighting.

I don't analyse it in that way. What has influenced me most is theatre lighting. I study lighting from China, India, but each country adds its own cultural element. What I really care about, like I said before, is conveying an emotion, like in the theatre. My thinking is theatrical.

It's like music: imagine you have to compose a song and you can't play it to check if it's good. What will you compose? Lighting is composition! There is light, there is dark, there is silence, there is noise.

Do you see different trends in the way countries like China or India approach lighting?

Oh, for sure. It's cultural. But everything is cultural.

Are these trends converging and unifying?

Yes, but fortunately there are still some countries putting up a bit of resistance. The Czech Republic, for example. Prague's lighting is extremely theatrical. You think you're going to hear an opera. Everything is scenery. It's the emotion of watching a theatre play. Prague and Budapest are still that way, while in the rest of the world just about everyone is doing the same thing.

You don't make a building stand out because of its architectural value: you create an ambience. It's a different school of thought.

A different school?

Yes, but it's a minority one. The majority tendency just now is to make the architecture stand out – I'm talking about outdoor urban lighting, which is now called city beautification.

And what do you see as the main trend within that?

Today it's colour changing – that's quite obvious. This will last for another three or four years, or maybe more.

What emotional need do you think this trend addresses?

Novelty! It's curiosity, of course! Why do we change cars? Now, if you produce a car with 8 wheels, everyone will want it. That's just the way it is.

Still on the subject of emotional needs, can you share with me any final thoughts on the use of light to create emotion?

In the theatre you have to help create some emotion: you are not there just to light up the actor. An electrician can do that! You learn how to contribute emotionally to the act. That is different from being simply a light projectionist, you know? I'm not a lighting designer. I am a theatre lighting professional, a scenographer. I don't think of myself as a lighting designer because their role is limited to placing light on the scene. I introduce emotion. For me, rule number one is to ask myself – what kind of emotion can I put into the scene?

Education	Scenographer
Design experience	49 years
Field of work	Stage and architectural lighting
Projects discussed	Palácio do Planalto | Brasília | Brazil
	Museu do Paraná | Curitiba | Brazil
	Ibirapuera Auditorium | São Paulo | Brazil
	Metropolitan Cathedral | Brasilia | Brazil
Agency	Peter Gasper Associados

Peter Gasper

Paul Gregory

At the end of the day, it's a matter of coming up with ideas that trigger an emotion, *says Paul Gregory of Focus Lighting in New York.* That's what we're always searching for, something that will make a project meaningful and lasting. Our projects vary greatly – we work on many retail and hospitality projects, educational and entertainment venues, and specialty works like the Times Square Ball or the historic Tivoli Theme Park in Copenhagen. We have six senior designers each leading a small team. When a project begins, I meet with each lead designer and help guide the initial designs. We try to use an unconventional approach to push ourselves for creative ideas every step of the way.

How did you get interested in lighting in the first place?
For me, lighting design is a combination of art and physics. My first passion was theatrical lighting design. I loved the challenge of trying to create an emotional response in the viewer by lighting the stage. It was exciting and so much more fun than physics. I trained at the Goodman Theatre School of the Art Institute of Chicago and then studied Architectural Lighting Design at the Parsons School of Design in New York. What really intrigues me is that 'all we see is reflected light.' You do not see the paint on the wall, the fabric upholstery on the furniture, or the stone of the fireplace, you see the light reflecting off of those surfaces. It is an additive process where we move from a black pallet, to a fully revealed setting full of colour and texture. We are painting the environment with light, and thus creating the image the viewer sees. We prioritise the most important features of a space and bath them in light to improve the functionality and beauty of a space.

An architect's training is all about being inside a space, feeling the volume, the proportions, whereas theatrical lighting designers are trained to be outside the space looking in on the patrons' experience. It is the culmination of these two designers' points of view that can create a great project.

This makes theatrical training a delightful place to start because it provides this different point of view. You have to consider how people move through a space and coordinate how to make the movement more pronounced. From the experience of lighting people, our expertise flows into emotion. We find that emotion can be created in architectural lighting just as it can in theatrical lighting.

Can you expand on this a little?
The success of a Broadway show, for example, is determined by whether the audience feels an emotional attachment to the characters, and the same is true in architectural lighting. You have to create a situation where there is an emotional relationship between the viewer and the space. But how do you do that? It's as if you're sitting with someone on a beach looking at a beautiful sunset, and if you feel something for the person or the sunset, the image will be engraved in your memory.

Tavern on the Green, lit by Ken Billington, here on the West Side of New York is the kind of place you don't forget. Why? Because it's nature wrapped in light. One hundred year old, beautiful, big oak trees with lamps on two-inch centres, articulating down to the finest branches throughout the whole tree create a stunning image. It's incredible; it moves you and you remember it.

Can you walk us through some of your projects and tell us about the emotion or mood you were trying to convey and what techniques you used to do this?
The Marcus Center for the Performing Arts in Milwaukee is a good example. Bursting with the creative energy of performance found on its 3 stages, our aim was to mimic this creativity on the façade of the building.

Marcus Center | Milwaukee
→ *Colour, p. 088*

We considered what Milwaukee is about, who comes from there, and its beautiful natural landmarks. Georgia O'Keeffe is a Wisconsin native, so we did an analysis of her floral artworks and of the Northern Lights and Aurora Borealis seen from this state. Inspired by O'Keeffe's painting technique, we drew from her careful blends of colour to recreate a painterly feeling with light. Photographs of the Milwaukee sky also informed some of the light blending and tonal choices for the final design.

So how do you want people to feel when they see this building?
We want patrons of the Marcus Center to appreciate the colour and the beauty found in nature from every exterior view of the building. Using solid colour blocks of light seemed repetitive and mundane.

People have already seen that. It doesn't spark the imagination. So we sought to do something subtle, to render the blank façade with a selection of 'light paintings'.

The LED colour-blast fixtures allowed us to get multiple points of different coloured light all simultaneously reflecting off of one surface. To mimic O'Keeffe's Red Cannas we cast orange, yellow, red, lavender and off-white light onto the surface of the façade. For the recreation of the Northern Lights image, we used blue light with green and lavender twists that run through it, it's really beautiful.

So do different colours project different moods?

Barbara Horton

I think having that neutral experience on an everyday level and then those moments of something that changes, that's what makes colour exciting.

There aren't really any concrete rules of colour as far as I'm concerned. There are theories like 'red makes you hungry' etc, but I just don't subscribe to it. If you stand in an area that's filled with red light for ten minutes, it starts to look pink and then looks whiter. Your eye tries to acclimatise, to make an area white. But then the blue at the other end of the hall looks incredibly strong, rich, beautiful and intense. And if you walk down there, once you're bathed in the blue light it starts to become lighter and lighter, and the red that you were in before appears rich and strong…and yet nothing has changed except for the way your eye perceives things. How a colour makes you feel depends on many different aspects of the environment you're in at the time.

Mall at Millennia | Florida

Let's talk about Mall at Millennia…

Mall at Millennia is a covered mall that is supposed to feel like an exterior space. It's too hot in Florida to have an open-air mall, but this feels very airy and open, as if you are outdoors. To imitate nature inside, blue light is projected onto the ceiling to represent the sky, and blue light is cast inside the elevator cabs and the main hall to represent the ocean. Ceilings are covered in fibre optics to resemble stars. Everything from the warm accents on the palm trees, to the subtle reflections off of the glass windows, serves to bring the outside within.

We wanted to create a space where people want to be, where they look and feel good. The warmth and glow of amber light – a bit like the light when you sit around a campfire – makes you look good, and when you notice everyone else looks good you feel good. We have taken what you see outdoors in nature and brought it inside to trigger those positive emotional memories of the beauty found in nature.

Paul Gregory

And what feeling do you want people to have when they see Macy's?

When New York natives and tourists see Macy's during the holiday season, I want them to have a sense of vastness (the sense that it's the largest store in the world). We proposed a glittering band of light that goes all the way down to Seventh Avenue. It completes the entire building and adds unity to what are, in effect, three different buildings.

Similarly, in the case of the Saks holiday windows, we wanted to create a feeling of a holiday extravaganza. We wanted it to seem 'over the top' and exciting. There are 120 seconds of music with 450 light cues set to the music, so it is unique and special for the passer-by. It's all about a sense of celebration and nostalgia.

In contrast, the Social House in Las Vegas was designed to make people feel like they were in an opium den; to feel they are in a mysterious place. We did this by using a bit of red light among amber and warm white light. The suspended bird cages above the main dining room have red light coming through and filtering onto the faces of the diners.

Social House | Las Vegas
→ Emotions, p. 174

Creative lighting design requires the spark of inspiration. Where does your inspiration come from?

I get my inspiration from everywhere – from the World's Fair, art exhibitions, Broadway shows, even a walk through Central Park. I try to see a show once a week and visit as many galleries as I can. It's just a matter of seeing more and appreciating something new. By adding more to my visual memory, I am constantly expanding my ability to be creative and introduce something interesting into my work.

Education	Theatrical Lighting Design, Architectural Lighting Design
Design experience	27 years
Lighting association	IESNA, USAA829
Field of work	Hospitality, Restaurants, Education, Museums, Healthcare, Retail, Residential, Entertainment Venues, Offices
Projects discussed	Marcus Center for Performing Arts	Milwaukee	USA
	Mall at Millenia	Orlando	USA
	Macy's	New York	USA
	Mansfield Hotel	city	USA
	Saks	New York Millenia	USA
	Social House	Las Vegas	USA
Agency	Focus Lighting

Paul Gregory

Jürgen Hassler

What I find interesting about lighting design is that time and space melt together, *says Jürgen Hassler, of Hamburg-based Hassler Entertainment Architecture and Make It Real.* It is three-dimensional painting in light and space. I try to see what can be expressed with light and how you can paint pictures with it using all the different tools.

It is always a question of how you can change the atmosphere – the way surfaces creating that atmosphere look. That is one example of light design. It also means concentrating on how lights are positioned, which kinds of beams you use, which colours – how the total composition looks. You can create the illusion of a room using media, and I try to combine surfaces of an actual, existing room and change it with different colours, different shapes and also through the different pictures that are projected on it. That is time and space – and they are always changing.

What do you mean by media?

For me it means having different tools. And to create, using all these media, different pictures. Let me give you an example. We were asked to handle an award show, and for every person who received an award I created their own hall of fame, hall of glory. The recipient was standing in the middle, and there was a carpet behind the recipient, and the design framed him or her and made them look special. We used lower resolution LED in the floor and everything could be changed, making the whole event very emotional. It demonstrated how dramatically space can be changed by using pictures or atmosphere and how design can be used to enhance the award and the winner.

German Movie Award | ZDF
→ Emotions, p. 168

Can you tell us something of your background?

I studied stage design at the academy in Munich and then worked in international opera houses. But after five or six years, I began to feel restricted and I decided to take an art-oriented study. I wanted to widen my knowledge to enable me to express my ideas and thoughts more clearly. Design on its own is art and sculpture; what we are trying to do is communicate using design. Light and media are very good tools for communication and therefore interior design and architecture are very close to light and medium design. I have two distinct companies here: Hassler Entertainment Architecture is a design company that specialises in concept, design, 3D motion and everything connected with that. And I also have Make it Real, which handles budgets, does project management and is specialised in LED development. We do this not only for events and shows but also, with Make It Real, for retail projects. We handle both interior and exterior projects.

Do you have a certain style?

I think it is a very clear style. Everything we do, we try to develop from a point. The end result can be extremely complex. I will always try to start from a very simple and powerful point.

If we are doing light design, we just want to create one light that is strong enough, then add all the rest. So that could be the red line that runs through the project. We also follow a special theory when we develop a public building. It is that everything you find on the outside must also be found on the inside as well. So if we are dealing with the light on the outside, it must also be found in the inside. When I develop interior lighting, I base it on the exterior and on the red thread running through the concept. For example, for the design of a shopping mall, I produced an entrance where I made use of the idea of a red carpet – but then I had that carpet on the ceiling. It featured strip lights with different animations to lead you into the interior world. It's animated, but it changes very smoothly and lifts you up. You look up and see that little light. Light always opens my heart; it is so positive. And everybody feels this. I wanted to use the façade as a means of conveying mood management, colours, even structures for information, such as breaking news.

This carpet is there to have different colours, movements and an interaction with the façade; this means you are bringing the movement from outside into the inside.

Kiyoung Ko
We wanted people to feel they were watching outside, not inside. And so for the artificial light, we had to create a feeling of 'natural sunlight'.

Kaoru Mende
In Japan, we didn't have lighting from the ceiling and we always have daylight coming in from the side.

Stadion Center
Shopping mall | Vienna
→ *Dynamics in colour, p. 116*

Jürgen Hassler

271

Stadion Center
Shopping mall | Vienna
→ *Dynamics in colour, p. 116*

We also use the architecture to display colours from the morning to the evening. We change the colour every hour: for a winter morning, it's warm, in the summer cooler. If I were to go to a shopping mall at 8 in the morning, I don't want it to feel cold. So I made it warmer. At midday, when perhaps you're coming for lunch, you want it to be inviting. And maybe between 10 and 11.30, it could become a little cooler again. There is a rhythm. It's a feeling I tried to put into the project. We chose warm and cold colours, and others just for the evening. They are sympathetic colours, inviting. The interior has a lot of wood, so the lighting must complement that. I start with a particular atmospheric look and then maybe introduce some power with a blue and the colder looks. It creates a rhythm: warm, cold, very warm. And for the evening, we make use of what I call entertainment colours – red, purple. Entertainment always makes people interested in the shop. There are also eight video walls and they are constantly changing. Sometimes there are strong colours, but also very soft colours. It's all about mood management. Three of these video screens are visible at one time. As you move through, your mood becomes relaxed and you want to stay there for a long time. One of the aims of the lighting is to keep people in a space. Then they try to become involved in the whole environment. The whole impression is sympathetic. You watch things and you're interested. It's always our aim to get people interested. You don't have to look at the screen, but you want to. It is about mood management. You can sit down and think about something else. But it also creates movement. Sometimes, there is a shape moving from one place to another, and this makes people move more quickly. That's one part of what we have to do when we work in public spaces. We ask ourselves: what result do we want to achieve. These things do have an influence, but the question is: how far do you go? You feel better when the sun is shining outside.

Many designers think interior lighting is different from exterior lighting, because it shouldn't always be a show.
I agree. Buildings shouldn't be compared to shows, but they are staged places. So by designing them you are using similar techniques. One famous architect told me once: 'My architecture is like a church: you enter and go "wow".' But I see it from another side. I want to go in and feel comfortable, not say 'wow' and never come again. So it is a show, because it is about creating emotions. After all retailing is a type of stage and because it is about creating emotions it always will be the case otherwise – what is the point of going?

Retailing, of course, does not create such concentrated emotions as a TV show. There you have to put everything into 30, 60 or 90 minutes. With retail properties you have ten or twelve or fifteen years before refurbishment and during that period you have to perform almost every day.

You frequently use media façades.
I use them because they can interact with and enhance the surroundings. They can communicate and change. I love looking at a building that is going to change, especially at night when it can have a totally different type of attraction. It can show me a secret about the building, maybe related to its other uses or it just looks more interesting or special. And I like that.

*Final Draw for the 2006
FIFA World Cup | ARD | Germany*

Education	Academy of Fine Arts, Munich
Design experience	27 years
Field of work	Television, stage design and architecture
Projects discussed	Final Draw television show	ARD	Germany (2005)
	German Movie Award	ZDF	Germany (2007)
	Stadion Center Shopping mall	Vienna	Austria (2007)
Agency	Hassler Entertainment Architecture Make It Real

Jürgen Hassler

Jonathon Hodges

My background is in architectural lighting, *explains lighting designer Jonathon Hodges,* but that is not really what Jason Bruges Studio, where I currently work, is primarily about. We do all kinds of lighting, often interactive projects.

Did you train in architectural lighting?

It is still reasonably rare for people to be trained in that. I actually studied chemistry, but while I was at university I became involved in lighting concerts. It was a good way of getting near the people making the music. It was exciting. But towards the end, I felt I wanted to do something more enduring, something that would stand the test of time. I noticed that people around me were starting to move from rock and entertainment lighting into architectural lighting. It was becoming something of a high-profile area and was enjoying a lot of coverage in the press and on TV. I also saw an increasing number of beautifully-lit buildings around me and I began thinking this may be a direction for me to take. I worked for a manufacturer for a number of years and then as a lighting consultant. It was mainly about selling an idea, explaining how lighting could be applied to a space, what equipment would be required and then setting everything up.

And what about your work with Jason Bruges Studio?

This is a different type of studio. It's a crossdiscipline practice; there are architects, product designers, people who work with furniture. Everybody has his or her own take on what we do and can contribute towards using light as a medium.

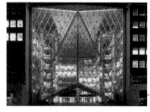

55 Baker Street Façade | Public Artwork | London
Architect: Make Architects

Can you tell us something about projects you have recently been involved in where lighting has had an effect?

I think that is always the intention. The work I do is rarely just functional lighting; of course, light always has a function, unless it is purely artistic. At the moment we are working on a project with Make Architects on Baker Street, in the centre of London to light a façade as a public artwork. The façade is a very interesting structure and acts like a mask to the building. It is very geometric and the lighting has been done in a very grid-like way. Our idea was to pick out all the structural members very carefully and to bring out each section of it very gently. It has become a metaphorical mask for the building – a party or carnival mask.

Did it start out as an artistic project?
Yes. The company that owns the building was required, as part of the planning permission, to provide a public work of art.

So it is explicitly artistic...
It certainly started with the concept. The structure is hollow, so we felt that the light could be easily contained by it and that by lighting each diamond we could get a stained glass effect. But that proved impossible, because at some places the structure is solid. We tried many different ways to fit lasers, projection, different patterns on the glass and we spent a lot of time developing optics that would make a very narrow beam. And, of course, LED technology moved on considerably, and that was convenient for us. It is an arduous process, because there are so many technical constraints on it, and we are still in the process of installation.

Will the lighting be static, or is it important that it changes at certain moments?
That's something we are still considering. We have to ask whether it is important that that happens. Is it a novelty? It is good? Do you what something that people can set their watches by – something that happens regularly on the hour? Or is that crass. The art is finding the correct balance.

And how will you know whether you have achieved that?
In a few weeks time, enough of the project will have been completed to allow us to sit there for a couple of evenings and get used to what is happening. We will then see what kind of impression it leaves when a certain colour changes how it looks. How the gradient or the patterns change. Whether there is an animation of some kind. We will all sit down and address what the artistic content is, how it looks, how it performs during the week, should it be different at the weekend, what tone we can set for things. And we will ask ourselves just how outrageous can it be.
We have created a canvas but then we will need to experiment with it. We wanted to create something which would echo what happens during the day.

Earlier you mentioned interactivity...

Yes, we find that extremely interesting. One example is a project we undertook in Soho, in London. We were commissioned to produce a public artwork for the Richard Rogers building, Broadwick House.

'Recall'
Broadwick House | London
→ Colour, p. 076

The narrative behind our concept is that the building is dormant during the evening. There is nobody there except the security guards. The architect has a philosophy that buildings should have a life after the working day is finished and within this vibrant part of London, the building almost looked lonely in the evening. So we wanted to create something which would echo what happens during the day. A reminder of the building's activities, even when it's empty.

So what we did was retrofit the lift shaft – which is a striking feature of the building – with LED panels between some of the floors. Originally these were just blank bits of metal, but now they are translucent panels that hide features. During the day, a computer program monitors the lifts and records where they have been and in the evening, these are 'replayed' by the LED panels to show that the lifts move up and down. The colour we chose is sympathetic with the orange of the steelwork, which is such a striking feature of the building. It has brightly painted, big exposed metal surfaces, and orange is an indicating, warning or signal colour; it grabs the attention. The whole effect is magical, as you don't really notice the panels during the day. They only reveal themselves at night.

What reaction were you hoping to achieve?

We wanted to interest people. Intrigue them. Make them wonder what it does, what it is for.

I understand you do some work that is more environmental or socially oriented.

Last summer we were asked to provide a temporary installation with a sustainable idea behind it. And we produced 'Wind to Light'. The budget was very small, but it gave us the chance to develop two ideas we had been thinking about: first, is it possible to visualise the elements by using light, and second, could we encourage people to think about energy saving and new sources of energy?

'Wind to Light'
South Bank Centre | London
→ Emotions, p. 176

You know, everybody understands the wind: you cannot see it, but you can see the ripples it leaves on a lake. The way it makes the trees move. You don't see it, but you see the effect. You can actually see where the wind is.

Now in our installation, the wind outdoors drives a series of miniature turbines, which lights up three LEDs inside each one. When the wind blows across the balcony where the installation is erected, it leaves a trail of light behind. I think it says, in very simple terms, that you can turn wind into light – and so also says that alternative energy is possible. There may be many technical problems or things you have to solve, but we can do it.

So you like making people think through your lighting?
Certainly. This was the basis for a project we undertook for Switched On London. In that project, we used the movement of people across London Bridge to feed an installation on Tower Bridge. We were able to lock in on blue-tooth enabled phones carried by people crossing London Bridge and our sensors would detect whether they were moving north or south and at what speed. Each person was allocated a colour and these colours would then move across Tower Bridge.

Tower Bridge | London

And did people understand what was happening?
There was some press coverage at the time, but I don't know if people actually made the connection. We are planning a new installation on London Bridge for this year. People cross it daily, but I think that few ever really stop to consider what a wonderful location it is. We are planning to light the footways – and we are thinking of seeing whether we can influence the way people walk on the bridge – fast, slow, marching, strolling – with light and so make them think about the view around them. At Jason Bruges Studio we think a lot about this and have carried out a lot of research. We've learnt that architecture can exist beyond a building. A soundscape or a lighting effect can shape the space so that it becomes a much more pleasant place at night, an environment that people would want to use. You can create a new environment using light.

Education	Chemistry
Design experience	10 years
Lighting association	PLDA
Field of work	Light art, landscape, bridges, interactive, urban, facade
Projects discussed	55 Baker Street Facade, Public Artwork	London	UK (2008)
	'Recall', Broadwick House	London	UK (2007)
	'Wind to Light', Southbank Centre, Architecture Week	London	UK (2007)
	'SWITCH ON your Bluetooth', Tower Bridge, Switched On London Lighting Festival	London	UK (2007)
Agency	Jason Bruges Studio

Jonathon Hodges

Barbara Horton

I think I got into lighting by osmosis, *says New York-based lighting designer Barbara Horton.* I was actually an interior designer, but just happened to be married to the founder of the company. He was extremely passionate about all he did and this rubbed off on me. I came to understand that lighting really combines art and science. Atmosphere is created by blending physics and psychology and all those other things. I realised that as an interior designer I was only affecting the tangible things; I wasn't really affecting the environment and the experience that people have through light. Today, the opportunity that lighting affords me is that I get to work with great architects and great interior designers all over the world.

What sort of projects do you undertake?
Extremely varied. We do offices and airports, but also monuments – just about everything in fact. Lighting is such a fascinating part of architecture. But so often it's approached purely from the technical point of view. A lot of times, when we work on a project, somebody wants to know how many foot candles there are. Foot candles – measurement of light. And we try to explain as best we can that it's not about measuring light, it's about how the room feels. I sometimes use a slide-show and ask them: 'if I had seven foot candles in this space, which space would you rather be in? The white space or the black space?' Well, if it's a theatre, people prefer to be in the black space, and if it's a school they may prefer the white space. So it's about trying to help people understand that you can transform the space by bringing out finishes, textures or whatever.

National World War II Memorial | Washington
→ *Direction, p. 132*

Doing conceptual boards, renderings, models, whatever we can to help them feel the space and see what the alternatives are – that's really important. I go to the owner or architect and say: 'Let's look at the floor plan, or the model or the building: what is it that you want to feel? Let's walk through this and create an experience. Is it light? Is it dark? Do we have shafts of light? Do we use colour? What do we do to make this space become something that people can interact with?' It's not about the technique, it's about how people feel in the space. I am very much a people person.

Can you give us an example of your 'people approach'?

We did a project for the Phoenix Public Library – not the entire library, but the Teen Center. The problem was: how, in this computer age, do you get people to take books out of the library, or even visit one? Libraries are quiet places, yet also places where people meet. But they're transforming themselves. Phoenix was one of the very first progressive ones to try to get the teenagers back in.

Burton Barr Central Library | Phoenix
→ *Dynamics in colour, p. 110*

We played around with dark surfaces. We made it very moody, very theatrical. We also created lighter areas, where necessary bringing in natural light. We wanted it to feel like Starbucks. Starbucks feels like a living room: it's a place where you relax, meet your friends, have a cup of coffee, and more and more libraries these days do have coffee, so that's kind of interesting.

There isn't just a sea of downlights in the ceiling. It's accented, with little highlights, adding to the drama. And the lighting is interactive, with dynamic colour-changing effects. Kids find it a fun place to go, and I think that's partly because they can control and change the lighting as they need to.

What emotions or moods do you want to create in your work?

It really depends on the project. Retailers want drama, theatre, or they want to be the brightest boy on the block. If it's an airport… you know, it's funny, some of our staff are like, 'airport … there's no emotion in an airport'. Oh yes there is! If you've ever gone and watched what happens: people arriving, people departing. It's the biggest soap opera you've ever seen, so many people moving through the space. It's our job to use light to offer them a degree of comfort. So even in the, let's say more mundane projects, we always try to get inside the head of the client or architect to elicit what they really want to feel there.

Recently, we went away for the weekend, down to Annapolis. While everybody else was shopping, I was really stepping back and watching. How were people moving through the streets? What were they attracted to? I try to make sense out of it all. I've always been like that, so this isn't just my 29 years of experience. I say to everybody here: 'We live in New York City, it's the biggest experimental pot you could ever have. Get out of the office, go see what's going on in the world. Don't read it in a magazine when it's down the street. Get out there and feel it."

Do certain colours create certain moods or emotions?

Well, yes, lighting really can change our mood. Let me give you an example. Within the range of white, you can have a warm colour or a cool colour. If you're in a restaurant and everything has a very warm tone, you feel warm, relaxed, enveloped. The kitchen door opens and they've got a cool-white lamp in there. This still happens, sadly. When that door opens, what does it feel like? It feels like you've just looked into Siberia. And nobody wants to sit next to that when you've just had this wonderful warm candlelight glow.

Again, cool and warm: if you give people down south a choice, they want the cooler white every time because psychologically it feels cooler to them. Hospitals are another place we're starting to see it. We're seeing children's wings using light to make youngsters feel more at ease; there's a huge amount of emotion in a hospital environment, one way or the other.

What about colour and colour changing on the exterior of a building?

Colour on a building can put a smile on our face or make us think 'I've got to go find out why it's that colour'. But if you have colour every day, it's not fun anymore, it's not special. I think having that neutral experience on an everyday level and then those moments of something that changes, that's what makes colour exciting.

You do work in lots of other countries, are there cultural differences that affect how you design lighting in those countries?

Absolutely. The Middle East is a great example. Many years ago we did a project to light a water tower. We – the American architect and us – wanted to light it very white, very beautiful. Well, through some fluke of technology, the lamps used all had a slightly different colour. Some were a little pink, some a little green, some a little blue and some were white. They got installed and this tower now has streaks of all these different colours. The architect called and said 'These lights look terrible! Get them changed!' So we go back and get all the newly tested lamps: everything more consistent, everything white, we put them in and the local people say, 'We hate this, we liked all the colour'. Now the colour was by accident. It was not intended that way, but that was a rude awakening: our culture had wanted that white light, everything perfect, but the culture we were designing for said, 'You didn't give us anything exciting'.

All the projects we're working on right now in Dubai and Cairo are so much about colour change… but not because they want to be Las Vegas. I think it's because in their culture, it's important to find colour, vibrance, in everything. Think about it – everything is neutral, their clothes are black or white. So to create something that makes people feel good or becomes celebratory or is just different, I think is really important. I can't explain why that same phenomenon exists in Korea or Taiwan or Japan, where colour and light are so significant, because they don't have bland environments. I don't really understand that, other than I think there's a tradition of bigger, brighter, better, more vibrant, more colourful, more animated gets you more attention.

Finally, what inspires you in your design work?
I draw inspiration from nature – there is no single architect or designer or anything like that that I would say moves me to the core. It's really about being in the Muir Woods and seeing the light filtering through the trees and seeing all the reflections – that's probably the most spiritual thing I could ever feel.

Education	Interior Design
Design experience	29 years
Lighting association	IALD
Field of work	Interior, exterior, master planning
Projects discussed	National World War II Memorial | Washington | USA
	Burton Barr Central Library | Phoenix | USA
Agency	Horton Lees Brogden (HLB)

Barbara Horton

Philippe Hutinet

What attracts me most to lighting is its emotional potential, *says Philippe Hutinet of Agence Hutinet, Conception Lumiere in France, a lighting design company that has been active for over twenty years.* There is a magic which lighting brings to the interior and to urban space. Light is, by definition, emotion. The only light you can look at and still feel the emotion is a candle; for the rest, light simply emanates, it is there, it exists. It is the application of light to a space – to a surface, to architectural characteristics – that creates the magic.

You came to lighting after a long career in the theatre.
I spent 20 years in 'show business' – at the end of that time I was director of production at Lyon Opera and at the Aix Festival. I had had some experience of the occasional lighting enhancement work – castles and rather specific prestigious places – but lighting urban space did not really exist as a profession when I started my company in 1988.

How would you describe what you do?
Lighting design, purely and uniquely. We have always wanted to undertake different types of lighting applications – interior, exterior, festive or otherwise. It's a philosophy, an approach, a behaviour in relation to the lighting tool. For each project, we start at the drawing-board. It's not about saying 'we know this works, let's do it again', because each project is different. It fits into a different environment, because there is a cultural difference between north and south, and between east and west. In the south they're attracted to a more violent, whiter, rawer light that is directly associated with sunlight; it is part of their culture.

As you move farther north, it is more about light colours closer to sodium, because the common culture is linked to the idea of interior, and so a warm light is more convivial.

Every time we start from scratch. We consciously want to avoid falling into the trap of habit. If people want to make use of a lighting designer, it is because they want something different, something unique. And which is the result of reflection, real reflection.

Do you have your own style?
Generally speaking we tend to make use of warm tones. Most of the time, when we work on a façade, it is generally the Haussman style, which has been restored using light coloured, golden stones. Even the slightest light makes the stones sing. I'm not there to create a live show on the façade; I am there to enable the façade to reveal itself. And so, in a sense, I have to embrace the façade, embrace its forms, its roughness, its rhythms, its structures.

And the relationship between light and shade?
Light only exists in relationship to the darkness alongside it. If you only use light, there is no point. If you make sure there is light and shade next to each other, the shade will help to emphasise the presence of the light. It's a relationship of contrasts, a game of contrasts between volumes, surface contours, architectural details.

And what about the use of colour?
I use colour when it has an emotional reason. For example, we undertook the lighting plan for the City of Valence. The Grand Boulevard is almost the Champs Elysées of Valence. The aim of the project was to give back the city square to pedestrians. In an urban space, emotion stems from the quality of the light dispensed onto the space, but also from the capacity of that light to allow pedestrians to see what is around them.

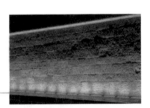

Grand Boulevard | Valence
→ Emotions p. 166

Each individual is given the chance to experience emotions, to grasp the space, breath it in, understand it, re-appropriate it for himself. In the square, we made use of a soft, fairly warm light. We also took considerable precautions to avoid glare, because by doing this we increase pedestrian comfort. The other end of the Grand Boulevard is close to the river Rhône. There I decided to use bluish lighting. The same light is also applied to the fountain. I created the idea of an entrance to the Grand Boulevarde with blue, reflecting the presence of water and the river Rhône. It is about suggesting not

Philippe Hutinet

demonstrating. We suggest emotions through the use of blue; that was the basis of the concept.

So to return to your question: I do like colour but if I apply it somewhere it has to have meaning. You shouldn't put colour in for colour's sake, because then it doesn't mean anything. At least, that is how I see it. I think at the moment there is an excessive use of colour, without any conceptual basis. Then all you create is something which people may find pretty or not and that's it. It doesn't make them feel any emotion.

You also used blue in the Jean Jaures metro station in Lyon.
That was a choice we made together with the architect. We worked with linear lighting which turned from blue to white. It is a dynamic scheme, connecting the entrance and exits of trains in the station with systems. What is interesting, however, is the use of hundreds of dots of light in the ceiling. There are about 1000 dots of light, produced by fibre optic generators. The quantity of light dots was inversely proportional to the number of people in the station: the fewer the people in the station, the more dots and vice versa.

What was your idea behind this?
A metro station is below ground, and that is an alien environment for people. I wanted to create a playful environment – not slapstick, but something that was playful, reassuring. If there are few people in the station, having a large number of dots makes them feel less alone. If there are a lot of other people around, you don't necessarily need that reassurance.

Saint-Joseph | Reunion Island

It is very suggestive.
That is what lighting can do. Another recent project was for the town of Saint-Joseph on Reunion Island. What I wanted to express was the feeling of a Creole house. We again used soft, warm lighting. And we introduced transparency through the varangues – overhanging archways. There are French windows and we placed lighting inside the building so that it would shine out. Even if nothing is happening inside, the back wall is illuminated and this creates a presence.

How do you create the feeling of presence?
You light inside, within the space. It creates notions of warmth, lighting linked to the use of the building, the life that may be in that building. Whenever we light a project, we take such considerations

into account. When we lit the Renault Trucks factory in Bourg en Bresse, we wanted to stress the connection the factory had with vehicles. And so we used red lighting, because this suggests the lights of a truck. The building is pretty isolated on an industrial site. From the national road, the lighting turns it almost into a contemporary painting. It makes people ask themselves: what is that building? It is punctuation. It is the vocabulary of the road experience.

At the same time, you also have to be humble about your design. You have to be honest with yourself, but you must also realise that the public may not necessarily feel the emotions you are trying to convey. You have to remember that you are delivering something to the public and they will use it, read it, interpret it, and experience it in their own way.

Renault Trucks
Façade | Bourg en Bresse
→ Colour, p. 072

Education	**Theatre lighting**
Design experience	**44 years**
Field of work	**Urban, architecture, interior**
Projects discussed	**Grand Boulevard	Valence	France (2009)**
	**Saint Joseph	La Reunion (2005)**
	**Renault Trucks façade	Bourg en Bresse	France (2004)**
	**Jean Jaurès metro station	Lyon	France (2000)**
Agency	**Agence Hutinet**

Philippe Hutinet

Mee Jeong

There is no boundary between lighting and space, *says Mee Jeong of Seoul-based Eon Sld.* I've never thought that light exists separately. In our everyday life, there is always some kind of lighting, whether that is natural light or artificial light. We use the word 'lighting', but it is something that lives and coexists with us at all times. I'd like to see lighting as something that is naturally amalgamated into our daily lives. People do not need to be excited by it all the time, but I would like to have people recognise and appreciate the existence of light. I do not want them to recognise the lighting itself; I would much prefer for people to find their space warm and comfortable because of light. I want them to realise that the reason they find their space comfortable at night is because of the light. I would like my lighting to be the climax of the space.

Can you tell us a little about your work?

We undertake a wide variety of work. For example, we've done most of the master plans for the big cities in Korea: Seoul, Kwang-Ju, Choon-Chun and Bu-chon. We basically plan how the lighting of the whole city's going to be designed. A city is composed of individual buildings but this causes an imbalance. If you have a big picture and a plan for the whole city and look for variety within the city, it is possible to give it a personality and an identity. From that, we develop it further. Some of the work is done by us on each building; some is done by other designers or other companies. Basically, what we do is the most fundamental job in developing and growing the market.

There are restrictions on illumination and luminance; the authorities want it to be lower than a certain level. Guidelines are very rigid things – they are not really fun. But we are the ones who introduced this kind of culture when we returned from Japan.

The second biggest job we do is art works directly requested by various clients. The characteristic of Korean works is that they are a mixture of European and Japanese concepts.

Konkuk University Business Area | Seoul

Japanese projects generally have a strong sense of belonging to the building rather than being a separate identity as an art work. On the other hand, European projects show the very strong individual character of the artists themselves. Korean works have both these qualities.

There are twelve of us in the office and our motto is 'Let's create something we've never seen before. Let's try something nobody has done before, something totally new and let's have fun doing it.' If we are not having fun or if we do something that resembles something somebody else has done before, that is a pity and it hurts our pride. As an artist, I tend to emphasise creativity.

When did you start your company?
We started it in 2000, when my husband and I returned from Japan. We both studied at the Tokyo National University of Fine Arts – I received a doctorate in space design and he received a doctorate in architecture. My major was industrial design. When I went to graduate school, I wanted to combine design and industrial design and that's why I went to that school in Japan. Tokyo National University of Fine Arts in particular is especially interested in raising and producing an artist. There is no boundary – you can do anything you want to. You cannot graduate unless you are able to create and portray your own colour and your own world of art in its uniqueness. It's a very special purpose they have and that suited my personality which is why I chose that school.

And how did you become interested in lighting?
I became convinced that you must have artistic perspectives. My works for example constitute movement. If there is no light, there is no movement. You cannot see it unless it has ample lights. It's a very subtle movement – in dark spaces, it needs a spot light and that's how I ended up working together with my husband. Lighting requires an object and lighting all depends on how you present the object using the light. I was focusing on presenting the object and this involved strength in light. That's when I realised that light is enormous fun and my husband also realised that light cannot be apparent unless there is space. We continued to work together and we were continuously complementing each other's weaknesses which stirred more interest in lighting and studying it. My husband is already part of the office and I feel our differences create synergy. But lighting design cannot be just working on art works. My colleagues in the office have a lot of work. I think it's because I started with space and I coordinate all my

colleagues' works in their decision of flooring, colour, placement of signs and sizes. They appreciate it because it involves the complete big picture. When you say you do lighting, it can sound very two dimensional but because I take care of everything within the given space – for example, recently I even include sound and images.

When this is three dimensional like this, it becomes a piece of art work. When you say you are a 'lighting designer', people underestimate you and think that it's a very simple job. But it's not that easy. It's science. Would you like to know what lighting is? It's a perception that natural environment and men are the same creation. It's not something people need to develop but we need to learn from nature and find ways to live without being invasive and harmful to our environment. You need to work together.

So how would you define 'lighting designer'?
For me it means lighting the finish of an architectural structure. There are two different concepts of a lighting designer in architecture: one is as a partner to the architect and the other as a partner who creates a new work with a nice finish. To the non architects, the lighting designer is someone who sells the new dream and the new world. You have to show the world of night. When you see the same building or environment during the day and at night, the night view brings more sensitivity. People become more sensitive at night. Depending on the environment, one may have a different sensitivity, emotional state or a different thought process. In some cases, it may be therapeutic, healing, or it may be stimulating or uplifting. You need to give hope depending on the needs of different projects. The most difficult thing as a lighting designer at presentations is that I have to show something invisible. Your presentation must stimulate the imagination because you are only showing your concept with images/pictures. It's very important what you portray. A client will not be moved unless the presentation is thought/emotion provoking. I don't want the client to be just the owner or the person who only sponsors the project financially. I want them to participate in the project, being involved in creating something new so that he can feel a sense of accomplishment. I tell my clients that their project will provide a world for other people to come and enjoy the space we create and that's it's a very rewarding.

Can you give some examples of your work?
We are currently working on a project for a plan within the four gates of Seoul. It includes Kwang-hwa-mun and Sung-nye-mun. The theme is: 'Let's walk through the historical city'. We wanted people

Sung-Nye-Mun | Seoul

Mee Jeong

to experience the history within the four gates that surround the ancient Seoul with quietness. When you take a leisurely walk from Kwang-hwa-mun and reach Sung-nye-mun, you feel the symbol of Seoul. It's important that the pedestrian feels the space – the light provides the sense of the space. But the light should not be too prominent so that you feel it dominates the space. We also did the Seoul N Tower. It is the symbol of Seoul. It was lent to a private company for 10 years, but because it belonged to the city, they were not allowed to make it look too commercial. The biggest challenge was to balance the private and public aspect of the building. Each hour, the first 55 minutes bathes the tower in white light. The white colour represents the highest technology. The final 5 minutes is a lighting show. The concept is a flower, and we therefore made all the laser rays visible. The tips of the rays are colour-coordinated. So those five minutes return the building to the investor.

Seoul Tower | Seoul
→ *Dynamics in colour, p. 112*

And finally, there was a FIFA VIP reception held in the Kyoung-Bok Palace. I was in charge of the lighting installation and it had to be submitted in advance for approval to the FIFA office. The special thing was that it did not have any cables or wires. Everything was battery operated. We had special hand-made lighting units, made of traditional Korean paper, which floated on the water. We also created lighting in bamboo trees, made of fabric, which created an overall feeling of calm, but still very suitable for a party. It received a rave review from the FIFA VIPs – they really liked it.

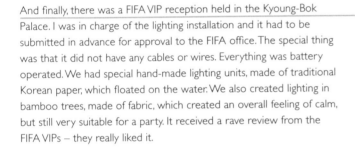

Kyoung-Bok Palace | Seoul
→ *Emotions, p. 190*

Education	Design
Design experience	21 years
Lighting association	KSLD
Field of work	Architecture, landscape, city lighting master plan
Projects discussed	Seoul Tower	Seoul	South Korea (2005)
	Sung-Nye-Mun	Seoul	South Korea (2005)
	Kyoung-Bok Palace, FIFA VIP reception	Seoul	South Korea (2002)
Agency	Eon Sld

Mee Jeong

Yann Kersalé

For me, as an artist, light is sensitive, *says Yann Kersalé*. In fact, it is not light that primarily interests me but the night. I am fascinated by the way things which appear so normal, so common-place during the day, can take on a different personality at night. You can see an object, a building every single day. But then at night it can suddenly become completely different. It raises a philosophical question: how can things be so different at night?

What really interests me is being in the landscape. My business is almost the business of cinematography. I am first and foremost trying to move the individual, who is 'called' by something which is free. It is there to be seen. You don't have to go to a museum to see my work; it is outside. I work with architects and landscape artists who are conceptual. They are determined to give meaning. They produce architecture which is not yet another tower which could quite easily be in Tokyo or New York. The conceptual architect who creates is always contextual.

So your ideas are about being in the night?
You are not always what you think you are. And people aren't always what you think they are. What interests me is that the night is an area of life that is different from the one to which we are accustomed. And I am also interested in man's fragility. It is this delicacy and fragility that interests me. My projects interest me because they are not peremptory. I do not disturb civilisation too much, as I only use a small piece of time.

Do you describe yourself as a lighting artist?
I am first and foremost a creative artist. I studied at the School of
Fine Arts in Quimper where I concentrated on plastic art. I was interested in changing the concept of art itself. I was extremely interested
in innovations, even political ones. I spent several years floundering
– engraving, painting, assemblies, installations – but I was determined
not to limit myself to one single artistic expression. I did not want to
live in an ivory tower.

Lighting, for me, is something I can use to explore my fascination
with the night. Night, with all its parameters, its sociological and
geographical parameters. And I develop things which I think of as
geo-poetic. When I use light, I do not make lighting plans. We do
not have any equipment. What we do is create the synopsis. And
that, for me, is the greatest freedom.

Synopsis?
A synopsis is really the entire work. There is the original creation,
always done on-site, looking for meaning. The synopsis is made up as
if for a film, a book. It is my firm conviction that the creation must
come first and that technology and all the competencies of people
available in lighting today should be put at the service of the creation
and not vice versa.

Can you give us an example of your projects?
I recently completed Quai Branly and the concept there was to
create a garden of shadows, inspired by the forests in Amazonia.
When you sit on the terrace of the restaurant, you will look out
on a sea of vegetation. And the shadow below will be even more
intense. I created a virtual lake using 1,600 canes. It is like a musical
composition, but without sound. It is a concerto for piano in
which the piano is the large virtual lake and the orchestra is the
different forms of light that are dispersed throughout the garden
like clearings.

L'Ô | Quai Branly Museum | Paris
→ *Colour, p. 086*

The canes are blue, green and white and the intensity of the colours
changes according to the ambient temperature. It is, in fact, based on
a very simple pluviometer. If there is rain, the blue canes are dominant
at 100% power, with the green and white canes at 81 / 75%. If it is
very cold – say 5 or 6°, then the white canes are at 100%, and the
blue at 81%. And if there is evaporation, then the green canes are
dominant. The three colours therefore also represent the three states
of water:

solid, liquid and gaseous. In this way, you create meaning, you tell a tale. You're not obliged to put up a sign saying: 'This is how it works'. It is for people to decide.

There is something else: concentric circles are projected on the surface of the building, reinforcing the idea of a lake. They are like the effect you get when you drop a stone into a puddle and see concentric circles. But there is also a random element that had not been predicted: there is an automatic watering system which starts at fixed times and also at night. Droplets of water become attached to the canes and so the concentric circles on the ceiling start to vibrate, as if someone were really throwing things at them. These are co-incidences that come at the right moment.

L'Ô | Quai Branly Museum | Paris
→ *Colour, p. 086*

I am currently working on the concept of geo-poetic trails. I am creating a geo-poetic trail at Château Chasse-spleen in the Bordeaux region. I'm taking the notion of a vineyard throughout the year, with its pruned vines, its vines in leaf, its wine cellar, its various processes and I want also to create meeting places. There is a dynamic you can program into your lights that can provide breathing, impulses, fade ins and fade outs, to allow you to orchestrate your lighting.

Let me return to the parallel with music. Everybody knows it is about tempo and also about sound and silence. The breathing is a game between fortissimo and pianissimo, and you can use this statically by implanting a beacon system which is pianissimo and a chorus that is fortissimo. There is also something that musicians call texture. I use this in light, comparable to the musical range. The variations between pianissimo and fortissimo. And you can also introduce play elements where you trigger something. You can have systems recording the passage, the motion, which then automatically triggers other things.

What interests me is, a little like Tom Thumb, to see the light over there at the back of the woods. So, it is when you are in the dark and suddenly see something light up over there. Perhaps when you reach it, it is a 200-year-old oak and a rock lights up. You can't see the rock, because you are 350 metres away, but you see it because there is a path and that invites you to discover what it is. And when you reach the tree, something else is triggered. It is a game of composition.

When you make such a trail, how do you choose the colours?
That is a bit like asking a painter why he chooses certain colours.
I want white light. Or I am going to use extremely radical mono-
chrome things. But I do not choose the colours; the subject determines
which colours should be chosen. Let me give an example: in the
Bordeaux region, it is going to be red. Bordeaux red. Light is an accompaniment. I am tempted to believe that it could be a sensitive, poetic,
pleasant accompaniment to creating something at night that is different
to those fears we have of it that are ancestral and atavistic.

Kaoru Mende
the lighting transforms the
architecture into some-
thing it never is in day-
light.

Education	Fine Arts
Design experience	27 years
Field of work	Architecture, urban, landscape
Projects discussed	'L'Ô', Quai Branly Museum | Paris | France (2006)
	'Théâtre Temps', Opéra de Lyon | France (1993)
Agency	AIK

Yann Kersalé

Kiyoung Ko

The first thing I want to do is to make things seem natural, *says Kiyoung Ko of Bitzro, Seoul.* I do not want lighting to be exaggerated, but I do want to create something which generates a feeling of emotion. I feel the origin of light is natural light, daylight. There must always be space for natural light; even when I design artificial lighting, I want it to look like natural light. Let me try to explain: when I am in a park, the street light or the underground artificial lighting can make me feel uncomfortable. But the light shows that if I stay there for a long time, I would feel comfortable. I hope the user will create a new space from the feeling which combines the comfort provided by the light and the user's own feelings and emotions.

Light controls people, people's behaviour and emotions. It can make them even happier. In my lighting projects, I think about the people; about what they are doing, what they do here and why they do it. I put myself in the position of people working in that place. I am now concentrating on human beings, on the environment. I like to think of my lighting as 'Human Centric' and I am concerned about including human life in my light. Even if the lighting seems very functional, I do not design it in that way. I imagine people working and the movement and I think about the music in that area. We hear a lot of different sounds in an area. Music is the combination of beautiful sound and a lot of noises.

Does music inspire you?

I played the piano for 15 years, but I then changed my major to design. Music is four dimensional. The art is merely a question of time. Design is about space and it is three dimensional. One day I attended a lecture given by a stage designer. In stage design, light is a four-dimensional project, because light changes over time. I heard there was nobody specialised in that field and I joined an internship programme in the architectural department. When I asked questions about lighting concepts, nobody could give me an answer.

I searched for a school and got some information about the Parsons Lighting Design School. I went there after I graduated. My thesis was about the interrelationship between music and design. Music is space. I found that we need light to make space four dimensional. I read a book which said we should embrace the light into the space. I found that fascinating. And I became aware that light can make space four-dimensional. Light makes people change. People see some kind of emotion when they see the concept or the time of value, which is more like feeling the space. There are lots of tunes and music about moonlight, by, say, Debussy or Nocturnes. When I play that music, I can feel the moonlight. Light changes over time and the environment changes. And because of those changes in the environment, people feel different. If I hear Debussy's Claire de lune at night or at day or in the moonlight, the change of environment effects my feeling. I want the user to observe the sound in a space and feel the emotion. I try to find the sound in an area and then I visualise that sound into lighting. There are certain sounds people like, others which they don't like. That is the same with light. There are some kinds of light people like and some kinds of light people don't like. So I try to imagine how the light can be acceptable to people and I try to visualise sound in light.

Mônica Lobo
I really think that lighting has the power to reveal that essence. It makes the intangible tangible.

Can you tell us a little about some of your projects?

My first project after starting my company in 1998 was the 'Club Nine Bridge' golf resort on Jeju Island. The main architect was Denniston, a British company, and I supported the main architect with local ones. I wanted to give the main entrance a welcoming feel. Trees lined the pathway to the entrance and the architect wanted to erect poles next to the trees. But I didn't want to use artificial poles; I wanted to see just the landscape, the purity of the material we were highlighting. The space concept is like the Korean traditional partition. When you close it, there are more areas that are closed. But when you open it, it becomes one big space.

Club Nine Bridge' golf resort | Jeju Island
→ Emotions, p. 158

This is like the sections of music. Each section indicates a different kind of meaning. But when they are all connected, it is like one piece of music.

Dark and light is repeated to contrast the different sides of the building which make up the main whole. The landscape's welcoming feeling harmonises and mixes well with the welcoming feeling of the light. The idea was to create the feeling that you are approaching a place with something precious inside, and that you are happy to approach that place. The trees are at the same time guarding the visitor and welcoming him.

You mentioned the Korean tradition. Does this influence you?

I first want to discover what genuine Korean lighting could be. And then ask myself how can I globalise our Korean lighting? I've been working on overseas projects. I have a construction in Dubai, have worked on the Intercontinental Hotel in Angola, and I am also working on small projects in other countries, including China. I want Korean lighting to take its place in the world of global lighting. I found that the Arab emotion is quite similar to the Korean emotion. There's no boundary in lighting design. There's no border to sharing the value of lighting.

National Museum of Korea | Seoul

I think the breakthrough in Korean lighting came with the lighting I produced for the National Museum of Korea. The concept is a castle wall. The whole building's walls are 200-400 metres — very long indeed. And the layered walls are very thick, like a real castle's walls. In addition, it is next to the Han River and on lower land. The design was by a German company, and nobody had expected the lighting to be handled locally. But the project changed the concept of lighting design in Korea. At that time, we did not have lighting design and people did not know why they should pay for it. Through this project, we came to realise that lighting is important. In conservation terms, there should be no light. But this is also an artificial area, therefore we should not ignore the light. The question was: how to maintain a balance. And we should also tempt people. For this, natural and artificial light are important. Within the museum, there are indoor streets, like the back-streets of New York. So it was important that things be 'naturalised'. We wanted people to feel they were watching outside, not inside. And so for the artificial light, we had to create a feeling of 'natural sunlight'. And because of this, people said it was a landmark in lighting history.

Who or what inspires you?

My favourite composer is Beethoven – I often play his music. For imagination: Debussy and Paganini. I also do a lot of projects with students, getting them to analyse the fine details of a project in terms of light. For example, I get students to compare the differences between Rembrandt's and Monet/Manet's approach to light. People can have different emotions from the same piece of music. And the same is true of the impressions of light in an artist's painting. I also get inspiration from fashion, interiors, architecture magazines. And from movies and reading books. I used to design theatres.

And do you like any particular architects?

I like Louis I. Kahn and Tadao Ando. I can hear the music in the space they design.

Education	Environmental Design and Lighting Design
Design experience	16 years
Lighting association	KALD, KIIEE, IES, IALD
Field of work	Architecture, interior, landscape
Projects discussed	Club Nine Bridge golf resort | Jeju Island, | South Korea
	National Museum of Korea | Seoul | South Korea
Agency	Bitzro

Kiyoung Ko

Heayun Lee

For me, lighting is not about decoration, *says Haeyun Lee of Maverick's Lighting Design in Seoul, South Korea,* it is about making people feel comfortable. It is like meeting a girl: some you meet for just a moment, others you want to spend a lot of time with. The impact I want to achieve with my lighting is to make people want to stay a long, long time with it. I want to catch their attention and stop them feeling bored. I want them not to be able to take their eyes off it. And, at the same time, feel completely comfortable. This is also coupled to conveying the emotions and feelings that the architects are trying to transmit through their buildings. It is my job to understand the architect's objectives and intentions and to support them. My philosophy is that light is a soul of the space and the environment.

The environment?

I think the environment is crucially important to Korean architects. From a Western point of view, there seems little difference between China, Japan and Korea. But there are actually many differences. China, for example, is large scale and very proud, and this is reflected on the scale of its architecture. In Japan, they focus on how things look and try to make things blend in with the surroundings. In Korea, however, architects try to derive their concept from the environment. This applies to architecture, but also to lighting. It has the quality of naturalness.

Was it this that attracted you to lighting as a profession?
Not at first. I was originally an interior designer and worked for a
company called E-Land. At that time, lighting design was regarded as an
additional service provided by a lighting equipment company. Most
interior designers did not really take seriously the idea of lighting as a
means of entertaining people. The customers were also not very
sophisticated towards accepting lighting design. I didn't take lighting
design seriously either. I generally worked on very small projects, but
then I was given a relatively large project, and at that time I started to
become curious about lighting. In small-scale projects, you know the
principles. When I worked on the large-scale project, I tried to apply
the same rules, but I found the rules were quite different. The principles are very different. So I studied things for myself and finished the
project.

From that time onwards, I started to feel that lighting design was
important in my design work. At the time, I travelled a lot on business.
I went to Asia, Europe, Japan and China, and I gathered a lot of
information about lighting from those trips and passed it on to the
designers. Thanks to those trips, I learned that there was one special
lighting design education centre in the United States, so I resigned my
job and applied to study there. I saw a future in lighting at that time.
And I wanted to be the first one to know and share information about
lighting with people. I studied at Parsons School of Design in New York
from 1996 to 1998 and I then joined Brandston Partnership, which is a
very famous lighting company.

When I worked in the US, everything was so easy. Everything was well
organised and well located for the job. Everybody was responsible
for the work and it was kind of easy. But then I returned to Korea.
People here did not have the emotion that they need to pay towards
design work for lighting. It was a challenge. Nobody wanted to pay
for design lighting work because until then, people thought that the
design work was for free. They thought the lighting equipment
companies offered it for free. I first think about what the client wants
and what kind of emotions and feelings they want to convey. I don't
think about what kind of materials I have and how much profit I could
get from all the equipment I was planning. I always think about what
the client wants and the client benefits before I think about materials
and other things.

Heoyun Lee

Seoul Museum of Art | Seoul
→ *Contrast in colour, p. 100*

Haevichi Golf Course | Jeju Island

Can you tell us something about some of the projects you have undertaken?

When I returned to Korea, I undertook the lighting for the Seoul Museum of Art. It was located in what had formerly been a Supreme Court building, so it was a renovation project which had to retain all that had happened in the past. I think I was successful in retaining the balance between focus and the harmony of the other elements. It allows the viewers to feel the whole thing. I am also pleased that I have apparently created areas of comfort for the people; they now stay around much longer in the evening than before. For the exterior, I used a different lighting for the front and the back of the building. At the back, which is contemporary, I use cooler lighting. The front seems to be of stone, like an old building, so I tried to highlight that by using warmer tones.

I also undertook the lighting for the interior of the club house of the Haevichi Golf Course of Jeju Island. The background is the Halla mountain. I highlighted every element of the building, but this underscored the harmony of the whole building. The elements do not stand out individually, so all the other elements combine together well. I think the lighting is in line with the concept of Korean architecture. Here there is peace. A department store is very commercial, so that must be given a different impact. In the latter, I want to create movement, dynamic movement, which attracts people from the outside. Lighting helps attract people's attention.

From your experience, what makes Korean lighting special?

There are big differences between lighting in the West and lighting in Korea. The Western style is very direct and strict. There are differences between direct and indirect lighting. For example, when somebody is doing something at night: Western lighting is highlighting the room, the candlelight, that person's whole picture.

In Korean lighting, it is more like what you see through a window rather than through a door. It is a projection, without hearing or seeing the actual scene through the use of shadow. You can feel what the person is doing and what the situation is like. That is one characteristic of Korean lighting in comparison to Western lighting.

Where do you get your inspiration?

From nature and life. From the characteristics of the environment. Rather than highlight one aspect, I focus on how the light design goes well and harmonises with the whole. I use natural effects to make people feel a sense of comfort.

Education	Design and Lighting Design
Design experience	12 years
Lighting association	IES, KALD
Field of work	Public and private architecture, retail and urban
Projects discussed	Seoul Museum of Art | Seoul | South Korea (2001)
	Haevichi Club House | Jeju Island | South Korea (2007)
Agency	Mavericks Lighting Design

Heayun Lee

Ta-Wei Lin

○ Taipei | Taiwan

Whenever we start a project, I always give it a title, *says Ta-Wei Lin of CWI Lighting Design, Taipei.* That's the key point, the scenario. I always start with the vision, and only then move into the technical side. Most people think simulation and 3D-modeling is the best way to communicate a project. I think you should communicate with users about a scenario or idea. I make the concept short, for example, just a gold or white box.

I try to narrow everything down and crystallise our thinking into just a few words. Of course, we also have to care for the users, their environment, and we put that in our scenario as well. It's not easy because sometimes you could go too far or become too abstract. That's the challenge we face. You cannot tell real estate developers that you are going to turn their houses into museums. They want to hear something else. But then we have the simulations and 3D-modeling to back us up.

What is the basis for your philosophy?
It is largely based on the ideas of Howard Brandston. He sees the whole environment as a lighting environment. He doesn't concentrate on objects. He sees the whole city as a plan, no matter how big or small an individual project may be. He always looks at it from a total view. I worked with Brandston in New York for one and half years and then came back to Taiwan to open a branch office for Brandston here. We turned independent in 2002.

On the other hand, I think my approach is also different. After I finished school – I studied interior design – I initially worked with artists. I worked, for example, with Su-chen Hung as her assistant. She created an art work called Weeping Wall: she used a very narrow slide to project light on a wall. And then she allowed drops of water to fall on the slide so that light and shadow appeared on the wall. This was the first inspiration I got from an artist. Then Brandston, and later Chou Lien, gave me a broader view. They taught me to focus on the concept.

So you could say I have a mixed background. Lighting is one of the methods I use to communicate. I often ask myself a question: If I did not use light as a communication tool, what would I do then? Maybe I can become a movie director or novelist, writing with light or something. In fact, when I was at school, I nearly dropped out to become a movie director. There is a film by Fellini called Roma. His use of lighting in that film is very special. At the end of the film, a group of bikers ride through the city. There is no lighting, except from the motorcycles. We always think lighting should be fixed; but here, it was from a group of motorcyclists, so the light is moving. If there are no people there, why would they want to see?

Do you approach your projects in this way?

I see every project as a movie. I think about the users and the story you want to tell them. It's a performance. But it is also an attitude. I experienced a breakthrough when we undertook the Chung Tai Chan Monastery. I approached it as a lighting professional, but working on it taught me something different: how to look at the roots. In that project I had to give up a lot of the things I believed in. For example, they wanted a system with minimum light and easy to maintain. I thought a dimming system would be a good tool for such a large project as a temple. But they didn't want one. I didn't understand why. We spent weeks together with three interior designers trying to find a good lighting plan. In the end, the designers quit. But then I was invited to spend a 7-day retreat in the temple.

Chung Tai Chan Monastery | Nantou

I learned that they had a nun to turn the lights on and off. That was work for the nun, training. They had a rule, a guideline. I realised their practice was more important for the material or the physical feelings.

Users know what they want, but they do not know how to use light. Instead of educating them, I think we should discover their real need, rather than sending them information about lighting technology. Mr. Chou always says: 'Think about the light you don't need and get rid of it.' He says that we want to show clients what we can do, do something to wow them. But sometimes it is probably better to do much less.

How important is Asian culture to you?

I think there are two sides to Asian culture. One part is noisy, living in the street. The other is culture, Buddhism, Taoism. It is not easy to balance the noisy and colourful with the inner attitude.

But I realised that we have to be able to change to satisfy different needs, different clients. We cannot use one format or one way of thinking. The biggest challenge is to find what is most appropriate. We create shiny buildings and then may do something very low-key. My response is that the owners are different. You would treat a building in Shanghai differently. But also treat a building in the next street differently. Lighting can be anything. It all depends on the building and its environment.

In 2005, I gave a speech at Milan Euroluce. I spoke of culture and that Buddhism and Taoism are the most important influences. Buddhism is more inner, very simple, minimal. Taoism is broad, more colourful and elaborate, like Rococo.

Can you tell us about some projects?

Bei Gan Pedestrian Bridge | Yunlin
→ *Emotions, p. 180*

We did a project for lighting the Bei Gan Pedestrian Bridge. It is very simple: we light it up from below with high-pressure sodium. The architect designed the bridge in silver. But from a lighting and Feng Shui point of view, we suggested painting it red. The bridge is part of a temple. So we used four patterns, meaning blessed characters. So I wanted to use these themes, such as dragon and cloud. But there is a Chinese meaning to it – go higher and higher at each step, calm weather, sufficient rain, excellent breeze. These transform into lighting patterns inside.

I understand you particularly like the Chung Tai Chan Monastery project.

Chung Tai Chan Monastery | Nantou
→ *Brightness, p. 028*

I like it very much. I probably won't get another chance to do a project like this. There are three Buddhas in the monastery, and three Buddha halls. Three temples, actually – one on the first floor, one on the second and one on the third. And these represent the three phases of enlightenment. There are also three symbols, one for each phase, related to the sun. The first phase is the shadow of the sun, and so the first floor is dark, with dark stone. The second level is the sun itself, and so the second floor is all gold. And the third symbol is radiant light and so the top floor is white. On an even higher level, the sun is yourself and as the sun moves, the shadow changes. That shadow is your true self. But it changes, because you are yourself, but also the father of your daughter or the employee of your boss. When you reach the highest level, everything is white, because this is your pure self. They used these three phases of enlightenment to explain what type of light was needed. I actually used the same lighting technique throughout – incandescent light bulbs. Very simple. Yet they all look different. And this is because of the material. And also because the face of Buddha is important. They always want to show the Buddha smiling, so the location and angle of the light is critical. It was a strange experience working on this project. I would suggest something but I do not know whether they like it or not. And they would tell us to do something. Without any reason or comment. For example, they stipulated 300 lux, but I didn't understand why. When I visited, I realised they brought all the sutras to read. So they needed this light. So in the meditation room, they needed a bright light at the centre but dark in the corners. They need light to read the sutras but for meditation, they cannot have eye contact. So after reading the sutras, they turn off the light and walk around the room meditating. Incidentally, all the lighting fixtures are designed by the nuns. They have a lot of architectural background. There are professional monks and nuns in the temple. It was a break-through for me. I think I am more influenced by Taoism: it's always decoration. You have to show that a lighting designer has put something here and here. But there is no need to do that.

Being a lighting designer is almost like playing the psychologist. You have to listen to the architect. They always say: 'My building is not good enough and I want this and this or whatever.' And they start to talk and I would say: actually you need this. We are not talking about light. It is about how I feel and how you feel. This is the most important part: not discussing lighting, but about how he feels. Lighting is always about compromise at any given time. I hate to see myself as a beautician or a make-up artist. But somehow that is what I do. We always have to find the good part of the building. When you become a lighting designer you are very sensitive to bad lighting. But I think bad lighting can really inspire me. It is unbelievable.

Education	Architecture, Interior and Industrial Design
Design experience	20 years
Lighting association	PLDA, IESNA
Field of work	Interior, exterior lighting design, lighting Master Plan, light fixture design
Projects discussed	Bei Gan Pedestrian Bridge, Bei Gan	Yunlin	Taiwan (2004) Contemplation Walk, National Chiao Tung University	Hsin-Chu	Taiwan (2007) Chung Tai Chan Monastery	Nantou	Taiwan (2002)
Agency	CWI Lighting Design

Ta-Wei Lin

Mônica Lobo

I studied architecture, and after graduating I moved to São Paulo, *says lighting designer Mônica Lobo.* By chance I saw an ad in a newspaper for a position at Esther Stiller and Gilberto Franco lighting design consultants. It was my first job after graduating and, although it was to do with lighting, it felt as if I had rediscovered architecture. You analyse and interpret a building in the same three-dimensional way when you get involved in lighting design.

But you didn't stay in São Paulo, did you?

No. I have strong ties to Rio, that's where my roots are. I wanted to return, so I set up an office in Rio for the luminaire manufacture Lumini. I worked there until 1996, when I came to the conclusion that I would prefer to develop projects. I therefore joined the IES (Illuminating Engineering Society). I took part in trade exhibitions and international workshops. At one of the first exhibitions I attended I bought a lot of books, one of which was particularly fascinating: Light Design for Designers. It discussed everything from technical issues to design considerations, which at the time was very helpful. It was also a great way of learning from other experts in the field.

Lapa dos Mercadores
→ *Brightness, p. 026*

In 1999 we were asked to carry out some work on a church called Lapa dos Mercadores in downtown Rio. Very early on we became aware that lighting a church was very rich and symbolic, because you're dealing with something that is intricately linked to people's emotions and beliefs. There's also so much symbolism in the architecture of the church itself. So then you start seeing the building in a different way, from a more detached perspective, than if you were going as a believer. And you also think about the kind of process that people go through when they visit the church. We saw it as a kind of awakening.

An awakening? Of what?

When people enter, the first thing they experience is the ambience of the place as a whole. As they walk into the church they probably start noticing the decorations. Further on, the main focus is the altar in the nave, as well as the ceiling in the main chapel. So you are aware that you should guide them on this journey, as they discover one thing after the other, through the creative use of light. But at the same time you are also aware that there is a spiritual aspect… that people believe there's something bigger than them, so it's more than just architecture.

Michael F. Rohde

I mean, if you are inviting somebody to enter the building, you have to design the story further so that in each corner of the building you have the feeling of 'Ah, this is something I would like to explore'.

Does this mean that you would take a different approach for, say, a church than you would for an office or shop?
Actually, no matter what we're doing, we always try to define the essence of the project. We then work out how to translate that into something intangible, which is light. I really think that lighting has the power to reveal that essence. It makes the intangible tangible. That's why I think that we have a huge responsibility in our hands when we work with lighting.

One of the most attractive things about lighting design projects is that you are constantly facing new challenges. Whether that means coming up with innovative ways of solving problems or applying new technology, nothing ever stays the same.

It's funny, because after the Lapa project, I thought: 'Hey, it's too simple!' It felt like the light had always been there. I was asking myself why I hadn't put more drama into it, more colour, more contrast… but then I went to have another look and thought it was fine, everything was in the right proportion after all.

Lapa's not the only church project you've been involved with, is it?
That's right. We carried out a project on an old cathedral in Rio, the Sé, which was being renovated to celebrate the 200th anniversary of the (Portuguese) royal family arriving in Brazil. The first design we came up with for the façade was really audacious. There was a lot of lighting, plenty of effects; everything was a bit over the top – possibly because it was part of such a big event. But then, step by step, we simplified our approach. And I'm happy with the end result. We worked together closely with the city government to come up with something suitable for this historical building.

Were there any special considerations in this project?
Part of the church backs onto a very narrow street, in downtown Rio, called the Rua Sete de Setembro. The façade has several small windows, repeated in a neo-classical style, and we lit each one to emphasise the transparency of the balustrade. We also then had to illuminate the entire façade to make the overall impression softer.

Mônica Lobo

But because the street was so narrow there is no possibility of getting a good perspective on the huge façade. We therefore came to the conclusion that we should use the street lighting lampposts to help light up the front of the church. For this we used a really old technique, prismatic glass, which makes the light go whatever way you want; downwards, upwards, whatever. So the lampposts illuminate both the street and the façade. It's interesting because there's another façade of the church that has a large square in front of it, so you do get the wide perspective on it. We therefore treated that one differently, more in a classical, monumental building kind of way.

What kind of emotions did this project evoke?
The important thing is the atmosphere in the building. In this example, a church, it's all about contemplation, tranquillity, respect…

São Francisco de Assis Church | Pampulha
→ Brightness, p. 036

We were also invited to light another church – Igreja de São Francisco de Assis da Pampulha. Personally, I felt quite emotional because I was illuminating a masterpiece created by Oscar Niemeyer, who was a fabulous architect. Then I discovered there was even more heritage in this tiny church; Paulo Verneck was also involved, and there's a panel by Portinari. The gardens were designed by Burle Marx. The whole place is a treasure. The people of Belo Horizonte really love it. So we really felt the responsibility.

Basically we worked out how to light the church through using computer renderings. It was such an unusual shape – with so many curved shells – that our first instinct was to highlight these curves. We used light coming upwards from the floor to do this. We also mounted projectors on the existing lampposts. We used halogen lamps inside, and installed luminaires in the floor to provide complementary light. This was part of a larger renovation project, and when the church was finished the lighting gave everyone a surprising new view on it. It was like a kind of rebirth.

Hotel Fasano | Rio de Janeiro
Architect: Philippe Starck

A contemporary project like Hotel Fasano no doubt presents a different set of challenges…
The thing is, you always have to try to evoke an ambience that is appropriate to the kind of public that will be using the space. In the case of Hotel Fasano, the 'cool' people who go there want to feel they're in a really special place, a place that is, let's say… HIP.

The architect – Philippe Starck – saw this space in a movie-like way. He made the sketches like a storyboard: you know, where you draft the scene exactly the way you want to have it filmed. The drawings gave us a clear idea of what we had to do: everything had to be fancy... singular... to have a differentiated design. Nothing could be simple. It had to produce that 'Wow' effect.

Have you a particular way of working with coloured light?
We often use coloured lights to illuminate surfaces that are themselves already coloured, because this creates a greater depth, a sense of saturation. There is an element of fantasy in this. For instance, if you have a skylight in a shopping mall you can emphasise the glazing by adding some blue light. You could imagine doing the same thing, obviously using different colour lighting, if you wanted to emphasise moonlight.

Do you draw inspiration from different regions, or would you consider yourself very much a South American lighting designer?
I was heavily influenced by Americans in the beginning. I think they are very professional, and they have a vision of both the artistic and technical aspects of working with lighting. They are very businesslike. With the Europeans I have observed and learned the poetic and inspirational approach. At the end trying to produce good lighting has no boundaries. We always learn, are influenced and follow internal an external references.

What other areas influence you?
Cinema – I always pay attention to the lighting when I see a movie. Ridley Scott is a director I very much admire because of what he does with lighting. Tim Burton is another one. With him it almost seems like the lighting is actually another character.

Education	Architect
Design experience	22 years
Lighting association	AsBAI, IES
Field of work	Architectural Lighting Design
Projects discussed	Nossa Senhora da Lapa dos Mercadores Church | Rio de Janeiro | Brazil (1997)
	Nossa Senhora do Carmo da Antiga Sé | Rio de Janeiro | Brazil (2008)
	Hotel Fasano | Rio de Janeiro | Brazil (2007)
	Matriz de Santo Antônio Church | Tiradentes | Brazil (2002)
	São Francisco de Assis Church | Pampulha, | Brazil (2005)
	Centro Comercial Los Moliños | Medellin | Colombia (2005)
Agency	LD Studio

Mônica Lobo

Luis Lozoya

Lighting is the only thing in architecture that is intangible, *says Luis Lozoya, of Mexico City-based lighting company Luz + Form.* The rest of the elements are material, you can touch them, feel them, smell them; light is not material, yet it is the element of architecture that modifies the perception of spaces, makes them smaller, larger, warmer, colder. And that ability to modify space, or modify the perception people have of space, is what so attracts me to lighting.

Was this something you always felt?
The first official project I did was the lighting for a discotheque in the Hotel Nikko here in Mexico City. Basically I was given a black box and I could paint it in different colours, make it bright or opaque. And I could change things instantly. Yes, it was the ability to modify space with light that attracted me right from the start.

Did you study lighting?
You know, lighting in Mexico is a very young profession. Until recently, it was largely handled by companies who manufactured the fittings. They seemed more interested in selling their products than under-standing the power of successful lighting. I went to work and study in the States and Europe and then the States again. I worked mainly with lighting designers and those in the States taught me that lighting is really made up of two parts: there's the subjective part where you dream and then the objective part where you try to put your dream into reality. These designers really inspired me. I finally returned to Mexico and I started the company in 1994. We initiated a trend that was completely alien at the time: we handled projects rather than selling lighting equipment. It was very exceptional for an architect to pay somebody else to tell him what sort of lighting he needed and how it should work.

What about working with interior designers?

I think most interior designers have a great ability to perceive space.
They are normally in charge of the project and want to communicate
a sensation about the architectural space. Often their concept includes
ideas about lighting. I learned a lot from them. And now I try to
contribute to that design or lighting concept.

I like to think of the company as a workshop, a sort of lab. We consider ourselves nothing more than light craftsmen. The architecture is
always the foundation for our work and that should define the lighting
solution. When we receive a plan from an architect it will tell us – if it
is a good plan – what the project requires, what the intentions of the
architect are in terms of space and formal function. Then it is for us to
formally understand the space. How does it work? What does it look
like? What materials are used? And then we take a decision, generally
in consultation with the architect, about which space element should
be emphasised, which should be disguised, what we should do to
modify visual perception. That defines the language of the project.
Each project is, of course, different and we try not to repeat ourselves;
we try to innovate every time and achieve a harmony between the
architecture and the lighting.

Casa Fifield | Nayarit
→ *Direction, p. 148*

Any project is the sum of many talents – the architect, the engineers,
the decorators. For the Nikko disco, the architects were Japanese, the
designers Mexican, and the engineers American. Our meetings were
interesting: three languages, three ideologies, three different ways of
thinking. But it was the way we channelled all this into the final project
that made it so fascinating.

Could you tell us something about a more recent project?

My projects are my children – I love them all, even the ugly ones. But
one of our recent projects was in Japan, the Kin Chi Cho project,
meaning the golden floor. It is an area of Tokyo with textile factories, so
we wanted to play with the idea of textiles. We had an enormous floor
which we lit in one colour. But we made the floor pressure-sensitive.
Every time somebody walks across the floor, the sensors produce a
thread of colour, a trace of light. As more people move across the
floor, the lighting threads create something almost like knitting. We also
produced a bridge, again with the idea of textile and fashion in mind.
When somebody crosses the bridge, the electronic eyes we installed in
it allow the lights to follow that person, whichever direction they move;
the bridge becomes a fashion catwalk.

Luis Lozoya

Casa Helfet | Nayarit
→ Direction, p. 148

A very different project was the house we did in Panama. A beautiful house on the beach. The owner said he wanted a house that wasn't conventional. At the rear there is a patio and, in consultation with the architect, we constructed a way of flooding it. At night, the patio floods with water and lights come from the drains in the walls and when it is illuminated it creates the impression that the columns and all the elements of the architecture are somehow merged into one.

A mirror of water?

Yes, exactly. It was about creating something unusual. The architect thought about materials, spaces, details. And lighting played a very important role. Of course, there was also the technical problem of having to be able to drain the patio whenever the owner wanted to use it. But the effect is stunning. Once the client got over the initial shock, he finally loved it.

It sounds almost emotional.

It was the emotional aspect of lighting that I found initially appealing. The artistic part. But I realised that I would need to learn to solve the technical problems if I wanted to meet the expectations I created. Emotion, though, is still very important. I think it is because of the way I perceive architecture. For me, it is a gut feeling rather than a head feeling. And I think that is appearing more frequently in the work we are doing. I think that every space, both interior and exterior, generates, like music, its own notes. Lighting can play those notes or reinforce them, and turn the space into a symphony.

Gustavo Avilés
You do not design light, you compose, hide, remove, introduce it. For me, light is deeply related to music.

Ray Chen
For example, when you listen to music, a higher volume doesn't necessarily guarantee good sound. This is the same with lighting.

Is the same true of urban lighting?

I think we have to be very careful there. We must not abuse things, particularly when we use colour. I think colour in architectural projects should arise from a clear intention and must reflect a specific logic in communicating an emotion or an architectural concept. I think we are in danger of losing control because coloured fittings are now becoming so widely available.

Another element we must be careful with is the urban tones. I think lighting plays an important role in cities, not least in making us feel like human beings. But there are so many possibilities in lighting that I believe we must show considerable self control and not go over the limit. A focal point can be great, it can catch people's attention, but it can also turn against the design of the project. People must understand the sensation that a city wishes to communicate.

Luis Lozoya

312

If you have an important cultural heritage, important buildings, important churches, you must be very careful how you light them within an urban reference.

When you think of light, what is the image that comes into your mind?
When I became fully aware of the implications of light, I was struck by the use of light in art. The paintings of Joshua Klum with the candles lighting the scene. And the use of light and shade in paintings by Carabollo. These are so dramatic that they create an emotion.

San Josemaría Escrivá
Iglesia | Mexico City

But for me, light will always mean the candle. That is what I think of. It has been the lighting tool of mankind for thousands of years. Today, I specialise in artificial light; but in my mind, in my sub-conscious, light still means the candle.

Education	**Architect**
Design experience	**22 years**
Lighting association	**DIM, IES**
Field of work	**Hotel and resorts, corporate, shopping malls, residential**
Projects discussed	**Casa Helfet, Punta Mita	Nayarit	México**
	**Casa Fifield, Punta Mita	Nayarit	México**
	**Iglesia Santa Fe, Santa Fé	Mexico City	México**
	**Kin Chi Cho shopping mall	Tokyo	Japan**
Agency	**Luz + Form**

Luis Lozoya

Martin Lupton

For me, architectural lighting is the perfect balance between science and art *says Martin Lupton.* What we do can very often be artistic, but it is not art. Over the last few years we have been collaborating a lot with artists and they bring a real conceptual, contextual depth to the work; we often cannot achieve such depths in commercial activities due to the timescales involved. But I strongly believe that our work must be based on a strong conceptual basis. There must be a reason for doing what we do – something that extends beyond simply creating something that looks good.

Was this what attracted you to lighting?
Definitely, being involved in a creative concept process with a team of people is one of the most rewarding experiences you can have. In fact the human aspect of lighting on the whole is very important to me. One of the reasons for that is the ability to promote social interaction. You can change the feel of a place with light. You can, in fact, change it from a place where people don't want to be into a space where people are happy to come out and talk to other people, to socialise and interact. I originally wanted to be an architect, but when my faith in my drawing skills wavered I decided, instead, to take a course in Environmental Engineering. It concentrated more on what happens inside buildings, how to make them work for the people who occupied them; it was, I suppose, creative problem-solving. At the end of that course, I had the chance to take a Ph.D in lighting, which was the start of my awareness of light and lighting and design, and I went straight from academia into a light and design consultancy.

You are now very much involved in the Professional Lighting Designers Association.
Yes. I originally joined PLDA because I really believe in the profession we work in and I liked the message that they were promoting – establishing the profession of lighting design with a big emphasis on education. Perhaps the best example of this is the week-long workshop we hold annually in the Swedish city of Alingsas. Sixty students are divided up among six designers from different backgrounds and to-gether they work on a site chosen by the designer concerned. It is all about learning the concept process. The designer doesn't make the design, but acts as mentor and helps them through the whole concept process, hopefully making sure they avoid making too many big mistakes.

It was the experience of one of these workshops in Sweden that really inspired me to become even more involved with PLDA. I worked with 9 students in an apple orchard attached to a small house – essentially a private garden. On the first evening, I took them into the garden and had them test various fittings and look at some effects. I wanted them to understand that pointing light at things is not the same as a concept. While we were out there playing with our lights, a little girl came into the garden and started running through the beams of light. She was having a great time, laughing her head off. Some of the students took photos and one even made a video.

Apple Tree Garden
PLDA Workshop | Alingsås
→ Emotions, p. 172

We went back inside around midnight and I asked them what ideas they had. They started throwing suggestions around, but then I asked them to play back the video clip of the little girl enjoying her-self and suggested that this could provide some inspiration. And things just went from there. They created a fairytale land for this little girl. It was incredibly conceptual. It was all about the harsh outside world and this fairytale world where the little girl could play.

I've seen photographs – it was pretty magical.
Yes, it was. We also had a little trick up our sleeves: it was October, so the ground was covered with apples. We buried some fibre optics in the ground and stuffed them into apples, and they just glowed. It was just like a fairytale – and I think people saw it for the emotion that it had.

On that level, I see the emotion of light as something theatrically artistic. But you must also consider emotion in a social context. Somebody once told me how proud they were of a scheme they had just completed. It was really very simple – they had just improved the lighting along the edge of a run-down stretch of canal. But because of the lighting, mothers would now take their children down there, because it was a shortcut on their way home. The lighting had created a place where people would now go – whereas before they would not have dared. This is the power of light to transform things socially.

It can, in a sense, be profoundly optimistic, because it actually makes a difference to people's lives.
Yes, but rather than a big emotional rush, you're actually affecting them in a very small way. But it affects them every single day of their lives, because you've created a space that they now go into and have transformed an area that they would otherwise have avoided. I think that this social side of lighting is not being addressed to the full.

I suppose you actually have functional lighting – where you need to be able to see so that you don't get mugged – and there's a different kind of lighting where you try to create some kind of emotion.
It's about promoting social interaction. You could take a space, for example, and simply put the same amount of light all over it, flood-light it like a football field and people would hurry through it. But you could also create areas of interest and pockets of intimacy where people can stop and sit and talk to each other. In such a situation, light does not exist by itself, but must be supported by a strong landscape concept, a strong architectural concept.

Can you talk about a project you have done that illustrates this?
We were recently involved in exterior lighting for a retail urban regeneration project in the centre of Exeter: a new block with re-tail spaces on the ground floor and residential and offices above. The space is actually active, because people live there and restaurants and bars stay open longer. It's an occupied city centre. We brought our experience with similar projects to this one and a lot of what we did was building the lighting into the buildings and letting the light come out in a low-key soft way, and then having accentuated areas.

Princess Hay | Exeter
Architects: Chapman Taylor, Panther Hudspith, Wilkinson Eyre

So having the light coming up from the interior of the buildings and using that to light up the more public spaces.

Yes. And this produces patterns of light, shadows and shapes, some of which are like a graphic design language. We have done that in a couple of schemes recently, using the light fittings to light the space and also using the lit feature as a graphical key. It not only accentuates the architecture, it also creates a rhythm in the space. It is not bland uniformity. Under one of the canopies in Exeter you have what we call a bar code. We used simple linear fittings but we've adjusted the space between them so that it appears like a bar code. It lights up the street but when you look at it, you've got this interesting rhythm of light fittings that doesn't really relate to the architectural rhythm of the building but adds interest to the view and draws your eye into the space.

Roger Narboni
The very essence of working with light is the relationship with people, with what they feel.

Ulrike Brandi
Lighting is not just for the building, or for somebody's ego. It's not to make the building more commercial. It's a social task.

And is there a mood, an emotion, you are trying to achieve?

I suppose we are trying to make things intriguing but in some cases also add a social contact. We want people to look and think about what is there so that it sticks in their minds but we also like to try and make sure people the people who 'own' the space understand the logic and have the knowledge of the concept that they can share. We're also looking at using bar codes in another project we are currently developing. There is a Victorian stone viaduct which runs through the centre of Birmingham. We have developed a design based on bar codes – vertical lines of light and shadow. Rather than continuously lighting the viaduct, we have created a horizontal line of vertical lines. The spacing and colour of the lines is determined by translating a word into a bar code and we plan to collect the words from the local community. Each vertical bar code line is connected to an individual wind turbine, so that when the wind blows the bar code becomes brighter. It will make the viaduct come alive in different ways as the light reacts to the urban wind patterns. When a train passes, the turbulence will make the turbines spin faster and the bar codes will also respond kinetically to the passing of the train.

Eastside Viaduct | Birmingham

So you're not just lighting the viaduct, you are adding fun to it.

Yes, we're drawing attention to the viaduct and saying: take a new look at this amazing Victorian engineering.

Westminster Academy | London
→ *Emotions, p. 154*

You often talk of natural lighting design.
Do you mean large windows?

Designing for natural light is much more that just big windows.
I think I can best illustrate that with another project –
a school in Westminster. When we first met the architects we
showed them some research on how daylight can improve the
performance of students in schools and they reacted in a very
positive way and daylight become a high priority for the project.
However, designing for natural light is not a stand-alone activity –
it is always a series of compromises with other environmental
conditions. Big windows mean you lose more heat from the building
in the winter and in the summer sunlight provides thermal gain, so
it is a balancing act to get good daylight conditions. In this project
we also influenced the roof design and suggested one that was completely glazed, but which has a series of vertical louvers which
maximises the daylight coming in. It also allows sunlight at certain
times of the day.

For me sunlight is definitely the most emotionally charged type of light.
Sunlight is happiness, don't you think? When the darkness of night
turns into day, there is a big evolutionary association with positive
change. It's morning, a new day. All that is so emotional in light is born
out of evolution and ingrained within our psyche. If you ask me what
the best type of light is, I would say natural light or firelight. Such
primitive light generates strong emotional responses. Look at the great
cathedrals or historic buildings: you walk in and the space is dramatically lit by shafts of sunlight through stained glass or even simply
sunlight filtering through dusty windows. It's an immediate emotional
moment. The strength of the light is solidified by the dust particles in
the air and the reaction is always emotional.

Education	Environmental engineering and lighting
Design experience	18 years
Lighting association	PLDA
Field of work	Indoor and outdoor, architectural space
Projects discussed	PLDA Workshop, industrial façade and garden | Alingsås |
	Sweden (2004)
	Princess Hay | Exeter | UK (2006)
	Eastside Viaduct | Birmingham | UK (design in 2007)
	Westminster Academy | London | UK (2007)
Agency	Light Collective | UK

Martin Lupton

Paul Marantz

We're a lighting design firm, and at least 90% of our work relates to architectural lighting for new projects or for restoration and renovation projects, *explains New York-based lighting designer Paul Marantz.* We do a lot of retail projects, and recently retail has become theatre. High-end retail, in particular, is strictly theatre. And it's probably closer to our roots than anything else because it's all about show business.

What, in your opinion, are the key factors in lighting design?
First of all, there has to be a single architectural vision. The way the project looks is really communicated by the light, so light is in effect the medium through which architecture communicates. Lighting in the theatre has traditionally been more creative than in architecture because the theatre is all about illusion and changeability.

How did you get into lighting design in the first place?
When I was about eight years old, I got involved in a puppet and marionette activity and I was immediately drawn to the scenographic elements of it. What attracted me was the idea of creating a world separate from the real world. I love the fact that light is so flexible and mobile. I mean, architecture is heavy stuff and it's static. Most stuff that is corporeal is static. Light is not static. It can change from one second to the next. Natural light teaches us just how variable light can be. Electric lighting offers the greatest potential for kinetics and change. By changing the light you can make a space feel different. If you turn on the light when it gets dark in the evening, everything changes, so you can reinvent your environment. For me it's about control: controlling what you see and what you don't. You have to work with both light and darkness because light is only revealed by dark. Light and shadow are all part of the toolkit.

What do you get out of being a lighting designer?
Well, aside from making a living, I get a lot of satisfaction from finding a way to become one with the architect on some spiritual or at least intellectual level, and achieving a result that I could never have imagined at the outset. And it feels great when you get it right. Listen, every time you come up with something new, you know you're still alive.

What kind of emotions do you want to convey through your architectural lighting?

That's hard to say, because I don't approach emotion as a fixed concept. Emotion is a human response. Light isn't an emotion. Architecture isn't an emotion. You have to ask yourself: 'What experience should the building give the viewer?' Let's say we were engaged to design a police station. You have to think what the aim, the ambition, of this police station is. It should probably convey the rule of law, authority, stability – all those things that government is supposed to help you with. You also have to think about where the police station is going to be.

So you have to consider regional differences and cultural differences?

Yes, for example if it is in California it could be relaxed, a nice building with no hard-edged materials. You look at all these aspects and try to condense the ideas you want to convey. Again, it's the architecture that will convey it, and the lighting that helps the architecture to do that.

How do cultural differences affect the lighting?

To give you an example – one of the things lighting designers think about is glare. Glare interferes with what you're seeing, so we think we have to prevent it. In Japan, however, they use bare fluorescent lamps because this is more efficient. That's a cultural difference. Is it just because this is the cheapest way or does glare really not bother them? I don't know. Regrettably, cultural differences are starting to fade, what with TV, movies and the Internet. Nowadays things look remarkably similar wherever you go.

When you did the lighting for Richard Meier's Jubilee church in Rome, Italy, what emotion were you trying to convey, and how did you go about achieving this?

It is based on three identical shells separated by glass and is lit purely by natural light during the daytime. We wanted to make it warm and inviting at night. Most churches are more opaque, but this one is supposed to be more transparent. So we had to make it warm, inviting, soft. As in any other building, here the light comes in through the openings, and at night it comes out of the openings. This makes it more welcoming and inviting at night than in the daytime. We didn't have to work very hard to achieve this because the building was already telling the story. We just had to find the best way, and this was to light the surfaces of the three stone walls. At night a building is basically a lantern. The way you design the lantern determines whether the building welcomes people or tells them to stay away.

Susanna Antico
Sometimes, if we are in the town centre we don't know where we are, and I think this is really bad. In this sense, I am against some kind of globalisation.

Dolly & Anil Valia
Globalisation means there is more interaction between the various countries and cultures, giving rise to the same modern architecture, so there should be no difference in terms of lighting parameters.

Jubilee Church | Rome
→ *Direction, p. 134*

Paul Marantz

You say it was easy, but you don't see a single source from the exterior.

That's true, there are hardly any sources in the church. The only thing we did was to light the walls. There were a few little things in the roof that you can see, but almost all the lighting is at the bottom and that's what makes it really glow. You know, good architecture tells you how to light it, how to think about it. The important thing is to get the essential idea down on paper.

Postcards – The Staten Island September 11th Memorial | New York
→ *Emotions, p. 184*

We also worked on the Postcards project, which is the 9/11 memorial on Staten Island and probably the most emotional thing we've ever done. It shows silhouettes of every person on Staten Island who was killed in the World Trade Center disaster, and it is supposed to represent two postcards that may have been sent to loved ones. We lit it from the ground because it is just these two wing-like shapes that glow.

What does lighting it from the ground do?

Well, it anchors it… If you stand between the two 'postcards' and look across the harbour you see where the Twin Towers once stood, so it was very much about framing that view. The mood we wanted to create was one of simplicity and quiet. If you come to this kind of monument you don't want something that competes with your own emotional process. The lighting had to be unobtrusive so it didn't interfere. We achieved this by keeping things simple. There is no colour, it's all white. And nothing moves, nothing changes. So it creates a very quiet, simple, minimalist atmosphere.

Let's talk for a moment about colour and light.

Colour and light can be difficult, but you look to nature for instruction. Nature does colour and lighting, but it does it in a very sophisticated way. And in nature this is connected with the atmosphere, the time of day, the weather conditions or the season. These all affect the colour of natural light. In architectural lighting, the dilemma is to find a rationale for the use of colour.

Ulrike Brandi
I'm glad we found that inspiration in the surroundings.

Let me give you an example. We did a project in Columbus, Ohio – the beautiful science museum by Arata Isozaki, the Japanese architect. It is very long, narrow and symmetrical, with an upright cylinder in the middle. There is a theory in impressionist art that you must paint shadows in purples because in nature shadows are always filled with light and this light is from low in the horizon. It's a cooler colour. So we made the entrance, where there's this cylinder, bold and bright.

The building is entirely opaque and we decided to let the ends of it evoke shadow at night, so it is lit in a rich indigo blue at either end and there is virtually no other lighting. The way we've used colour here really focuses the eye in the middle. The colour doesn't change and the light didn't have to be white because this would have made the building look too big – it is about three blocks long! So this was a solution that used colour for a specific, clear reason.

We've also just finished designing the lighting for Suzhou Museum in China. As you know, all the great Chinese houses are built around gardens and these have water, trees and things like that. This was purely about serenity. Here you have a kind of stylised, idealised relationship with nature. So we worked very hard to make this as simple and quiet as possible. One thing good lighting designers are supposed to know is when to stop. It's a question of how little do you have to do to tell the story!

Suzhou Museum | Suzhou
Architect: I.M. Pei

So how did you convey serenity through the lighting?
Through reduction and simplification. By lighting only a specific sculptural tree, a strand of bamboo, we connected the various elements of natural plant material to form a sort of basis. We had one object in the middle – the garden pavilion – and the museum around it. There are tiny little lights under the water that cast the gentlest of lights on the building. That's all that's required – so that's all you do.

Education	Architecture, Architectural lighting
Design experience	52 years
Lighting association	FIALD, IESNA, LC
Field of work	Architectural lighting
Projects discussed	Jubilee Church (Dio Padre Misericordioso)	Rome	Italy (2003)
	Postcards – The Staten Island September 11th Memorial	Staten Island	New York	USA (2004)
	Ohio Center of Science & Industry (COSI)	Columbus	Ohio, USA (1999)
	Suzhou Museum	Suzhou	China (2007)
Agency	Fisher Marantz Stone (FMS)

Kaoru Mende

Lighting designers have to learn from natural light, *says Kaoru Mende of Lighting Planners Associates based in Tokyo and Singapore.* Every important aspect, every important emotional scene is hidden in natural lighting – daylight or light from a fire. I teach students and the first assignment I give them is to observe natural light, to collect beautiful natural light scenes. I think today, in the 21st century, natural light should play a very important role. It is a very challenging goal for architectural lighting. We also have to learn how to create comfortable lighting using natural light. This is very important for lighting designers: how to apply the latest advance in technology to human life. If we do not do that, technology is just technology. I hope that we, as human beings, never forget to use natural light or the light of a candle.

Paul Marantz
Natural light teaches us just how variable light can be.

Hiroyasu Shoji
I thought that the change of natural light is the strongest power source to touch and move the hearts of people.

Can you explain your philosophy concerning architectural lighting?
Lighting must be interpreted or incorporated into the space that the architect wants to express. It should be used to complement the environment, to bring out the space. Architectural lighting design is not about the big statement, but about expressing feelings. Those feelings may be the result of the statement, but lighting is not an artistic gesture in itself. I always try to emphasise the architecture with light, to make the architecture appear much more elegant at night. Sometimes lighting seems to deny that architecture can be beautiful during the day; the lighting transforms it into something it never is in daylight.

Were you inspired by specific architects?
I studied Industrial and Environmental Design in Tokyo. I tried to become an environmental designer, but nobody knew what that was! My teacher had planted an idea in my head when he suggested that I try to find a job with Yamagiwa, the lighting manufacturer. At that time – this was 1978 – they had laboratories which were developing the idea of lighting design. And this was my first step towards getting started in architecture lighting design. At the time, I was not really interested in lighting design; to me, it seemed all about the shape of the lighting fixture or designing a decorative chandelier. I do not think lighting is about the shape of fixtures. I decided I wanted to concen-

trate on designing light itself. My first task had nothing to do with designing light; it was all about publishing a very beautiful book – an application manual of architectural lighting. It was about the importance of lighting design for people. I subsequently discovered I was not the first person interested in that direction, and I got in touch with my lighting ancestors, Mr Edison Price, Mr Claude Engle, and Mr Paul Marantz, all of whom were living in New York or Washington, DC. These three gentlemen are very important people who led me to architectural design. I learnt so many things: how to cooperate with architects; how to achieve some lighting atmosphere without exposing the lighting. We architectural lighting designers want to create a beautiful atmosphere without the lighting sources being visible. We try to make the architecture into a huge piece of art, without installing any decorative lights. It is sometimes hard to find the right lighting materials. And, of course, we also need ambitious architects who are willing to cooperate with the lighting designer.

You know, when I started, I tried to use other words to convey the profession – luminous environment. I had studied many aspects of lighting, including theatre lighting techniques. I met Tadao Ando and Toyo Ito, very capable architects, and also Mr Isozakii and Mr Maki of a slightly older generation. They are special people who concentrate purely on light.

Are you able to influence architects?
It depends on the architect or the project. Sometimes Toyo Ito has an original initial idea about the lighting – an ambition, just for the image – and sometimes just needs some technical assistance. Most of the capable architects ask me to cooperate as early as possible. This means that architecture lighting design is not just about lighting fixtures location or some final lighting adjustment. We collaborate, talk with architects about the materials to be used. Architectural material is very important, and equally important for the lighting material. They ask me about colouring, how to allow the material to be seen nicely or to change nicely during the day and at night. I remember collaborating with Toyo Ito some 20 years ago regarding the project of 'Tower of Wind'. He had some images in his mind. He likes to change the atmosphere completely at night. I suggested not one scene but several, and that these should be operated by small computers and sensors of mind and sound. So this was cooperation based on exchanging ideas. Tadao Ando, on the other hand, sometimes never said what he had in mind and simply asked me to give him some images of what the night scene could be.

Tower of Wind | Kanagawa
Architect: Toyo Ito

Kaoru Mende

National Peace Memorial
Hall | Nagasaki
→ Dynamics in brightness, p. 064

Lighting Masterplan for Singapore's
City Centre

Can you tell us something about a specific project?
The lighting design for the Nagasaki National Peace Memorial Hall
for all the victims of the atomic bomb was a very emotional project.
More than 70,000 people were killed by that single bomb. The
architect wanted to create a place of prayer. The lighting is intentionally
very mysterious, like the wind blowing flames. I needed to make a
strong impact so that people would know what the tiny lights signify:
the dead people.

You also work in Singapore.
We were engaged to develop the master lighting plan for the city
centre. When we started the project, we were not sure about the
cultural influences, but we did understand the climatic conditions, the
geography, and the fact that Singapore is a multi-racial culture. The
master plan was founded on five concepts: comfortable tropical
climate, light and shadow, enhancement of lush greenery, the melting-
pot culture and the enhancement of the waterscape. We proposed
a warm light at street level and at the top of the skyscrapers we introduced a must higher colour temperature, such as white or blue white,
to reflect the tropical cosmopolitan culture.

**Your use of various colour temperatures of white is different
when compared to other cities such as Hong Kong or
Shanghai, which have lots of colour.**
Each city has a different latitude and climate. I recently visited Copenhagen. They never use such white light there; the colours are much
warmer. In this tropical city, people like to have whites or blue whites.
Tokyo or Osaka has a much whiter landscape than Paris, New York
or London. Colour temperature is largely based on climate. I don't
know why the Japanese like to have white light while Europeans and
Americans like to have warmer colours. Today's technology can
achieve both warm colour and brightness. We wanted to reveal the
characteristics of Singapore and not imitate Paris or Tokyo. Different
cities have different feelings. People in Osaka have slightly different
feelings or images to those in Singapore or Paris.
It is very important to find out what is the original character of the
light. Each city has to have some original character of light.

**Can you explain a little further the difference in character
between cities in terms of lighting?**
Japanese lighting is completely different from French or English light.
The architecture, design, climate and history are different. In Japan,
we didn't have lighting from the ceiling and we always have daylight

coming in from the side. Architectural lighting always comes from the side, sometimes hitting the ground and reflecting upwards. This is the big difference between Japan and Europe. And Japan is also different from Korea and China. In China, they use many light sources; in Japan we like just one light source or one shadow – very simple. In China they put lights everywhere. In Korea, they make similar use of rice paper, but their's is more like board and not transparent. In Japan we are more interested in not having a strong contrast between light and shadows.

Can you explain this further?
Basically there is sunlight. If you turn on a light – a candle or a bulb – you will have daylight penetration alongside these lights. The beautiful shadows should be located together. In the 20th century, we tried to make everything even, without shadow. Nowadays, shadow or dark-ness is important to allow us to feel bright images or even the light itself. We very often do not design light alone, but draw beautiful shadows as well. We now want to have contrast between beautiful light and shadow. We no longer want to keep everything even. Year by year, people are coming to understand the importance of light. Not only in terms of quantity, but also in quality. Today, lighting design can be imitated so easily. So we must develop more sophisticated and advanced design ideas. And for this the lighting industry should be much closer to the user.

Howard Brandston
It is very important
to see shadows but you
have to be careful how
you control them.

Vannapa Pimviriyakul
Many times, we blend
shadows into our design.

Education	Industrial and Environmental Design
Design experience	32 years
Lighting association	IES, IALD
Field of work	Architectural, Urban, Commercial to Residence
Projects discussed	Tower of Wind, Kanagawa, Japan (1986)
	Nagasaki National Peace Memorial Hall for the Atomic Bomb Victims | Nagasaki | Japan (2003)
	Lighting Masterplan for Singapore's City Centre | Singapore (2006)
Agency	Lighting Planners Associates (LPA)

Kaoru Mende

Francois Migeon

My vision of light is that it is not a continuity of daylight, *says Francois Migeon, partner in the French-based design group Grandeur Nature and 8'18".* Nocturnal light should give a building a different aspect than the one it has during the day. I am given an architectural backdrop on which I am free to use light. I have the freedom to disagree, to hold a prejudice against the medium I have been given. It is a hand-to-hand fight with the building. I work a great deal with colour and the way I use it is, I believe, rather exclusive to me. I work very little with primary colours; I prefer secondary colours, shaded whites, colours blends, combinations of colour. Using blends gives us more freedom to give the building its own unique colour. And there is also the movement of light. I think that's another aspect very specific to us.

Have you always worked with light?

I actually studied Applied Arts. It allowed me to become involved in the urban environment. I worked as an artist for a number of years, making sculptures, fountains, painted walls. Plastic arts allowed me to be in contact with architecture, something that has always fascinated me. As I developed, light became one of the materials I worked with, just like steel and wood. It was a component we incorporated into our work. But over the years, light got the upper hand. It became the favoured material, the essential element in our projects. Our first project was a water tower, and I think that had a link to sculpture. I accidentally came across a competition for a water tower. I went to see an architect friend and together we developed a light project. We won the competition and were also presented with an award from the Ministry of Culture. A water tower is normally something people want to hide. But designing it with an architect turned this one into an

Francesca Storaro

I believe that there is a story associated to every colour, an emotion, a significance that you want to give to that particular building.

interesting object. What's more, opening it up, clearing the trees around it and lighting it makes it much less oppressive. It is on show.

You have undertaken several water tower projects during your career.
Yes. We have just completed the water tower in Ploubazlanec, in northern Brittany. Water towers are always located on the high points in town and are visible from a great distance. In addition, this one was near the sea, and I wanted to make it a point of light – something like a lighthouse. I also wanted to turn the concrete mass of the tower into a mass of contained water. Movement of the light became important. The volume of light shifts with the level of the tides. The light swells with the tide; it is almost as if the tower is breathing.

Ploubazlanec Water Tower
→ *Colour, p. 082*

Did you make use of colour?
Yes. The design is based on the idea of an enormous shell. So I wanted the colour of a pearl. When the light is at its brightest, it is virtually white. As it dims, it has a pink or yellow sheen. The light arrives gradually, just like the tide coming in. I love to take buildings into the shadow so that the light can flood out. It is almost as if the building is keeping watch.

You did a lot of interior lighting for Fabre Museum in Montpellier.
We've been working on the museum for several years. And just recently we also undertook the exterior lighting. We were asked to work on the façade of the building and on Daniel Buren's new entrance. We lit the entrance by channelling a flow of light – it is like a carpet of light unrolling. The façade itself had to make an impact. The museum does not have an easy relationship with the space around it and we wanted to bring it alive.

Fabre Museum | Montpellier

You use colour again.
I was hesitant about it to begin with. It is a 17th century building and some people do not welcome the use of colour in such cases. And I will admit that I do not always agree with the way colour is used in our cities. But I want to give people an image at night which is different from the one they see during the day. Flooding the building with colour is not enough. We did a lot of research into colours and blends, and ultimately produced a three-colour concept with a warm white that changes into amber. The timing is so slow that people don't realise it is changing. Yet they know it is different. We also added floodlights on the top left. Light must have a direction and the way light is positioned changes the way people look at the building.

What about the interior lighting you did for the museum?

I think it is important to remember, in a museum, that you are not interpreting the exhibits; you are providing the light in which people can view them. A poorly lit museum will only get a small number of works and few visitors. Museum curators and collectors would not lend out their art works for exhibitions if the basic rules were not respected: good lighting level, good uniformity, good colour rendering. In the columns room, for example, the architect takes the natural light into account. We designed a series of relays so that as daylight declines, artificial light increases. It provides a sense of continuity. We cut out a lot of the natural light, but you still need the sensation of natural light. And it must be handled so that the lighting never becomes poor.

Pierre Soulages' new building
Fabre museum | Montpellier

Poor?

For me, that's when you enter a room and don't feel right. Rich light, on the other hand, is all enveloping, it makes you feel good.

People don't think about it – they just know whether they feel good or not. Much of what we do as lighting designers depends on the space we are given. There are times when we have to be discrete and melt into the surroundings. At other times, often with exterior lighting, you can be more assertive, and create a stronger image corresponding to a stronger creative act. Colour is being used more extensively – largely thanks to new technologies. We know we will be able to do things that we couldn't have done in the past.

We are moving towards a more festive atmosphere in our towns. The outdoor environment is more and more a shared space. Town planning is allowing more space for pedestrians and cyclists.

I believe the trend is towards more shared space. We are opting for people to flow and come together. Who would want to picnic on an empty motorway? The lighting there is high, harsh. We move towards light where we would like to settle, to talk. We see closeness. And light can create that environment. We are currently working on a project where there are open salons in the town. Light is essential in creating the right atmosphere. Because it is light that can make you feel comfortable. And emotion is often linked to comfort.

Education	Applied Arts
Design experience	17 years
Lighting association	ACE - President
Field of work	Architecture, interior and exterior
Projects discussed	Ploubazlanec water tower | France (2007)
	Fabre museum | Montpellier | France (2007)
Agency	8'18"/ Grandeur Nature

Francois Migeon

Antonio Mingrone

I have a degree in Engineering and Architecture and have been a professor in architecture at the University of São Paulo since 1977, *says Antonio Mingrone.* For the past twenty years my partner and I have been running a consultancy, focusing on indoor and outdoor lighting for residences, shopping malls, museums, theatres, stores, supermarkets and churches. We currently have 13 people working with us, most of whom are architects, and we never advertise because all our work comes from referrals.

When did you discover your passion for lighting?
My introduction to lighting design came when I worked on a study for the Ministry of Planning in Brazil with Juan Mascaron. Two years later I started working as Lucia Mascaron's assistant, teaching Natural and Artificial Lighting, the same course I teach today. I taught myself lighting design from books. I particularly love the International Lighting Review; I have every issue since 1950. I am currently a member of AIDI, an Italian Lighting Association, and a founder member of ASBAI, the Brazilian Association of Lighting Architects.

What motivated you to work in this field?
I learned about light as a presence in architecture and the potential of advanced technologies from books. That's what moved me. Light is sometimes referred to as the fourth dimension of space, with space being the fundamental matrix. What captivated me was seeing the huge potential in this tool, both for natural and artificial light. In our work we always try to use natural light whenever possible.

What is it about lighting that interests you?

What I love about lighting is how it can bring ideas to life in the architecture as a whole, changing the fundamental character of a space. We focus on three main points: visual comfort, enhancing the emotion associated with the relevant activity – for example making shopping more enjoyable or making it more pleasant for people to wait in a hospital – and enhancing the architecture itself or the ultimate purpose of that particular space.

How do you approach a project?

We first do some project-specific research. For the Alzheimer's hospital, for example, we used just three books, that's all. We found out that the patients need constant lighting levels that resemble daylight and by understanding how they perceive the world around them we realised we could not use marked point light sources, for example, because this would create disturbance. I always read a lot of journals, scanning information and recording it for future reference. Sometimes we use photographs, just as a reference, for example to show where the shelves will have certain details, what will be lit up, what the effect will be like. We develop special luminaires for all our projects and pride ourselves on covering every aspect of the building, from the machinery house to obstacle lights, ensuring everything is in technical and aesthetic harmony. When we do churches, for example, it is essential that the atmosphere can be varied according to the purpose, e.g. service and emergency lighting, lighting for prayers, major festivities, solemn celebrations, and even to enhance works of art.

What about your projects?

One of the projects we did was Alto do Ipiranga, the last subway station in São Paulo. This is the region in Ipiranga where the declaration of Independence of Brazil took place, so we used green and yellow light to reflect the colours of the national flag. The green part is on the platform, with the T5 fluorescent bulbs in asymmetric luminaires in long, continuous lines, and the façade is being commissioned now. The glass entrance area will be lit in yellow.

Alto do Ipiranga Station | São Paulo
→ *Colour, p. 078*

The station had to have great architectural value and create a sense of wellness and satisfaction for users. It also had to be a place of beauty, even though the users are only passing through. With its reputation as one of the best subways in the world to uphold, the São Paulo subway company strives for excellence, using the best granite, stainless steel and aluminium panels, etc. The stations are in a fantastic state of repair and there's hardly any graffiti. It's as if people recognise the high quality and want to preserve it.

Antonio Mingrone

Alto do Ipiranga Station | São Paulo
→ Colour, p. 078

What sensations did you want to convey through the lighting?

Light has a huge impact on the human senses and we wanted to create a real element of surprise. There is a 30-meter difference in height between the platform and where the trains ride. Our problem was how to light this drop. We used theatre switches and mechanical furniture, with scenic switches inside the station that come down with the lighting. We focused on this hole and managed to take light down there using effective but low-power projectors on an electro-mechanical switch. It was difficult, but all our hard work paid off and I am proud of the result.

Another indoor and outdoor lighting project is the Pinacoteca Station museum, which used to be called Museu do Imaginário do Povo Brasileiro. This was an old building by Ramos Azevedo, a renowned Brazilian architect born in São Paulo. We used dichroic halogen bulbs to accentuate the little arches in the façade and 90-series fluorescent bulbs to enrich specific areas. We also brought out the colour of the sandstone and the bricks themselves. The aim was to use light to reveal the aesthetic beauty of the building at night.

What emotion did you want people passing through Pinacoteca to feel?

We wanted to give the building an identity at night by revealing its architectural features under artificial light. It looks totally different at night from how it looks under natural light. We wanted it to make an impact against the surrounding scenery.

Why did you highlight details rather than using lighting that resembles daylight?

We felt it would be better to enhance and reveal details that the architecture itself brings out from the design. Light and dark details create their own effect, almost like some sort of 'dynamic statics', because light and shade create a rhythm, irrespective of whether the light is uniform.

What other projects have you done?

We did the Parlamento Latino Americano (Latin American Parliament) for Oscar Niemeyer, and the Partido Comunista Francês (French Communist Party). In 1990 we worked with Niemeyer on the theater in Araras and we did some work for Julio Neves as well as two beautiful fashion stores, one for Carlos Miele in Cidade Jardim Shopping Mall, with no bulbs or luminaires in sight, and one for Daslu.

Carlos Miele – Cidade Jardim
São Paulo

Antonio Mingrone

We also did the indoor and outdoor lighting for a Ferrari showroom, the architecture of which was inspired by Zaha Hadid's School. We wanted the lighting to reflect the permeability of the structure itself and tried to use maximum natural light whilst also ensuring thermal comfort. We placed projectors in long, rectangular fixtures instead of having a rail stuck to the structure, and positioned them in different ways to allow a range of programmable scenarios, such as general lighting or specific highlights on the vehicles.

What changes have you seen in lighting concepts over the past five or ten years?

Things have evolved a lot, especially in Brazil. These days the client is more aware of lighting. Light can add an exhilarating component so valuable to the product that the client becomes enthusiastic about it. It's great when the client is delighted with the solution.

Jaspreet Chandhok & Vilas Prabhu

People principally buy with their eyes…

Where does your inspiration come from now?

I try to combine a mixture of things. I may pick up some detail from a fashion magazine that then inspires me to choose fabric for light diffusion. I always live the process like that, holistically. I read a lot, flicking through magazines to keep up to date with what's going on here and abroad.

Are there people who influence you?

I mirror myself in what the great architects are doing – Foster, Roger, Renzo Piano, Antonio Citerio.

What do you see yourself doing in 10 years?

I just want to continue developing. I love what I am doing. Federico Fellini was right, he knew that 'life is light'.

Education	Engineering and Architecture
Design experience	22 years
Lighting association	AIDI, ASBAI, CIE
Field of work	Internal and external lighting, natural light
Projects discussed	Metropolitano Alto do Ipiranga Subway Station | São Paulo | Brazil (2007)
	Pinacoteca Museum | São Paulo | Brazil (2002)
	Ferrari Showroom | São Paulo | Brazil (2008)
	Daslu – Cidade Jardim | São Paulo | Brazil (2008)
	Carlos Miele – Cidade Jardim | São Paulo | Brazil (2008)
	Philips Brazil Headquarters Building | São Paulo | Brazil (2008)
	Ugo di Pace's Residence | São Paulo | Brazil (2007)
Agency	Mingrone Lighting and Consultancy

Antonio Mingrone

Roger Narboni

I was born in Algeria. My ancestors had lived there for many centuries and I spent the first nine years of my life there before moving to France, *explains Roger Narboni of the French company Concepto.* I went on to study fine arts and electronic engineering in Paris. This was rather weird, particularly in those days between 1970 and 1975. I also did Math Sup, but realised this was not the direction I wanted to take. I dreamed of doing art – painting, sculpture. But there was still something about science that attracted me – and I didn't see why there should be a conflict between art and science. Today it seems logical to link art and technology; but at that time it wasn't. I then left for New York, where I spent three years painting and sculpting and doing part-time jobs. I think it was at that time that I really discovered the city at night.

Was this what attracted you to lighting?

I think I can trace the moment to an exhibition by James Turrell in 1979. Everything I was doing in painting and sculpture played on the notions of transparency, but I hadn't realised you could also play with light. I next went to Alaska for 6 months, chasing the aurora borealis. And I started to theorise. I wrote a theory on light, on what you can do with it, how you can express things, and I finally decided to return to France and devote myself to lighting.

And this was the start of your career?

Not exactly. There was no interest in lighting as art in France. I think I knocked on every door – right up to the Ministry of Culture – but nobody was interested. So I started up my own operations. I organised my own exhibitions, and gradually I began to become known. And in 1987 – I had returned to France in 1981 – I did an exhibition at La

Villette called 'Lighting in all its States'. It was the first exhibition of its kind in France. It was a starting point. I continued with my theories and I wrote about light and the city.

Lighting in all its States | Paris

What did your theories entail?
I asked myself why we didn't think in terms of whole cities. I wanted to work on the general topography of the city. The first one I did was Montpelier. I drew up a proposal for the whole agglomeration. Today, nobody questions the idea of drawing up a lighting plan for an entire city. There is always an important relationship to the site, the city, its history. I work increasingly on the level of people. The feeling, the social aspects. The very essence of working with light is the relationship with people, with what they feel.

Do you involve people in your lighting plans?
We try to take an interest in what people feel. We're moving from a culture of expertise – in which we did things despite people – to a culture in which we make more effort to share. Let me give you an example. For the construction of a park in Rouen, we talked to children. We told ourselves they were the future users. We held educational workshops, made drawings, had the children participate in the lights. We integrated them from the very start. They came up with the idea of a treasure island – and that is what we made.

There was a project we did in Toulouse. There was a big tree-lined walk-way running through an area with housing estate towers. The contractor wanted us to light the access to the buildings, leaving the walk-way unlit. But the residents wanted exactly the opposite. The walk-way had become a no-man's land. People wanted to feel safe at the foot of the buildings. They wanted to cross the walk-way in light, not darkness. We didn't respond to the contractor, but rather to the people. And when we presented the project, the residents were really happy. They're the ones who live there. So it is important that we find human dimensions.

Emaplot districk | Toulouse

How did you do this technically?
We created what we call micro-spaces – three of them. One is a small ring, lit with a ring with luminaires above it, where people can meet, but also where young people come to fight. There was also a lost fountain: people told us they wanted a fountain, so we did lighting for when the fountain will be erected. And the third is a space with benches and children's games. We created columns with coloured light inside, so that children can play there.

Roger Narboni

Garonne river embankment |
Toulouse

This wasn't your first project in Toulouse.
No. We had already drawn up a lighting master plan for the whole city. And this included a lighting project inside the Garonne River. We believed it had symbolic value for Toulouse because it links the two parts of the city on either side of the river. We also wanted to support with light the urban development policy. And also show the link between the right bank and the left bank.

What do you mean by symbolic value?
Historically, this is where the city started. There used to be a ford and that's where the original founders were able to cross the Garonne. It provided us with enormous symbolic scope. Our idea was to create a type of impalpable line under water. We decided to use a colour – cyan – to contrast the river with the urban environment. Incidentally, the colour we chose is based on stress levels in fish. At 510 nanometres, the cyan was the most de-stressing colour for the cryptochrome of fish. I was delighted, because it is also a colour I love. For me, cyan is a blue that is warm, not cold.

What has been the reaction to it?
I no longer ask myself that question. I think the result is amazing. So I tell myself it will amaze others as well. I mean amazing in the sense of dreaming – like looking at a sunset. There will always be people who do not like it. But it's a public work, so the more people who like it the better. But for me, as a designer, all the joy lies in the design process. The love story ends when you press the button. When you go back to a project, you never experience the same pleasure you had when you were designing it.

Design Center
PSA Peugeot Citroën | Velizy
→ *Direction, p. 138*

What about interiors?
I think a special interior is the one we created for the Design Centre of Peugeot Citroën in Velizy. They wanted to build a presentation room with 2500 lux of light yet with no visual disturbance for the people inside. We imagined that all the lighting would come from the back and the top, via an elliptical shape. The architecture moulded itself to the light. This place is the holy of holies. It is where they present the vehicles for industrialisation decisions and where all marketing decisions are made. Everybody – all the bosses – stay in the room for up to two days and the visual conditions must not change at all during that time, regardless of whatever happens outside. So you need a totally blind room, with no link to the outside world and which is not altered by external light.

Is there an emotional aspect to this?

Honestly, it's amazing. It's emotional and sensorial; you expect Nirvana. When you're inside, you are almost in a state of weightlessness. You're floating. You are in a world that is always exactly the same. If you leave it and it is night outside, your brain simply can't make the adjustment. There's nothing like it in the world.

You have also worked in China. Do you find it very different from France?

The Chinese want to do things the Chinese way. We worked in the city of Hangzhou and used colours and contrasts. They like violent contrasts. For them, it is never bright enough. In one case, we had proposed a simple shape for an underwater mast, but they wanted to add the symbol of a water dragon. It had to be included because it was supposed to stop flooding. Everything is linked to mythology. They put animal symbols everywhere. What they are trying to do is combine modern architecture with a symbolism of forms. It is their culture – and we should do nothing to harm it.

Do you often work with metaphors?

Certainly. I want to leave people the freedom to think. As a spectator, I don't want to be told what I should think. So I don't tell people what they should be seeing. The problem today is that the available products allow you to play with every conceivable colour. That's where the danger lies. It's a specialist trade. I spent 12 years painting. I worked in painting restoration as a colour specialist. I mastered colour. Before the introduction of LEDs, creating colour was a complicated business. Now all you have to do is press the button. I think the use of colour today is a real issue.

Vannapa Pimviriyakul
Thais are used to strong sunlight and they therefore want the same brightness when they come indoors.

Main Canal | Hangzhou

Education	Fine Arts and Electrical engineering
Design experience	22 years
Lighting association	ACE, AFE, PLDA
Field of work	Public spaces, landscape, architecture, museum
Projects discussed	Garonne river embankment	Toulouse	France (2005)
	Design Centre PSA Peugeot Citroën	Velizy	France (2005)
	Rion Antirion bridge	Greece (2004)
	Micro sites	Toulouse	France (study in 2004)
Agency	Concepto

Roger Narboni

Enrique Peiniger & Jean Sundin

I came to lighting from an interior design background, *explains Jean Sundin of the Office for Visual Interaction in New York,* and my colleague Enrique Peiniger is an architectural engineer. I'm fascinated by how lighting can transform a space without physically changing it. This room could look very different depending on what lighting solution you put in here – you could make it look bigger, more exciting, less exciting, simply by changing the lighting. Lighting is really powerful – you can do such complicated things with it.

How do you set about lighting a project?
Lighting design is based on dialogue. We maintain an intensive dialogue throughout the design phase to identify the owner's values so we can respond to these, and then start to add value. Every project has a story – you have to find out what that story is and then enhance it with light. It's about the character of the space, whether it's interior or exterior. For example, for the Air Force Memorial we used light to evoke the feeling of flight. Our job is to pick up this kind of metaphor and transfer it into lighting, *adds Enrique Peiniger.* For example, a piece of clear glass is transparent. There is nothing particularly beautiful about it. It's just a piece of clear glass. What's important is how it's used, how it is illuminated and what's in context with it.

US Air Force Memorial | Arlington
→ Emotions, p. 182

What is the best thing about being a lighting designer?
There are several things. You are free to design, it's open. You can use every colour there is or you can be very rational. We work on a variety of projects, so we are not bound to a certain medium or a certain type of building. We can use light and even fog – general fog and light fog – to blur boundaries. It can be very creative and very technical at the same time.

Jean: As our company's name suggests, our work is all about the visual interaction of surfaces and materials with light. We don't have one set style, and it's not restricted to interiors or exteriors – it could be anything. That's the challenge, it makes it fun.

In your work, what are the different types of emotions or moods you want to create?

Enrique: It depends on the project. With the Air Force Memorial the emotion is very different from something like the New York Times headquarters. That's the beauty of light: you can tailor the atmosphere to suit the project. The Air Force Memorial had to be respectful and very silent to allow people to contemplate. We can't control how people feel – a kid feels differently from an adult or a group of veterans – but we can try to influence how they feel, up to a point.

Jean: The Air Force Star logo embedded in the granite pavement in the centre is lit with LEDs to provide a glow in the middle of the space. It feels comfortable, it gives a sense of orientation, so you're not walking into a dark, open space. We introduced a low level of light in the paving to create that quiet moment. It's just enough to make you feel comfortable, without being distracting.

Enrique: In this project we actually concealed a lot as well. All the workhorse lighting for the tall spires is hidden behind the inscription walls, so to a visitor it looks very clean. All they see is the project itself and they just feel the effect.

The New York Times Building | New York
→ *Brightness, p. 020*

Another significant project in this respect was the New York Times headquarters, which involved a mixture of interior and exterior spaces. The architect was Renzo Piano and the first question was how to design an icon for New York City. What was the cultural context? How much brightness did we need to give it a presence on the skyline? Because it was in the Times Square District, the façade lighting had to provide so-called 'visual excitement'. It was a challenge to do this in an elegant way, without flashy signage boards like the other buildings.

We decided to make taxi-cab yellow fixtures, and create a wall-wash effect, with the light brightest at the base of the tower and tapering to a soft glow at the top. This was a real feat of technology because there were no ledges or setbacks to tuck away and hide lighting equipment - most of the tall buildings in Times Square have banks of lights every ten feet. The entire lighting for the New York Times tower was done with lights located at the base of the building. We used very precise and efficient optics to project light up the entire 850-foot façade.

What atmosphere did you set out to create for the interior of the building?

It was all about drawing the eye through the building. Lightness and transparency were the most important factors. So we had to enhance visibility through the layered spaces at night – the lobby, garden and a glass-walled theatre – without creating glare on all those glass surfaces.

Why did they want to enhance the transparency?

Enrique: The notion of 'transparency' can be interpreted in different ways. For the architect it was about openness, literally being able to see through the spaces and inviting the public into the lobby. For the client, transparency implied a democratic process, suggesting there's very open communication. They liked the idea of the newspaper being a forum, not produced behind closed doors. It's a sort of branding.

The New York Times
Building | New York
→ Brightness, p. 020

As lighting designers, we had to translate this into lighting terms. In order for the effect of transparency to work, we did a master plan. If we need so much light in the lobby as our starting point, then that means we recommend less light in other areas. We mapped and programmed the lighting levels for all spaces. It is quite unusual to develop the lighting scheme to such an extreme level of detail but we understand our role as lighting designers in a broad way.

How do you figure out cultural contexts and then integrate them into your designs?

Jean: Let's take the Scottish Parliament as an example. Our research led us to Charles Rennie Mackintosh and the Glasgow School of Art as a design icon for the region. So we based our custom fixtures on Mackintosh's architectural language from the turn of the century. A project should never feel like it was designed elsewhere. It has to be embedded comfortably in the local culture.

The parliament is a complex of nine buildings. The leaf-shaped towers serve as giant louvers, shielding the chamber from direct daylight during broadcasting hours. The architect Enric Miralles didn't want anything gimmicky, and he wanted spaces like the debating chamber to have views to the outside. He thought if people felt good when they were sitting in the debating chamber they would make better decisions. This serious building has a playful touch – in both the architecture and lighting – in order to make people feel comfortable.

Enrique Peiniger & Jean Sundin

Are there any trends you've seen in lighting concepts over the past five or ten years?

Enrique: One trend is about understanding how to use dynamic light. Since the invention of LEDs there's a lot of coloured light being used, but it's not always used appropriately.

Jean: The fact that LEDs weren't good at white light for so long has perhaps pushed the industry towards all this colour and RGB and dynamics. They're available, so people paint and do fun things with these colours. But you need the right solution for the right project. Dynamic lighting doesn't have to mean colour.

Enrique: Another important trend is, of course, sustainability. People have been making a case for bad lighting design on the basis that it is sustainable. Sustainable does not have to mean bad or ugly. The next trend will be for beautiful design that is also sustainable.

Finally, what inspires you in your design work?

Jean: Our inspiration comes from the project itself and from things we see, places we've been. But sometimes, it's important to forget everything you know and just think afresh.

LED Streetlight for the City of New York

Take the New York City streetlight project. What we did is try to forget every streetlight we ever saw, and ask ourselves, what's the light source of the future? Let's take that as the starting point. Everyone else started with the form of the streetlight. We began at the other end – looking at how to optimise the configuration of LEDs, and designing a whole streetlight around this.

We're not trying to create something different simply for the sake of being different. It's a case of understanding the most advanced lighting technologies so that we can use them effectively, to achieve the best performance and create the appropriate atmosphere.

Education	Enrique Peiniger: Architecture, Engineering
	Jean Sundin: Interior Design
Design experience	Enrique Peiniger: 24 years
	Jean Sundin: 25 years
Lighting association	IALD, IESNA, PLDA
Field of work	Interior and exterior lighting, iconic lighting
Projects discussed	United States Air Force Memorial | Arlington | USA (2007)
	The New York Times Building | New York | USA (2008)
	LED Streetlight for the City of New York (2008)
Agency	Office for Visual Interaction, Inc. (OVI)

Enrique Peiniger & Jean Sundin

Michel Pieroni

I think my attitude towards lighting is somewhat less artistic than some of my colleagues, *says Michel Pieroni*. Light needs a medium to receive it. And we are always working with a medium created by somebody else – an architect, a landscape artist, an existing monument. You're not trying to create a work of art on top of somebody else's work of art. You're trying to provide cohesion. If an architect designs a round building, I'm not going to mess around creating a square lighting scheme. I am going to enhance his round building. I don't want people to say 'the lighting is magnificent'; I want them to say 'that building is great'. Lighting must enhance what is there and bring cohesion. It should bring aesthetic added value.

What made you decide to go into lighting?

I left high school with a certificate in furniture making. Not connected to lighting at all. But I started designing lamps as an independent designer and realised that it would be more interesting to look at the function of the product. What attracted me was the way of channelling light, orienting it where you wanted, conveying emotions through the effects produced by lighting. I exhibited some of my designs at the Salon du Luminaire, where I met Louis Clair, who became one of my first employers. I stayed with Light Cibles for seven years and then started working for myself in 1993.

So you've seen a lot of changes in the profession.
Certainly. The technology is changing every day. Projects won't be
handled in the same way in 10, 20 years time. And people's sensitivities
are changing too. Today, people expect you to use colour. And perhaps
even animation.

Animation?
The fact that the colours change. A fixed image used to be enough.
Now we produce animation if the client specifically asks for it.
After all, it implies an additional cost and the funds for this are not
always available. Sometimes – as with the National Assembly, for
example – we created a fixed, serene image for the week, but built
in the possibility of doing other things, having fun. And then on festive
occasions – like July 14 – we can project revolving red, white and
blue around the building. It's fun. Lighting it with white is the standard
thing to do, so that the building can be seen from afar and act as a
signal. But I like to do fun things as well.

Did the neighbours share your opinion?
Actually there aren't any. But to be perfectly honest, as a resident,
I would much rather live next to a building that isn't always the same,
but livens up in the evening and weekends, rather than always being
the same white or orange. What's more, people are developing
just as lighting is developing. Just look at the way the lighting of the
Eiffel Tower has developed over the years. First it was uniformly
lighted, then more light was added to the interior, then some sparkling
effects, then they added a lighthouse. What is daring today is normal
by tomorrow.

**Do you think you would do things differently in other
countries?**
That depends on the country. I think here in France we lag behind
what is being done abroad, particularly in the US and China.
I have a lot of clients who say to me: 'Don't turn us into Las Vegas'.
Most of them have never even been there. Yet it's amazing,
the animated effects, the colours. Everything there is perfect.

Can we turn to some of your recent projects?
We recently worked with architect Laurence Allégret on the
Nestlé headquarters in Noisiel. The building used to be a chocolate
factory. We wanted to recreate the history of the place.

Nestlé headquarters | Noisiel
→ Direction, p. 122

Michel Pieroni

345

We had some magical spaces to work with, halls measuring around 400 m2. At the centre of the hall there was a mixer with holes through which they would pour the chocolate ingredients. So we drew the shape of the mixer on the ground using ultra-tight beams. There was also an area where the chocolate was allowed to cool, and we tried to produce a colder ambiance by lighting the ceiling indirectly with a glass roof.

What do you mean by colder?
We used white and blue, which are cooler lights, whereas warm light tends more towards yellow. We also lit the mill on the Marne which was the former power station for the factories. We had fun getting it to reflect in the water and having the water project the reflection onto the façade. The result highlights the fact that the mill is attached to the water.

Congress Hall | Paris

The Congress Hall in Paris is different. There the architect specifically requested us to use colours. We were rather restricted, because at the time we were only able to use the colours of the lamps available. We initially used green – but we changed that, because we found out that green brings bad luck in a theatre! We did things very simply because of the technological limitations. We didn't have LEDs which would have allowed us to do things differently today. What we did was mainly a wall-washing effect from the balcony. The aim was to have something as homogenous as possible. The changes in colour take place very slowly. There's also a safety factor there: the congress hall is in a very busy part of the city, and rapid light changes could cause accidents. Now, when you stand in front of it, it looks amazing. It gives me a buzz.

*Porte de Montreuil
Subway Station | Montreuil*

What about an interior?
Well this one started because we did the TGV stations for the Mediterranean line. And then we were asked to light the metro station of Porte de Montreuil. It's really rather simple: an arch in a metro station. But when you have 6000 m2 of illuminated arches, all that gives an impression of brightness, immensity. And that was exactly the effect we were looking for. You could say we tried to achieve what the builders would have liked to have done if they had had the necessary resources. What you have now is the recreation of a luminous sky – or at least a luminous ceiling. It makes people forget they are underground.

That sounds very emotional.

It is a basic emotion. People do not feel comfortable underground. And we have tried to create a comfortable area just through our lighting. I think it is successful. Yet it was achieved with very simple technical solutions. Our job, whether we are lighting old or contemporary projects, is to find out what emotion the architect really wanted to project when he designed the building. It is all about finding the strong element in the architectural project and trying to apply light on top, without ever wanting to redesign things.

Education	Art, Furniture-making
Design experience	22 years
Lighting association	ACE
Field of work	Cultural heritage, architecture, landscape, shopping malls, transportation
Projects discussed	Nestlé headquarters | Noisiel | France (1995)
	Congress Hall new facade | Paris | France (2000)
	Stade de France | Saint Denis | Paris (1998)
	Porte de Montreuil subway station | Montreuil | France (2006)
Agency	Aartill

Michel Pieroni

347

Vannapa Pimviriyakul

Thais are used to strong sunlight, *says Vannapa Pimviriyakul of the With light Co. Bangkok,* and they therefore want the same brightness when they come indoors. From my observation, Thais prefer more light compared to Europeans. If they have to adjust to dimmer lights indoors, they find it very dark. At the same time, Thais are not very keen on strong sunlight. They do not appreciate it. Especially Thai girls. They want to be fair skinned and are scared of sunlight and of getting tanned. So we take these factors and cultural perception into consideration when designing and limit the amount of sunlight. For daylight, we use sunlight indirectly because otherwise it can make the space very warm. Even though we like bright light, we prefer indirect light, because otherwise it becomes too hot.

Did you study lighting?
I went to Chulalongkorn University and graduated from the department of Architecture in 1990. I then worked as an architect for 4 years and by then, I had become interested in lighting and wanted to know more about it. I then got a scholarship from the government to study lighting. So I went on to get my master's degree in it. After I finished my master's degree I went to Texas A&M University to do my PhD thesis, which had to do with lighting in Thai temples.

Can you tell us something about that thesis?
Thai Buddhist architecture has very simple planning in a rectangular shape. It would normally have wall-bearing structure and we have

limited lighting in the space. It doesn't have skylights. Lighting is only controlled from the sides. We do not use skylights in temples like western places of worship. Those have light from the top and light represents God. In a Thai temple, the Buddha image would be inside, in the centre. The lighting inside is very, very dim and when your eyes adjust to the light, you first see the image or statue of Buddha which is golden in colour and only then do you start to notice the mural paintings on the wall. It's a philosophy. I learnt that in this culture: light does not represent god. In Buddhism there is no god. Light represents wisdom. I came to an understanding that light means peacefulness. People come in and they calm down.

The second meaning of light here is that it makes the place feel holy. Dim light gives people a sense of being protected by the Buddha, who is not god but a protector, a special person. I conducted an interview with the novices. They told me they liked to be in this space because it makes them feel protected; they can look out and see the sun while still being shaded from sunlight.

The third meaning of light is 'light of admiration'. Thai people paint on the walls and natural light coming from the side doors illuminates these paintings and this makes them feel connected to their ancestors. The light through the door gives them access to their ancestors and the fourth meaning is also very important: the light of modernity. In this temple, monks installed different lamp types to use for different purposes. They have incandescent lamps to uplight the Buddha images, and use bare lamp fluorescent tubes to give more light to mural paintings, and, the worst part in my opinion, they have two metal halide hanging lamps to give more light to the whole place. They told me that having these lights makes them feel that they adapt well to the modern world. This says a lot about the culture.

Can you tell us about your projects?

We designed the lighting for the Mantra Restaurant in the Amari Hotel in Pattaya. Mantra means spell and the interior concept was to create an Oriental / Indian / Chinese atmosphere. We had to create the mood. We used gold surfaces in display boxes together with uplights to make artworks floating in space. We also used lots of contrast. It is very precise lighting. It offers a stunning visual perception, using both dim light and directional light, gold and Asian art. These elements together make the place look magical.

Mantra Restaurant | Pattaya
→ Contrast in brightness, p. 050

Museum Siam | Bangkok

We have also just finished lighting Museum Siam that relates the story of the origins of the Thai people. It is a preservation building and we designed lighting for the exhibition inside. There is one room called Buddhism and it is themed around the concept of Buddhism. The exhibition designers created four columns and a sitting area in the centre. The four columns bring out the philosophy of the religion. They wanted to create light patterns on the columns in this rather dark environment. This I think was very nice. I personally liked it. It offers a sense of peacefulness. You automatically adjust your tone to fit the environment of this room. We do not do a lot of entertainment places. Active lighting is easy if you want to stimulate people. If you don't play with colour and movement, you can play with brightness. Brightness wakes you up.

For relaxation, we prefer warm colour light, dim light and indirect light. Relaxation can be created with natural as well as artificial lights. Humans tend to relate to natural light and shadow makes us relax so we need to mix the two. Many times, we blend shadows into our design.

Elias Cisneros Avila

It makes you realise that you must look for balance. Nature does this all the time.

Have you seen a change in the way people regard lighting as a profession?
Certainly. When I obtained a scholarship from the Government, my grant was intended for an interior architecture programme. Still, I applied for Lighting Design. My application was not approved immediately, and I had to explain to the ministry the significance of lighting design to the design profession. Back then, not many people studied lighting. There were lighting designers, but they did not receive any formal education and learned their trade from experience. Today, more and more designers from both interior design and architecture continue their master study in lighting design.

Where do you get your inspiration?
Louis Kahn, who puts a great deal of thought into lighting. I also like Ricaldo Legoretta from Mexico. They are masters of using daylight but Mexicans also use a lot of colour. I find their simple technique and use of daylight very interesting. As for Legoretta, his interpretation of sunlight, colour is very dramatic for me.

Does colour have a special meaning in Thai culture?

There are no clear concepts but some colours create certain moods. Some colours are associated with unpleasant feelings. Like red light might make people feel uncomfortable while blue makes you feel light hearted. Blue therefore, is the easiest colour to use. Yellow is warm, but too much yellow light might make us feel too warm. As I mentioned before, Thais tend to like bright light. But they are beginning to realise the importance of light in their home environment and how it can help them relax. I like to use cool colours in a monotone theme, like blue, greenblue to violet-blue. I like it to go unnoticed and to fill in the space lightly. Light seems to lift the space and makes the space appears wider. Thais are laid back people and therefore, I think cool and soft colours might be more suitable.

Education	Architecture, lighting design
Design experience	16 years
Field of work	Exterior and interior architectural lighting; hotel & resorts, restaurants, shopping malls, museum, offices, retails, showroom
Projects discussed	Mantra restaurant	Pattaya	Thailand (2006) Museum Siam	Bangkok	Thailand (2008)
Agency	With light

Vannapa Pimviriyakul

Michael F. Rohde

I really got into lighting because my gut feeling told me this was right for me, *says Michael F. Rohde, founder of the Berlin-based L-Plan Lichtplanung.* I studied architecture and worked as one for three years. And it was then that I became aware of the contribution lighting made to architecture. We would often discuss this among ourselves. And then one day we received a very prestigious project and we engaged Hans von Malotki, the famous light designer, and I was introduced to him as the lighting specialist, which I most definitely was not! We talked and he suggested I take a master degree in London. I thought about it and finally enrolled with the Bartlett School of Architecture.

After that, I founded L-Plan in 1998. We are, I think, specialists in the field of architectural lighting. We also like to include the background of theatrical lighting, because this has been an enormous source of innovation for architectural lighting. That is why I share my office with Herbert Cybulska, who is a prominent specialist in that area. I also teach at Wismar University, something I consider important, particularly in times like now, when so many revolutions in lighting are taking place. I think it is vital that I have insights into the day-to-day work. And it is important that we share our knowledge. I remember an incident at a seminar I was involved in some ten years ago. We built a light installation in a park and people came to see it. I was there, walking among the visitors, and I heard a little girl say: 'Why is this only here for a day? Why can't it be here forever?' I picked up a lot of what people thought about lighting, simply by mingling in the crowd. And you know something else I learned then? That everybody is interested and fascinated and captivated by light.

How is this reflected in the projects you undertake?

One project from which I learned a lot was for the
Ärztekammer Berlin (Berlin Medical Society). We eventually did
both the interior and exterior lighting, but initially the focus was on
the individuals in the offices. We created the possibility to choose a
warm, or cold light using an RGB mixture, and we also made use of
two colour loops. If you press a button, the colour will be fixed.
When we went to the office after two weeks, I discovered they were
not using the warm light, or cold, but all the colours instead. I actually
thought something was wrong with the controls! But then they told
me: 'today we feel like blue. Yesterday we were in red.' People were
using the light in their own way. And I think the success of this concept
is that it respects the individuality of each person. It was a big break,
because at the time, many lighting manufacturers were dreaming of
just one luminaire for one big office space and the automatics running
it all. But that's what people don't like. With this concept people realised: 'Hey, there's somebody taking me seriously as an individual'.
If people feel that, you get better results. If you feel happy, you will
be a better employee. This lady with a migraine thinks: at the office
I will be able to enjoy green light and that will help my migraine. And
though the colours look decorative, it's not decorative at all; it pro-
motes the feeling of individuality. We can talk about lux levels, but
at the end of the day it's what makes people feel good in their
home or the work place. I think that is highly individual. It is all about
creating well-being: when your body and soul are in harmony.

Berlin Medical Society | Berlin
→ *Emotions, p. 162*

Is this something you always try to create?

I think it is essential. You create interest externally, so that you attract
people in, but once inside they must have the feeling of well-being,
of happiness. This is why I always think that external and internal lighting
are part of the same entity. I mean, if you are inviting somebody to
enter the building, you have to design the story further so that in each
corner of the building you have the feeling of 'Ah, this is something
I would like to explore'.

I certainly wanted to create well-being and the sense of exploration in
a project we undertook in Pforzheim: a high-class shopping mall and
exhibition space called Schmuckwelten – worlds of jewellery. We did
this project together with Yann Kersalé.

World of Jewellery | Pforzheim
→ *Dynamics in colour p. 106*

Jaspreet Chandhok & Vilas Prabhu

In a jewellery shop you are made to feel special, as if the product has been made for you.

The client wanted something special, not only with sufficiently high lux levels, something important that attracts visitors in a shopping mall. So the colour concept was of vital importance. We created a light dome, which really is almost overwhelming. It features a back-lit ceiling and walls, and we made use of fluorescent and LEDs. I think today we would go for an LED only solution, but this concept dates back several years.

Colour seems very important in your work.
The combination of colour and light is very powerful. It can make you feel good – but it can also make you feel unhappy. I'm pretty sure that we will have to think very carefully in the future about how we dose colour. It's like a recipe: if you add just a pinch too much salt you can spoil the dish. That's the same if you have too much colour or too much direct or indirect lighting.

It's about balance. Balance between colour and white, between direct and diffuse, between general and accentuated. If you don't get the balance right, it is not going to work. The project incorporates a preset colour loop at the right speed.

Speed?
I think speed is a big problem in most existing colour-changing loops. Many of them are too fast, trying to mimic Las Vegas where you have an overload of dynamics. I think we are affected by colour loops because if you look at daylight, we pass through the whole spectrum in the course of a day. In the morning we have red, then we go through all the colours, and return to red again at the end of the day. This cycle regulates our hormones, our body temperature, our whole body. I think one of the reasons we like these colour loops is because they are related to the different colours we perceive during the day. But the natural cycle is typically a very, very slow process and you're usually not aware of it. I think it is important to allow loops much slower speeds. Also because I think it needs time to interact with your body.

One of the issues we are addressing at Wismar is the importance of health, which I believe will influence architectural lighting design a lot in the coming years and be a major source of innovation. We are already seeing colour being used very consciously in health environments and there is an enormous amount of scientific research into the beneficial impact colour can have on health.

Michael F. Rohde

You mentioned earlier you relationship with theatrical lighting.

They are more Herbert's projects than mine. He also does installations. Last year he produced something called the Tales of Light, in Milan during Euroluce. In theatrical lighting, there is a lot of contrast between light and darkness. A lot of drama. Much more than in public spaces. Do you want drama in an office? No, certainly not. But you might want zones in the building that create drama. It is all about context. Whether the context allows you more contrast. And I think one of our goals – both from my point of view and from Herbert's – is to get as close as possible to the genius loci. An architectural lighting concept will, of course, be totally different than a temporary, four-day installation for which everybody is expecting something more dramatic or more expressive. In an architectural lighting concept, everything must be much more reduced. It is all about showing the space and letting it work. But the most important thing is getting as close as possible to the genius loci. If we achieve that, then we are good. Very good.

A quote from Winston Churchill is making it very clear: "First we shape our buildings and afterwards, our buildings shape us".

Tales of Light | Milan
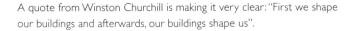
→ *Contrast in brightness, p. 052*

Education	Architect, MSc Light & Lighting
Design experience	24 years
Lighting association	PLDA, IALD, Deutscher Werkbund Berlin, Architektenkammer (Berlin)
Field of work	Architecture, daylight, indoor and outdoor lighting
Projects discussed	Berlin Medical Society | Berlin | Germany (2003) World of Jewellery Pforzheim | Pforzheim | Germany (2006)
Agency	L-Plan Lichtplanung Berlin

Michael F. Rohde

Tapio Rosenius

I was born in Finland and grew up about 100 kilometres from the Arctic Circle, *says Tapio Rosenius*. As a kid, I became interested in photography and lighting, and started doing things in an amateur dramatics theatre. That was my introduction to lighting. I first studied with a photographer who taught me that you first build an image with light and then capture it with the black box. I later discarded the box and went on to follow a fantastic lighting course at Tampere Polytechnic University, Finland. It was actually more of an art school, but it produced creative people for television and had a special lighting course. It was great. My teacher was very interested in architecture and we had unlimited access to an enormous range of lighting equipment.

And then you moved to the United Kingdom?
Yes. I first got a job with Kevan Shaw Lighting Design. Stayed with him for three years and then decided to take a lighting master degree at UCL. When I graduated, I joined Maurice Brill Lighting Design and have been with them now for seven years. The focus here is on the creative aspects, on the effect that light can have on people and spaces. Technology is there to facilitate that. Often we start a project and don't know how we are going to achieve it technically. But that is no reason for abandoning the concept. We like to push the boundaries and see whether we can be a catalyst for the development of new technology.

Can you give an example of your focus on people?
I think a good example is the Riverside Park project which MBLD did
in Staines. Now Staines is not one of the nicest parts of London and
the park was really a no-go area. What we wanted to do was to
create, in all its simplicity, two experiences in one. First, Maurice Brill
wanted to create a route through the park that was perceived as safe.
And then he wanted to create another route, one which was far more
romantic. For the safe route he used a classic approach: a relatively
high and even light level. The problem is that research seems to show
that higher lighting levels actually increase crime, because the bad guys
can see what they are doing. But other research suggests the opposite.
So we are actually in a position where nobody knows whether high-
level lighting actually increases or decreases crime. Anyway, in his
concept he played with the idea of a safe route and a more romantic
route.

Riverside Park | Staines
→ Contrast in brightness, p. 048

How does that work? How do you engineer romance?
The romantic route has a bit more shadow; it is also more theatrical.
Maurice began by limiting the light levels, so that things are not overly
bright. He played with the colour of light and moved towards warmer
light with shadow and accentuated features of the park, whether landscape, architectural features and even trees.

The result is pools of light and darkness. People like darkness because
you feel intimate. If you spotlight a seat, nobody feels comfortable
sitting on it. People like to look at light, but they do not necessarily like
to be in it. The lighting is mounted on top of a diagonally focused grid
across the trees and creates, at the same time, little warm pools of
light.

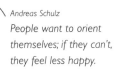

Andreas Schulz
*People want to orient
themselves; if they can't,
they feel less happy.*

What is the relationship between light and trees?
Maurice lit the trees very selectively. He picked out a few older trees,
almost in the way that you would focus on certain important features
in architecture. He gave a degree of importance to certain trees and
these also acted as focal and navigation points. Where paths cross,
there might be a lit tree there. We certainly didn't light all the trees.
What we do a lot in our projects with tree lighting is use little broken
tints of colour. We might, for example, use a very, very light tint of pink
or lavender, because this makes the bark look more healthy and lively.

Did you adopt a similar approach in the Broadgate project?
Broadgate – one of London's financial districts – was also very un-
inviting. It was built almost like a fortress. During the day, around

Broadgate | London
→ Brightness, p. 018

Tapio Rosenius

25,000 people work there, but previously, at the end of the day they simply packed up and left. The area became an absolute ghost town. Totally empty. Maurice wanted to do something to keep the people there for longer. And if we were to achieve that, we would have to make it more inviting.

So what did you do to make it friendlier?
Well first, Maurice opened it out. He wanted to turn selected parts into something of a night-time destination so that it became a much more pleasant place at night, an environment that people would want to use. There would be areas we called stepping stones, which would lead you into the area. Our overall approach was to play up the façades, but subtly, using what was there without introducing additional technology. It has become something of a high contrast environment, but it is nevertheless still very selective.

You don't need to blanket light the whole; if you see something that suggests you are going somewhere, it will give you a sense of safety. Maurice also used little wall features, picking up the façade very high up.

To soften it?
Yes, exactly. He wanted to create a softer, friendlier, more welcoming environment. Everybody knows that picking up vertical surfaces will give you a sense of an illuminated place. If the walls are lit, the space will feel nice.

Finsbury Square | London

Finsbury Square, which is just next to it, is a different story – although it was part of the same Broadgate project. During the day it is a very clean, quite simple space with a few benches. It's very open and it feels connected to the sky. At night, lighting tries to create a reason to go there. It is bold and strong enough for you to want to see it.

But it is a very different approach indeed.
Yes. Everything about it in terms of technology, detail is different. In the little square, every note, every line is separately programmable, using custom-written software. There is a different show every night of the week and these include various slow ambient light movements which move diagonally, which reflect the way people move through the square. Then every half hour and full hour, a new show kicks in which is slightly faster to wake you up and indicate that there is something to look at. It's not disco or going crazy – that would drive people nuts in no time. And people work in the square, so they see it at the end of

Tapio Rosenius

every day. Of course, there are different elevations from offices around the square. There are special shows for special days and so on. It's very kinetic, very dynamic. It becomes a totally different environment at night. MBLD actually made a film about it and interviewed people about the lighting. The stories were absolutely unreal. They were playing and jumping around like kids. And they still are.

And that's exactly what you were aiming for, I should imagine.
Certainly. We attempted to create something that was unique, unusual, strong enough to create emotional impact and to make you feel exactly like they did. Of course, the stories about it helping to meet a boyfriend or reminding somebody of a dragon – those are incidental. People make their own, individual interpretations. They are making the space their own. They are now taking ownership of it. And that's exactly how it should be.

Education	Lighting Design, Light & Lighting
Design experience	14 years
Lighting association	PLDA
Field of work	Hospitality, landscape, commercial, corporate and urban environments
Projects discussed	Riverside Park	Staines	UK (2002)
	Regents Place	London	UK (2003)
	Finsbury Avenue Square	London	UK (2004)
Agency	Maurice Brill Lighting Design (MBLD) 2001 - 2009
	Lighting Design Collective 2009 -

Tapio Rosenius

Andreas Schulz

People have a rhythm, *says Andreas Schulz of Licht Kunst Licht in Bonn,* and that rhythm has its roots in the development of human beings. During the day there was light, so our ancestors could move around freely, but in the darkness of night, they sought shelter in trees and caves to protect themselves from enemies. Then they learned how to harness fire – for cooking and protection, but also for light. So for a million years, our perception, our eyes and minds, recognise that artificial light is a different light source to daylight. At a candlelight dinner, we're happy with the candle, even though it produces little light. The movement of the candle, the punctual light distribution and everything, that's positive, because in our minds that's artificial light. For this reason, I think artificial light needs to be different than daylight – especially at night.

Galeria Kaufhof
Alexanderplatz | Berlin
→ Brightness, p. 016

Do you have a special signature in your lighting?
That we work with light not with luminaires. We try to create the atmosphere of a space, but not by working with chandeliers or lighting elements. Let me give you an example. We did the lighting for a big department store at Alexanderplatz. There is a large atrium with a cupola above it. We spent a lot of time on that cupola. We didn't want sunlight in the warehouse, because this would disturb the drama of the lighting we were trying to achieve. We illuminated the cupola and the light comes out of small gaps in the construction. We wanted the effect, but without seeing the lighting elements. And there's another thing: it is different by day and night. That interests us: how does a building look in the daytime and how does it look at night-time.

It's not our philosophy to create a night atmosphere that is like the day atmosphere. We think it's crazy to try to create a daylight atmosphere using artificial lighting. During the daytime, the department store has bright glass and the structural beams seem dark. At night, the glass is dark and the beams are bright. That's different. And it demonstrates the artificial light.

At the moment, the department store is changing its lighting to a system we developed, which is more for Gil Sander or Prada or Gucci. We are using punctual light sources – small dots of light – that can be easily adjusted. These are combined with a bright background.

People want to orient themselves; if they can't, they feel less happy – and then they don't buy as much because they are thinking about where they are and how to get out.

Is this also true for outside lighting?
Outdoors is different, because we are used to it being dark. I think the problem we now have is that it is too bright outdoors. You need shadow to express light, as I mentioned earlier. Some cities are now so bright that there are no dark corners anymore. Landscape design today is adopting lighting design to create spaces. We are currently working on one in Switzerland – for the Novartis campus. Buildings are springing up designed by a lot of leading architects. We are handling the whole lighting concept, including street lighting. We haven't followed the rules, because we think that following the rules actually leads to the problems we see in some over-lit large cities.

You are also handling interior lighting for Novartis.
We were involved in developing the underground garage. Garages are generally ugly and dark; women always feel unsafe, because you never know who may be lurking in some dark corner. The first thing we said was that we needed space. The architect Marco Serra eventually settled on three and a half metres – this is double the eye level and gives an enormous feeling of space. The down lights are fully incorporated into the cement ceiling, giving a very clean ceiling. And, more important, we created what we called illuminated walls. We used a special golden stainless steel in elements of 8 metres and integrated LED lines in the spaces between these elements. This helps create a very soft space. It also gives the impression of being very clean. Clean, but not antiseptic. People experience the garage as a nice area. They understand the area,

Francesca Storaro
With lighting, you can create a dual life for architecture: a daytime life and a night-time life.

Novartis campus, WJS-2099 Parking | Basel
→ Direction, p. 126

they have the walls, the golden light and they can see how the garage works. As long as you know where you are, you have a secure feeling about the area.

Feeling, emotion is important in your work?

I am certainly interested in drama. I think this is illustrated in the lighting we did for the Coal Wash. It is a building from the 1920s, influenced by the clean lines of the Bauhaus in Weimar. It was a very modern coal mine with high production. The coal was cleaned inside the building by bringing it to the surface and washing it, and then filling it onto trains. Rem Koolhaas, the Dutch architect, had the idea of turning it into a cultural object. He constructed an escalator for people arriving, so everybody is taken up and then they walk back down – the opposite to what you would expect. We felt the building had a relationship with two elements: steel and fire. So we decided to create a lighting scheme that would bathe the escalator in the colour of fire. There are glowing glass panels next to the escalators and this is the only source of light. It is very dramatic.

Former Coal Washer Zollverein | Essen
→ *Colour, p. 074*

What emotion were you trying to create?

I think fire reminds the visitors of energy. You see this glowing escalator behind the somewhat scary, dark object where the coal was washed, and this is somehow a reminder that energy can be warm and comforting. That's the entrance. But there is also the area with all the machinery. When I first visited it, it was dirty with oil and coal. I wanted to keep that atmosphere. It was somehow unreal and scary, so the light shouldn't be nice but should be strong, hard and scary as well. We used a power track with light sources inside, but it appears to be made of unpainted steel. The indirect light sources illuminate the ceiling and the machinery and tubes and gives everything a very cold, unreal atmosphere.

Don't you scare people?

No, we don't. We have a second light source which works directly, illuminating parts of the old machines with a very warm light. They become areas of warmth in the cold surroundings. It is a mixture of a cold atmosphere and being touched by the warm elements you see in your perception. And we also found beautiful surfaces: concrete pillars, now cleaned, but scarred with the pattern of 100 years of the working process. They are illuminated like a wall in a museum. They tell a story.

Andreas Schulz

Education	Electrical Engineering
Design experience	22 years
Lighting association	PLDA
Field of work	Architectural lighting design, indoor and outdoor
Projects discussed	Galeria Kaufhof Alexanderplatz | Berlin | Germany (2006)
	Former Coal washer Zollverein | Essen | Germany (2006)
	Novartis campus, WJS-2099 Parking | Basel | Switzerland (2007)
Agency	Licht Kunst Licht

Kevan Shaw

For me, Scotland is almost a Scandinavian country, *says Kevan Shaw.* We have particularly gloomy days in winter. In fact, we even have specific Scottish words for this: dure means dark and dull, and dreich is oppressive, grey, perhaps with rain or fog. On the other hand, we also enjoy very long days in summer.

What does that mean for you in terms of design and design ethics?

What interests me and gets me excited about light in Scotland is the nature of change. It changes constantly in quality, in brightness and this change affects the very nature of things. In the winter, people go to work and return home in darkness and from three o'clock onwards, work places are almost 100% artificially lit. It is important for us, as lighting designers, to understand this relationship between natural and artificial light. If you think about it, we have only had artificial light for the last two centuries or so. Before then, we depended on two natural sources of light: sunlight and fire. So for me, it is logical that the oppressive and constantly changing nature of Scottish light informs a lot of my design; it is all about the emotion and feeling that light generates.

How did you become interested in lighting?

My father was an artist who worked extensively in stained glass, tapestry and water colour. He was very interested in the way the colour, shape and form of glass reacted to light; he was fascinated by the nature of light and how the light would come through the window. I remember him being invited to design an exhibition entrance and for that he had a toy theatre with lighting in our house. I played with it and this got me really interested in lighting. But my career plan was to become a curator of Industrial Archaeology and so I studied that, with psychology as a side-line. Lighting, however, still fascinated me, and when, because of the economic situation, it became increasingly difficult to find work as a curator, I became more and more involved in all sorts of lighting activities. I started off doing stage lighting for rock and roll bands, did theatre lighting, a bit of film, some video, trade shows and I've been involved in lighting product development, so I had a broad background even before I decided to focus on architecture. And this is important, I think, because every time I have done something different, I have learned something new and this in turn is later fed back into new projects. This can be technology or an idea. We talk now about emotion in light, but we were using emotional cues in rock and roll lighting way back in the seventies and eighties. My core philosophy is 'light is light is light' and once you understand it, you should be able to apply your thinking in just about every arena.

Is this the same when you tackle architectural projects?
I think you have to be very careful. As lighting designers, we have the tools that can do almost anything to a building. A lot of the time, we have to understand clearly – more clearly, even, than the architect himself – exactly what he sees in the building, what he wants from the building. It is always very easy to use light to distort the building to an extent that the architect may not like. I think of it as creating a storyline; it is important to reach an architectural solution that actually adds something to the building. I always want to consider the user beyond the client – the people who have to live with the thing, not the people who take architectural photographs and then never see the building again.

Do you think there is a motif in your work? Something which makes it recognisable?
Our company is now 19 years old. We are deliberately open to any nature of project, in any area of lighting. What I like is when our projects don't necessarily win lighting awards but actually win architectural awards or recognition for the entire composition. I think there's something of the purist in me: I'm quite interested in getting ideas across but within the context of the building or the architecture or the architect's requirements or the users' requirements. We are open to a very broad scale of projects, right from the smallest church project to mega-structures in the Middle East.

Kevan Shaw

*Saint Mungo's
Church | Glasgow*
→ *Emotions, p. 186*

Can you give an example?

One of our recent church projects was Saint Mungo's Catholic Church. They have a lot of services, short ones, almost every day and in addition there's a large amount of casual use of the church for praying, for confessions and all sorts of other activities. We were asked to provide both the high lighting levels, so that people could actually read their prayer books, but also provide settings for people coming to pray in the evening. It's all scene setting, using very simple technology. But the idea is to change the mood and the focus within the church for the different kinds of use that the building provides. In the private prayer setting, there is a low light, because people are not expected to read, and the only focus is on the crucifix. And the lighting of the figure on the cross is, in contrast to the warm feeling throughout the church, intentionally cold, so you feel the sense of suffering. This is a private contemplation state, but it can be easily changed to a bigger service state. It is, paradoxically, slightly darker, because we wanted to create a feeling of intimacy by getting people closer to the action, so to speak. It's simply a matter of lighting the areas where you want people to come together and not lighting the other areas.

Centre for Health Science | Inverness
→ *Direction, p. 130*

A totally different challenge was presented by the lighting of the new Centre for Medical Science at Raigmore Hospital in Inverness. This design build for healthcare has a dual function: it is a training facility for both doctors studying at Stirling University and nursing staff training in Aberdeen. The design was originally made by Bennett's Associates and I wanted to produce an integrated lighting strategy as part of the whole design process. For example, there is a copper wall – it's actually a box that sits within the envelope of the building and appears outside. Instead of lighting it from the top, we lit it from the bottom. We took a standard technique – wall-washing – and inverted it so that it became visually more challenging, more exciting.

Gustavo Avilés

*In lighting design you
can start introducing
asymmetrical principles
that obey the funda-
mental principles of
nature.*

Why should you want to create excitement?

The point of teaching is to start with people with open minds. So anything you do to open people's minds, to challenge them, to make them think, is important; it's part of the educational process.

Emotional engagement?

Yes. Exactly. You see, natural light – and I come back to that every time – comes from above. When it doesn't, it's unusual and that brings visual challenge.

Kevan Shaw

Education	Economic, Technological History and Social Psychology
Design experience	35 years
Lighting association	ALD, PLDA, IALD MSLL
Field of work	Museum, event, public realm, leisure, historic, commercial, hospitality, healthcare and arts
Projects discussed	Saint Mungo Church | Glasgow | UK (2004)
	Centre for Health Science | Inverness | UK (2007)
Agency	Kevan Shaw Lighting Design (KSLD)

Kevan Shaw

367

Hiroyasu Shoji

In the early 1980s, I was studying architecture at university. At that time, I anticipated that a perception of light and lighting will be creating new architecture in the future, *says Hiroyasu Shoji, of Japan-based Lightdesign.* During my study, I noticed that many cabalistic temples built during the Heian Era did not have windows. It was part of the architectural style. Inside these temples, it is dark throughout the day. But there is a religious ceremony which involves burning lots of small wooden sticks, called 'GOMA'. That was their lighting. The light intermittently lights the ceiling and walls. There are religious drawings on the walls and ceilings called Mandara. The total space tries to convey cabalistic teachings, concepts and theories with the help of light. This underlines the relationship Japanese architecture has with light.

But there are other examples. Take the traditional Japanese tearoom. Tea parties are hosted at 4 am, so that the participants can enjoy the gradual light of the sun rising as they enjoy their tea. It is extremely sensitive. So Japanese space is a space of sensory perceptions. It is related to light, maybe sound and even aroma. I feel that current architecture is lacking those aspects. I thought that new architecture could be introduced again with lighting that utilises the traditional Japanese concept of space. That is why I decided to study lighting. I also had a feeling in the pit of my stomach that lighting design would emerge in Japan. So I decided to take a chance on this career.

How did you start?

I worked for an organisation called TL Yamagiwa Laboratory, where my immediate boss was Kaoru Mende. I worked there for seven years, and then – I think it was in 1990 – Mr Mende founded his company Lighting Planners Associates and I joined him as a partner. I worked with him until 2000 and then decided to become an independent and start this office. I now work here with seven other specialists.

Do you think architecture is influenced by lighting design today?

I think it has always influenced architecture. Even before artificial lighting and electric lighting, how to deal with light was a big theme in architecture. Now we have broader choices, including artificial lighting in addition to the daylight that comes through openings and windows. But in the past few decades, lighting has come to mean functionality. To secure a certain level of brightness. It soon became the brighter the better. Bright lighting was great. But it is not right, it is not soothing. Now even architects are starting to realise that it is an absurd way of thinking.

Can you describe some of your more memorable projects?

I think one of the most interesting results I was able to achieve in architecture was for the Matsumoto Performing Arts Centre, designed by Toyo Ito. The concept allows the light to ooze through the interior of the architecture. For example, during the day, light oozes in through a wall inlayed with amorphous glass. At night, the glass on this wall glows, creating a feeling of excitement, anticipation on the path leading to the performing arts stage. The inside of the spacious hall has small, sparkling lights which create a glamorous and glorious space like a chandelier. On the way back, after watching the performance, you follow the same path, but the light appears different. The environment is calmer, allowing you to live in the moment, enjoy the ambience longer. The space successfully synthesises lighting and architecture with natural lighting. The lighting changes naturally to uplift and prolong the emotion of the visitors.

Matsumoto Performing Arts Centre | Nagano
→ Direction, p. 124

NTT Docomo Tower | Osaka

Something different is the lighting we did for a mobile telephone mast. When mobile phones in Japan had built-in antennas, there was a small illumination tip placed on the antenna that lit when the phone was in use. It did not use power from the battery but instead from electromagnetic waves. In this tower, we put all the light units at the top and they illuminate depending on the level of phone use. And so the light fluctuates, changes.

Was there some message you were trying to convey?
The reason I made it this way is so that people in the cars and trains and hurrying on their way home can feel some comfort in knowing that they are not alone. That people are communicating with each other by phones. My approach is to treat lighting as a way to make it easier to identify the aim of the space.

You mentioned lighting changing.
I think change is very important in lighting. And also how that change occurs. We do not notice it, but designing light means either the light changes gradually in a matter of seconds or it makes a sudden, dramatic emergence. The way light changes makes a big difference to the way we feel. The sun rises in the morning. The sun goes up, casts a shadow. It moves to the west, turns orange and creates long shadows. And then the sun sets. It does not become dark all of a sudden, but there is a moment that is called the blue moment, and after that moment, it gradually gets dark. We take for granted that the light of the sun changes. It is abnormal for it not to change. I think humans would go crazy if they stayed in a high-rise building all day, where no change of light occurs. The only thing is that drastic change is not good. The important thing is slow and natural change. What is inspiring is the natural light in, say, a desert in Morocco. When I was there, I saw it in moonlight. The moon changed, casting a tiny shadow, and I watched for a long time.

I thought that the change of natural light is the strongest power source to touch and move the hearts of people. As I do many architectural jobs, I have many opportunities to see the work of leading Japanese architects like Toyo Ito. When I do that – rather than just seeing pictures – I see them with the light changing in the background. I feel touched. I feel the flow. Critics explain why this space is good and what is happening with the lighting in a given space. But this is quite difficult for the general public. What is easy for them to understand is, for example, an experience that the lighting is suddenly dimmed in an Italian restaurant at 10 pm. I decided to publish a book that targets the general public and talks about how to enjoy light at home. It is a book of lighting recipes. Eggs, for example, can be cooked in different ways. An egg can be made into an omelette or egg custard. There is also a big difference in the way you can eat. You can eat delicious food with your friends, and that becomes memorable. Or you can eat something just to fill a hungry stomach. These two are different. And this is the resemblance between light and food.

Is there another source of inspiration for you?

Music is also interesting. Because music already has its own time line. Because it is a change of sound. There are many logics to the way the sounds change. Music also has the power to make you feel comfortable, no matter where you are. I believe lighting has the power to have presence like music. Because just like music, light is important to life. Japanese people are not able to enjoy it yet. European people have a culture of using candles at home. But that tradition was lost in Japan. We have also lost the sense of enjoying natural light. Fluorescent lights are turned on as soon as they come home and this is what they are used to in their daily lives. There is a popular trend among Japanese men. When they go home, the lighting is very bright, with their wife and children around. When the other members have gone to bed, they create a different light, something in which they can open their hearts in a very small private place. Japanese values are based on change. Their aesthetics are visual. For example, Japanese people find it beautiful to see cherry blossom petals falling and the architecture of Ise-jingu (shrines) is rebuilt every 20 years, because it is not considered eternal.

Japanese culture has a background of actively accepting change. I think Japanese people have sensitive ideas towards the change of light. Their lighting environment has been getting brighter and brighter over the past few decades. My hope is that we will find a trigger so that that brightness is gradually reduced. It is the concept of better quality instead of greater quantity.

Education	Architectural design and Engineering
Design experience	26 years
Lighting association	IALD
Field of work	Outdoor architecture, indoor design
Projects discussed	Matsumoto Performing Arts Centre | Nagano | Japan (2004)
	NTT Docomo Tower | Osaka | Japan (2004)
Agency	Lightdesign

Hiroyasu Shoji

Francesca Storaro

Light has at least three languages, *states Italy- based Francesca Storaro.* The first, which is most commonly used, is simply functional lighting. It is created in order to allow us to see a monument or building, and is based purely on light. The second language is based on the interpretation of light based on the architecture. I call this architectural lighting. After you carefully study a monument, a cathedral, a building, you try to capture the history of that object. You want to show why it was built in this way – and generally this is what the designer or client wants. When I use this language, I can allow people to see things at night which they can see in natural light during the day.

Then there is the third language and this is one I am making increasingly my own. This is the communicative language of light, using light as communication. Light has a language, just as writing is expressed in letters and music is expressed by the seven notes of the scale. Light speaks by means of contrasts between light and shadow, and by means of colours, which are known as the sons of light. Using this, you can add communicative value. Nowadays, a great mistake is often made: colours are added just to create a scene. I believe that there is a story associated to every colour, an emotion, a significance that you want to give to that particular building.

How did you first become involved in lighting?

I started out as an architect and got a degree in Rome. During my studies, I was preparing for a lighting design exam. I produced a simulation, a model, a design. Around the same time, my father, Vittorio Storaro, who is a cinematographer, was asked to produce a lighting project for a square for Italia 90. My father persuaded me to combine the two things; I was responsible for the design part. We built a model and submitted our proposal. The whole thing fascinated me, because it became a language to me. I was acquiring all my father's knowledge, his language and culture regarding light. He had talked about light from my earliest days, but then applied to the cinema. It's a completely different technical and cultural approach. I have a different type of cultural training – technical, but at the same time a cultural, historic and philosophical approach. I become keen about the idea of bringing this knowledge, this cultural background, into a different environment. Not the cinema, but something that was specifically mine, the field of architecture. I wanted to take the past I had inherited from my father and turn it into something of my own: my own language of lighting in architecture.

You say you carefully study a project. Can you give us an example?

When I designed the lighting for the Campidolglio in Rome, I wanted to understand the concept which had been developed by Michel-angelo. It is based on the balance of forms, of horizontal and vertical elements. This concept of balance was translated into an architectural language. The piazza was virtually shut off from the public – there were no access routes. And so Michelangelo began creating them. He added a stairway, and this is the element of earth. To create inte-gration with the surrounding buildings and to impart symmetry to the square, he added a fountain, in other words the element of water. This is what Bernini called the poetry of the defect: an architectural element which appears to be an obstacle but actually gives you a brilliant idea. But Michelangelo went further: he used a balustrade as an innovative element, to create a link between the earth and the sky. The element of air. In the centre there is the statue of Marcus Aurelius, placed there as a symbol of power, of energy.

Thus you find the four elements – fire, earth, air and water – sym-bolised in Michelangelo's concept. In my lighting, I used a combination of four colours – ochre for earth, red for fire, green for water and blue for air – with white in the centre.

Piazza del Campidoglio | Rome
→ Colour, p. 068

Arnolfo di Cambio |
San Giovanni Valdarno
→ *Contrast in colour, p. 094*

Another example is the lighting concept I developed for the only building produced by Arnolfo di Cambio. It dates from around 1300 and is located in San Giovanni Valdarno. It is a very simple rectangular building. Subsequently, parts were added: porticos at the side, an additional façade element in the lower parts, and another façade projecting at the front. All these disguise the original Arnolfo di Cambio design. I have tried to make his original design prominent once more by means of light, by playing with its colour and using dual lighting. The building is protected by the Department of Monuments and Fine Arts and the use of colour could not be justified in this case. So I used white light – but used warm white light tending towards yellow and cold white light tending towards blue. I lit the original parts of the building with warm white light and the porticos with cold white light. For the rest of the building I used neutral white light, as this joins together the warm and cold colours. I was very pleased with that project.

What was your inspiration for these projects?
I was mainly guided by my lighting concept. Each project is individual. Light can be used in a new and different way each time. Each time, by changing the light, a building can be interpreted in a different way and is consequently enhanced. With lighting, you can create a dual life for architecture: a daytime life and a night-time life. And all of this can communicate to you the language of the architect who designed it.

And do you get the impression that ordinary people are becoming aware of this language, of this language of light?
When you see a place lit up, you may not know the reasons which led that designer to come up with that lighting, but you can always sense the emotion, even if you have no knowledge of the subject. Light completely changes the way you look at a place; it creates a certain atmosphere. Chromo therapy gives you the perception of what you are seeing. There is, it seems to me, a lot of discussions about the use of colours. I really think it depends on the way you use them. If you just add colour for the sake of it, people are right to resist it, because it makes no sense. If, on the other hand, it is a concept, a perception, then it is quite a different matter.

Bernini | Rome

Francesca Storaro

Are you influenced by other elements?

My approach is not purely technical, but also strongly historical. It consists of studies of philosophy and of the culture of light.

I have been lucky, because my father helped me a lot in this respect. I think that as a designer you cannot rely purely on a technical approach when handling a project. You must also have a solid basis in the history of art and the philosophy of architecture. In other words, the more humanist part.

Education	Architect
Design experience	20 years
Lighting association	PLDA, IALD
Field of work	Exhibitions, architecture, design, interior and outdoor
Projects discussed	Piazza del Campidoglio | Rome | Italy (2002)
	Arnolfo di Cambio | San Giovanni Valdarno | Italy (2004)
Agency	Francesca Storaro lighting design

Francesca Storaro

Satoshi Uchihara

For me, lighting design should be about designing the abstract ambience, *says Satoshi Uchihara of Japan-based Uchihara Creative Lighting Design.* Design is visible, but its objective is to design what is invisible as well. Lighting is communication; it is about the things we see with our eyes open. As soon as we close our eyes, we would have to imagine many things, such as feeling the air and sensing other people because we cannot see. Not being able to see is an inconvenient situation on the surface, but it is actually an environment where so many potentials can be explored for a human being. There is an amazing gradation of light between the worlds of seeing and not seeing. I am very interested in how to design that.

We often think that communication with words is sufficient. But it is actually not even close to enough. I believe that spiritual and emotional communication comes from cultural aspects. The Japanese traditional sense of beauty contributes to this spiritual and emotional communi- cation. For example, the sense of beauty that comes from the tea ceremony, a Japanese-style room or garden. Even everyday affairs, such as bathing and eating, as well as statues of Buddha, and historical and religious affairs. They have all helped our way of communication. I think we have it as our base. A beautiful thing is not necessarily complete in itself. Rather than just seeing the beautiful centrepiece, we have to understand the surroundings to allow us to understand completely the intent of others. We call this mitate (judgement) or saho (code).

Was this philosophy something you developed over time?

I am still moving forward – recognising more and more the possibilities of light. For example, as Le Corbusier said, we call a container in which to put water a 'glass'; for him, architecture is a 'receptor of light'. We pour water into a clear glass. The water fills in the shape of the glass. If you think of water as light, when you have finished a building, the last thing you pour in is the light. The light fills the architecture and oozes out. So one way to look at architecture is as a receptor, a container for light. This is not something that hit me in the face all of a sudden; it grew gradually. I spent the first 10 years of my life as a lighting designer improving my technical skills. During that time I worked as chief designer with the firm of Ms. Ishii. During the following 10 years, I became more positive about asserting my opinions and became more proactive about expressing my design. It was during that time that everything changed. It was the first time I reflected on myself, about what my backbone is and what it means to be Japanese.

Do you have a specific way of approaching a project?

The mission of a designer is to fulfil the terms of the client within the set budget. And although what I have said may sound like an artist talking, I believe we can achieve our design philosophy no matter what the budget may be. This is because, even if we were only able to use one lamp in a spacious area, we can implement various design controls to show how one lamp can be diverse and make a difference (unless, of course, people only want on or off). We are mainly involved in big projects, but what is crucial is to see if the objectives of our client and the needs of the end user are the same. They are often slightly different. It may demand difficult techniques, but we always strive to realise a comprehensive design for the end users when making a presentation to our client. Therefore, even if there is a budget issue, it does not concern the end users. The value of light ultimately perceived by the end users has to stand on its own without a consideration of financial factors such as cost performance.

Can you describe some of your projects for us?

We particularly value Japanese cultural and local projects, in particular ones in Kyoto. The Kinkakuji Temple (Golden Temple) in Kyoto is very unusual. It has gold plating on the structure and a finished gold surface, but inside there is a concentration of purity and excellent examples of Japanese art. We made the gilding into a silhouette. By lighting the surrounding mountains, we revealed only the silhouette of the structure. Actually, underneath the gilding there is the pitch black plaster temple. The concepts of 'inner space' or 'having a universe inside

The Kinkakuji Temple | Kyoto

Satoshi Uchihara

377

oneself' found in Oriental philosophy are not conveyed by looking at the temple objectively, but such a world of expression is made possible by using lighting.

What emotions were you trying to express?

Astonishment. Because it does not show the physical object. Lighting generally illuminates the object directly. When we undertook lighting for the Byodoin Temple in Kyoto, we achieved all the lighting through reflection from the water. What we were trying to achieve was to express and convey the flow of time – the 1000 years that this wooden structure has existed.

Byodoin Temple | Kyoto
→ Direction, p. 142

Another interesting project was the Beautiful Fukushima Future Expo in 2001. It is an environmental expo. We placed 3000 objects in a 24-hectare space. We used a combination of simple technologies, without any unnecessary wiring. All the lights of the pavilions are set to modulate periodically. Expos are for people and lights are necessary for humans; other living creatures do not require light at night. It generated a very negative response. People felt it was such a dark expo.

Beautiful Fukushima
Future Expo | Sukagawa
→ Dynamics in brightness, p. 060

La-Orchai Boonpiti
You go into the space
and you are fully
submerged into its
environment.

I wanted, however, to provide an environment in which people could feel that we live in a larger rhythm of things. Using an LED system, I achieved natural programmes of energy circulation without unnecessary wiring.

The illumination was linked with the sunset and the flashing was activated by the wind. Each unit has an individual microphone and the lights flash when the wind blows through it. It is very easy for humans to intentionally control a fake environment; it is difficult to produce a presentation to touch people's hearts while keeping it natural.

Have you undertaken other environmental projects?

We tried an interesting experiment in Ehime. It features old Japanese housing, which creates the ambience of this town. In order to create a night scene of the town, we proposed creating the light based on how light oozed from the windows. We called in 'window light'. But to realise this concept, we had to explain the concept to each of the owners. We went door to door, and finally received the cooperation of all 200 households. They also agreed to use their own electricity and the municipality agreed to reimburse the costs at the end of the project. It lasted for three months and then we went door to door again to pay them. All the 200 households received a few hundred yen

Houses | Ehime

and they all asked: 'Did it require such a small amount of money?' The point we made is that people do not fully understand what energy use really costs.

We all know we must reduce energy. Take illumination of offices. I think it is possible to reduce the light intensity from 750 lux to 500 lux. It would save the output of one atomic power plant. When people understand this, they can make a choice. In Asia, in Japan particularly, fluorescent tubes with more than 4000 Kelvin are used in the living environment. What has become noticeable in the past five years is that when you ride the bullet train from west Japan to Tokyo, the colour temperature of the residential windows goes down rapidly the closer you get to Tokyo. In those past 5 years, the lighting trend is changing from dense white light in apartments to warmer colours.

You mentioned Le Corbusier earlier; are there other people who have influenced you?
I am most influenced by the Japanese people. Buddhist priests. Gardeners. I learn a lot from them. I was first heavily influenced by the West, but lately I am more influenced by Japan.

One hundred years ago, we used to say 'hear the aroma'. The characters that represent the goddess statue of Buddhism mean 'see the sound'. Lighting designers have to create light that exudes aroma.

Saying aroma is sensed by the nose answers nothing. You have to widen your imagination fully to truly understand your feeling when you are in contact with a certain aroma. Only then, can you mount the steps of creativity.

Education	Design
Design experience	28 years
Lighting association	IES, IESNA, IALD
Field of work	Architectural, interior lighting design
Projects discussed	Omotesando Hills | Tokyo | Japan (2006)
	Tokyo International Airport (Haneda) | Tokyo | Japan (2004)
	Roppongi Hills Keyakizaka Complex (2003)
	Beautiful Fukushima Future Expo | Fukushima | Japan (2001)
	Kinkakuji temple | Kyoto | Japan (1996)
	Byoudouin temple | Kyoto | Japan (1994)
Agency	Uchihara Creative Lighting Design

Satoshi Uchihara

Dolly & Anil Valia

Bahai Lotus Temple | New Delhi
→ Brightness, p. 030

Our projects include outdoor architectural lighting for retail applications, office lighting and residential lighting with controls, *says Anil Valia, who works together with his daughter Dolly as a Lighting Systems Consultant in Mumbai.* The lighting design concept is very, very important in these projects. The essential element is the architect or client's brief – the lighting is just an add-on. We develop our lighting solution on the basis of this brief.

Apart from the architectural features, what other key factors do you take into account?
We also consider any strong material, painting or other aspects. If the building is old, like a thousand-year-old Hindu/Buddhist/Chinese temple, we may have to deal with archaeologists or preservation regulations.

Dolly: We also have to take the religious aspect into account. For example, for mosque façade lighting we have to use green light. Jainism does not permit façade lighting because many innocent flies will be killed – in some religions this innocent killing is not allowed, so this affects what we do too.

Are your concepts always realised exactly as you had intended?
Anil: The lighting design is subject to discussion. The concept is most important, it has to be realised quite quickly, and factors like power consumption play a role. Budgetary constraints often mean we have

to compromise. The availability of products to be used is a problem, but that has improved. We also rely to some extent on custom-built products.

Solid-state lighting is really taking off now. How soon will it be used on a large scale in India?
We started using LEDs in the year 2000, and most architects are using them now. The advantages they offer over conventional light sources are well publicised, so the future looks bright for them. The advantage of LEDs for architectural lighting is the strength of their colours.

Will coloured lighting and dynamic lighting catch on, or will people soon tire of them?
Dolly: Well, customers want their building or shopping mall to look attractive. It's a matter of personal choice. LEDs offer so many possibilities, such as interactive lighting, a lot of gimmicks to do with human perception… they can be programmed, so they appeal to the young. I would like to do a project with an interactive façade or an interactive lobby.

Asian Paints Colour Store, Mumbai

To what extent does the concept depend on cultural or emotional factors?
Modern buildings everywhere tend to share the same architectural features and materials. Wherever you go today you find coloured structures, atria, glass façades, etc. For an old building, however, you would have to consider the style or the religious context. Globalisation means there is more interaction between the various countries and cultures, giving rise to the same modern architecture, so there should be no difference in terms of lighting parameters.

Anil: In the case of the older styles, different cultures developed separately from each other, these differences were amplified and that's why older buildings vary more from one part of the world to another.

How do you usually interpret your conceptual themes in lighting terms?
We look at contrast and brightness. If the background is totally dark and the façade or other area is comparatively lighter, then even a little bit of illumination will help. But if the background brightness is higher, then you may need an even higher brightness level. This can be killing, and that's where colour contrast can be helpful.

How are different colours used to bring out the architecture?

After only having mercury and GLS lamps, which just gave flat flood-lighting, the introduction of the sodium-vapour lamp in India meant we were able to use contrast, enabling us to create depth and 3D effects. Now, with LEDs, there are lots of advantages – colour, long lifetime, colour changing, DMX control and so on. They make dynamic lighting possible, and all these advantages mean LEDs are becoming more widely accepted.

Dolly, do you use colour differently from your father?

On the whole, I follow my father's example. He's like my guru. But I did devise a concept for a silverware shop where the background was too dark to display the silverware effectively. I suggested dynamic coloured lighting, so it's not just the bright lighting but also the changing colour that attracts customers.

Do you think coloured lighting attracts more than white light?

They attract equally. It just depends on the requirements of the project. Dynamic lighting, which can be a change in colour or a change in brightness, attracts more than static lighting or mono-coloured lighting.

When choosing coloured lighting equipment, how do you allow for the interplay of coloured light with coloured materials?

Anil: You have to be very careful. If the façade is white, there is no problem, but if it is coloured, it will absorb certain wavelengths and reflect others. If you are using LEDs, you can program them to include only wavelengths that are reflected well. LEDs use very saturated colours and the way different wavelengths interact on different surfaces is fascinating.

What specific ways of applying lighting stimuli or lighting effects can be used to translate a concept into reality?

We've done at least 50 outdoor lighting projects, and the techniques we use include luminance or brightness, colour, contrast, brightness and colour contrast. The latter two are very important: they define the linearity / 3D effect, the profile of the building at night. We also use colour change – that comes under dynamic lighting.

We like to make our lighting interactive, which involves tailoring the colour of the light to suit what people like.

Do you think different colours convey different meanings, different emotions?

Yes. For us red would mean 'stop', but emotionally it is also associated with Christmas. Red is a warmer colour. In sound and light shows we use it to show a war is going on. Green, for example, is definitely a sign of peace, and we often use it to light Muslim architecture. These days, midnight blue is regularly used on façades, but in drama blue also means sorrow. We use different colours to evoke human emotions. In general, people tend to use blue a lot, and this may be because we are more sensitive to blue. I think dynamic lighting is probably also somehow linked to emotions.

Do you see regional or national differences in personal preference for a certain kind of light?

Brightness contrasted with mono colour is generally always acceptable to people, but when we did the Swami Narayan Temple in Gandhinagar way back in 1992 we only used halogen, hodium and metal halide lamps. However when another temple in Delhi was lighted by them after say 15 years, we observed a high level of acceptance for colour changing light, even among religious organisations! So things are changing.

Swami Narayan Temple | Gandhinagar

And have you seen a difference in preferences between the north and the west of India?

Anil: Yes. In the west, people prefer the light effect to be created by light sources that are hidden. But when you go to Punjab or even in the South, you find people prefer the light effect to be created by a light source that is visible like festival lighting. Colour is gradually becoming more acceptable and in the same way dynamic lighting will become more acceptable over time. It is up to us professionals to educate people about the benefits, about the link between the human emotional aspect and the colour changing.

I always like to implement something different. In one of the projects the architects wanted façade lighting with metal halide lamps. This would have highlighted the defects in the plastered wall, so we did a demonstration and they accepted my solution of blue and green 400 W coloured metal halide lamps. Since then, similar solutions have been used on many buildings in Mumbai.

Dolly & Anil Valia

So is there a preference for higher lighting levels these days?

Higher lighting levels are always liked by the people on the road, but when you take into account the energy and capital costs, it is better to use colour contrast, static or colour change/ dynamic background with white light focused on displays in Shop / Retail Lighting. The outlay for dynamic lighting is higher, but the total running costs are lower. People are gradually realising and accepting this.

Do you think we all interpret lighting in the same way?

I think there are certain lighting effects that are understood by everyone, such as accent lighting, uplighting, dimming up and dimming down, but there are others that tend to be more open to interpretation, such as silhouette lighting and the use of coloured light as opposed to white or monochromatic light. And then there are things like flashing lights that people don't really understand at all – because that flickering people see outdoors is normally only on top of towers: it's information for aircraft.

So, do you feel there is a need for a common lighting vocabulary?

It is important to publish documentation to guide the lighting fraternity, so they communicate in the same language with the users, specifiers and the public at large. In this way they will achieve the right type of result instead of creating something that is totally unacceptable.

Education	Dolly Valia: Interior Designer
	Anil Valia: Electrical Engineer
Design experience	Dolly Valia: 10 years
	Anil Valia: 37 years
Lighting association	IALD, CIE, ISLE, CEEAMA, MIE, FISLE, MIES(NA), FILE,
	MIES(AU)
Field of work	Outdoor façade, landscape, retail, offices, residential,
	temples, stadium, airports
Projects discussed	Bahai Lotus Temple | New Delhi | India
	Akshardham Swaminarayan Temple | Ahmedabad | India
	Asian Paints Colour Store | Mumbai | India
Agency	Lighting Systems Consultant

Dolly & Anil Valia

Patrick Woodroffe

When I started in rock 'n' roll back in 1972, there wasn't really a lighting industry, *says Patrick Woodroffe*, and the role of lighting designer didn't really exist. We invented it. Until then, they simply called it 'doing the lights'. Basically all you had was a very primitive fader connected to a couple of lights, and when we became very sophisticated, a flash button! I think that's where I learnt my trade; it was all very instinctive back then. You were really painting pictures with few lights and using small stages. Today the situation has changed completely. The rock music industry has the biggest budgets and we are the ones who developed all the automated lighting technology that's now used in films, theatre and architecture.

When did automated lighting start?

The first moving light was commissioned by Genesis. That was back in the nineties. They had an elaborate lighting scheme for their performances, but found that the follow spot operators were not reliable. They asked if an automated system could be devised, and Showco, an American sound company, made the first moving light.

You work with Genesis now, right?

Yes, I just designed their latest tour. They are known for having the best light shows and so we spent six months conceiving the show. I began with detailed discussions with the band and their manager to understand what the show was actually about before we began the technical process of designing the system. Then the process took place where the team all come together and there is a lot of collaboration between the various designers and supply companies to organise the technicalities of the scheme. Finally we all came together in Belgium for our full production rehearsals. It's at that point where you finally have your palette and your blank canvas in front of you.

Genesis Live 2007 | Europe

What do you mean by your palette?

We set up our lighting: 450 moving lights. Everything is working. And then you sit down with your programmers and start painting your picture.

So it's like having all your paints ready and your easel set up?

Exactly. You sit there are at your easel and paint your picture. In fact, you paint two hours of pictures, which, of course, are animated, and which move and evolve.

So this is the creative stage?

Yes. We spent three weeks on production rehearsals and worked something like 18 hours a day. You begin with nothing. The control board's memory is empty. And then you start: what will the first song look like? Now Genesis is known for its complicated lighting, but I wanted to start with an unusual statement. The first song was 7 minutes long, and I decided to use only 1 cue in it. The audience see this enormous lighting system and on the first note, every single light in the system comes on and floods the stage with white light. Even the video screen goes white. And we keep this lighting for the full 7 minutes. The band plays extremely complicated music, and throughout the opening number, the audience concentrate on the band. We are really saying: 'This moment is simply about the music' But nobody was disappointed. And then, when the second song began, we introduced incredibly complicated cues and colours and changes. If you do anything with enough conviction, you can get away with it. I think that is true of all art.

Genesis Live 2007 | Europe

We then look at each song, and I begin by saying to my team this song is the red song, this song is the blue song and so on. If I have any sort of signature in my style of lighting, it is that I tend to be very mono-chromatic. I don't like to have lots of mixed up colours; I like to make very simple statements. We do this for the 18 songs in the concert, and try not to do any other song in red or blue. Each song has a real identity, both visually and musically.

So in fact you're creating a visual musical identity.

You have the colour signature, but then you also have the dynamics. Some songs are incredibly dynamic and powerful with lots of changes. Now you could follow all those changes, but I prefer to vary the technique and so some songs will be syncopated and full of action and others will be completely static. I once did a show for Bob Dylan where he played 18 songs and there were only 18 lighting cues!

Patrick Woodroffe

Nissar Allana

The whole concept of scenography is that the actors, the lighting and the sets interact with one another; it is the dynamics between them that keeps the play alive.

The Rolling Stones
2005/2006 | World Tour

You play with the tension between what the audience is expecting and what actually happens.

Yes, exactly. Everything that happens must appear to come from the band. When I'm working with big dynamic performers such as The Rolling Stones, Mick Jagger can make a big move or Keith Richard can do a big guitar thing, and if I make a huge lighting change, it must appear as if it was because of what the artists were doing.

How do you do that?

I guess it comes down to putting the music first. One of the advantages I have is that I've done a lot of theatre, ballet, opera and architecture. I understand that it's all about the performance. Lighting is, in many ways, an addendum. You have the performance, whatever it might be, and lighting has to reinforce that, it has to discover and then reinforce the emotion coming from that performance. On the other hand, what we do is incredibly visual. A huge lighting show is very impressive, but it always has to come back to the music. One of the other things I do is always to make sure that the artist is lit, regardless of how dynamic the light show might be at that moment. A good example of this is The Rolling Stones. I've done their lighting for 25 years and I always put a white spotlight on each member of the band and I pretty much leave them on all night. I think it's up to the audience which band member they choose to watch. That's another part of lighting: illumination. You have to light what you want to see. Lighting design is very much a combination of craft and art, and you have to get both the practical and the artistic elements right. Unless you get to the point where you are completely comfortable with the technology, you have no freedom to be an artist.

I'm not underestimating the work of the lighting designer – I think it's skilful, artistic and involves taste and experience – but it doesn't mean anything without the performance. It's to do with drawing something out of the performance.

Automated lighting gave us a dimension we never had before. All you could do previously was to work with intensity: the light was either on or it was off. But suddenly we had a new dynamic. It was like discovering an extra undiscovered sense. It was really exciting.

Do you believe that there's a language of light?

I think the answer is probably yes. I remember when I first worked with The Rolling Stones, more than 25 years ago. I was taken to the dressing-room to meet Mick Jagger and I asked him if he had any ideas

Patrick Woodroffe

about the lighting. He said 'Well I suppose bright for the fast numbers, darker for the ballads'. And you know that still holds true. Ballads are blue, moody, and need a cool colour. If you have a blue stage and some strong white backlight on your star they will always look fantastic.

Brightness, though, is a factor of many things. Bright might mean you can see somebody from the back of a huge stadium, but in a smaller theatre, bright might mean something very different. When I did Genesis people said that nobody would want to sit through 7 minutes of white light at the start of a pop concert. But I was convinced that it was right and I followed it through. I don't know whether there are any rules as such – but it there are, they're there to be broken.

Andreas Schulz

We think that following the rules actually leads to the problems we see in some over-lit large cities.

In this business, the artists have to trust you. They have to trust your craftsmanship, your artistry and your judgement. After all, you are painting a very public picture of them; it's a bit like commissioning an artist to do your portrait and you'd want to make sure it was a good one!

Education	Rock 'n' roll lighting
Design experience	32 years
Lighting association	IES, IESNA, IALD
Field of work	Music, dance, theatre, opera, events and architecture
Projects discussed	The Rolling Stones | World Tour (2005/2006)
	John Madejski garden, Victoria and Albert Museum | London | UK (2006)
	Genesis Live | Europe (2007)
Agency	Patrick Woodroffe Lighting Design

Patrick Woodroffe

Research
Overview

Research Summary

Light triggers emotions in different ways and has a profound impact on the way people perceive and experience their environment.

Independent lighting designers' visions and ideas have shown that lighting affects people emotionally. The same lighting concept can be interpreted differently by people, depending upon their cultural sensitivities, individual taste and past experiences.

As new technologies make it possible to do things that were not previously possible the question, how lighting triggers emotions becomes increasingly important.

Main message _ All lighting designers interviewed indicated that the fundamental objective of great lighting design is to provoke an emotional response in the users of buildings and spaces. Lighting plays an important role in evoking emotions. The interviews indicate that this can be done in two ways. A lighting design can be used to make an architectural space more aesthetically pleasing or it can create an atmosphere in that space. Both affect people's emotions. In addition, the user's well-being can be directly influenced by light.

Influences _ A number of factors influence the desired emotional reaction in the creative process of the lighting designer: the context, personal profile and their inspiration sources. The interviews show that educational background or a role model can have a strong influence on lighting designers, especially in the first years of their career.

Approach _ Among the lighting designers interviewed, different design approaches can be identified: in some cases the lighting design supports the architect's original idea, while in others it actually changes the experience of a building or space in a positive way. The execution can differ too, the approach taken varying from, for example, an artistic content-based one to a technical expertise-based one. The style of a lighting designer – in essence determined by education, personal profile and inspiration – is reflected in the design approach as well.

Tools _ In the end, all lighting designers work with the same tools: brightness, colour, direction, contrast and time. More extensive background can be found in part two. Generally speaking, lighting designers also use similar combinations of lighting qualities for a given emotion. The wide diversity of lighting designs and executions is a result of the individual lighting designers' personal style combined with the specific context of the projects in question.

Whereas the interviews give insights into the way a lighting design can evoke an emotion, it is clear that the user's personal experience and the context will influence the perceived – as opposed to the created – emotion as well.

This was not part of the project, but might be of interest for follow-up research. Since light triggers emotion in different ways, the following pages present more specific findings as key aspects of lighting design.

Roos Molendijk

Emotion is fundamental in lighting design

The fundamental objective of great lighting design is to provoke an emotional response from the users of buildings and spaces. When generating an emotional reaction, lighting designers aim to offer an interpretation of a place. Lighting design is not just about displaying one's technical proficiency but about giving the users of a building or space something to think about.

Lighting designers consider lighting design as: a way to tell a story, a communication tool or similar to creating music. The perception and emotional reaction of the end-user is assumed to depend on context and personal profile. No lighting designer has just one emotion he or she wants to express. Emotions differ per project.

All lighting designers agree that lighting plays an important role in evoking emotions by influencing the atmosphere and mood. Light partly determines the atmosphere of a place, and through this, also the mood and emotions of the people in it. It is not so much about lighting buildings or spaces alone, but rather evoking reactions in people through the lighting.

Individuals are taken as a reference, as it is important to know how users will feel in a place. A design should enhance and optimise the experience of the people who use the space.

If a lighting design is aesthetically pleasing but has a negative effect on people – for example, if the lighting creates a negative mood, makes users feel unwell, creates fear and so on – it isn't doing its job properly.

Some environments ask for a lighting project that makes end-users feel more comfortable and want to stay in the place for a longer time. Others ask for lighting design solutions that focus the attention in the directions of a specific object inside the environment e.g. on the desk in an office, on a statue in religious places.

For some lighting designers the focus on people and their emotions plays a bigger role in their designs than for others.

Some lighting designers take the people-reference a step further by claiming that lighting design is not about lighting a space but about the people in it. In that case the approach taken could be: "How can my lighting influence how they will feel" or "How can my lighting trigger emotions?"

The perception of light and its effect on human beings is subjective. Lighting designers are often aware of the psychological effects experienced by the end-user when developing their designs. Lighting influences people in a subconscious way. It influences how users feel in a place. This also determines how people perceive, behave and use the place. It strongly determines the appreciation, and thus their behaviour: if people like a place, find it attractive, striking, relaxing, intriguing, inviting, they tend to stay longer.

The evolution of human beings is significant when understanding the emotional response to light. It is linked to the experience of light by people in the past. Firelight has an intimate, sensual but also slightly sinister quality.

Morning light fills us with optimism and energy. The light of late afternoon is calm and soothing. Moonlight is haunting and mysterious. Then people have a far stronger emotional response to natural light than to artificial light. The actual emotion experienced is determined by the personal profile of the end-user.

Context-focused design

Conveying emotions through lighting includes giving some 'information' or some indications about a place and its history. For this, an understanding of a place is needed.

The specific characteristics of a place include its history, culture (religion, symbols, attitudes) and surroundings (environment, nature, climate). Knowledge of these aspects allows the identity, the spirit of the place, to be respected and highlighted.

Light is a very subjective thing; its perception is always 'coloured' by the surrounding in which it exists and by the attitudes of the people who see the light. The same lighting design can be perceived completely differently according to the place and time.

Some lighting designers really want to gain a lot of in-depth knowledge about a place. This seems especially important for historical sites.

Personal profile

**Countries tend to want to develop their own lighting culture,
even though individual lighting designers might have been influenced by western lighting designers in the past. In western
countries lighting design has been around longer and is therefore
more developed than in non-western countries. Due to this
head start, western lighting design therefore tends to exert some
influence on or even act as an example to other countries.**

Education _ Some lighting design schools have a strong impact on future
lighting designers: Parsons School of Design in New York, Bartlett School of
Architecture in London, the University of Wismar in Germany are mentioned
several times by lighting designers. They have inspired and influenced them.
A other way of gaining knowledge of lighting is one's experience in an
established lighting design agency. These agencies influence the philosophy
of lighting designers, especially in the first years of their career. After
returning to their home country, lighting designers face the challenge of
applying their knowledge and experience in their own culture.

The European school is considered to be richer, more spontaneous and with
greater possibilities for expressing emotions, whereas the American school
is a pioneer in lighting, a master of technique, but colder and more methodical.
Brazilian lighting designers, for example, try to take the best from both
the European and American school. In the interviews Korean lighting designers
mention that they use a mix of Japanese and Western lighting styles.
By using the Japanese strong sense of belonging and the European individual
character of the artist themselves, Korean lighting is considered less direct
than Western lighting, using more elements such as shadow.

Lighting designers today are primarily influenced by three main cultural parameters: geography, religion and society.

Geography _ The geographical situation has an impact on preference for certain colour temperatures. In warm regions with very bright daylight and hot temperatures, people prefer cool white light. In colder regions, however, people tend to prefer warmer lighting.

Religion _ Religions have different meanings for light. This leads to certain values. For example: the Buddhist religion seems to lead to a preference for nature and tranquillity. In particular, Zen principles seem to lead to a preference for simplicity and subtlety. In the Christian-based religions, the colour blue is often associated with the divine.

Society _ Society determines the attitude and approach of lighting designers. Lighting designers are influenced in their opinions and their behaviour by the society in which they live. It influences their assumptions of how places will be used and also the relationships with their clients.

Inspiration sources

At the start of the lighting design process: the context, the history and the way a place will be used is usually taken into account. Like in architecture, this is the project foundation which will inspire the design. Inspiration sources can be:

Nature _ Recreating an element of nature by using natural light, the sky reference, has a huge influence on a project because it represents values that we are looking for, such as: rest, calm, light, freedom. Some lighting designers place greater emphasis on this aspect.

Everyday life _ Observing everyday life and situations leads to more understanding of people's habits and practices. Inspiration comes from walking in the street, when going to the office, eating out and other daily experiences.

Travelling _ Visiting other countries and cities, meeting other cultures helps to make lighting design daily. It broadens the horizon and allows for new and unexpected experiences and ideas.

People and their ideas _ Learning and sharing experiences with colleagues, brainstorming, borrowing elements from projects is an open field for inspiration. This works inside lighting design agencies but also across disciplines: architecture, engineering, landscape, art and music.

Media _ All expressions of culture e.g. music, shows, fashion, art, books, magazines, conferences are taken into account for lighting design projects. Inspiration is provided by pictures and drawings but also by the ideas behind them.

Completed projects _ Earlier projects or newly realised projects by other lighting designers can also prove inspiring. Poorly lit places can provide a motivation to improve a situation or underline the importance of lighting design.

New technologies _ New solutions that are smaller and more intelligent are of considerable interest to lighting designers. Also developments and new technology.

Honour original idea versus reinvention

Lighting can support and enhance the architecture or can present a completely new idea and experience. The approach depends on the project, its function and identity, but maybe even more on the lighting designer's background and profile.

Support and enhance _ Supporting and honouring the original idea of the architect by respecting the original intention of the architect means: highlighting characteristic elements and enhancing the architect's ideas and pushing them a bit further.

New idea and experience _ Creating a new emotional experience can imply reinvention. A new look and feel can be created for a building and thus reinvent it into something more interesting. In those cases a new idea actually changes the experience of a building or space in a positive way. But it can also overshadow the original identity of the building and place. It might distract and detract from the original idea. Reinvention is often linked to an artistic approach.

Artistic approach and technical expertise _ To enhance a building, space, or event using lighting, lighting designers clearly need understanding and creative imagination and therefore an artistic approach, but they also need technical expertise and the right tools for the job in terms of lighting systems.

Lighting designers consider themselves part artist and part technician. The defining ability of a great designer is not in technical capacity but in creativity. In order to 'bring out the magic' a designer must have a powerful conceptual understanding of what he wants to say to the people, an understanding of the essence of the space that is to be amplified using light.

Lighting design should be meaningful, judicious, instead of excessive, and related to the object: evocative colours instead of a random display of colours. As artists, lighting designers are proud of their more conceptual, creative and artistic work.

Balance _ Ideally a balance is found between the different elements. The best and most permanent work should involve coherence between respecting the original intention and creating a new emotional interpretation.

Location Index

Austria
> Stadion Center Shopping mall | Vienna | Austria | p. 116, 271, 272

Brazil
> Palácio do Planalto | Brasília | Brazil | p.032
> Museu do Paraná , NovoMuseu | Curitiba | Brazil | p.192, 263
> São Francisco de Assis Church | Pampulha | Brazil | p. 036, 308
> Hotel Fasano | Rio de Janeiro | Brazil | p. 308
> Lapa dos Mercadores | Rio de Janeiro | Brazil | p. 026, 306
> Alto do Ipiranga Station | São Paulo | Brazil | p. 078, 333, 334
> Carlos Miele – Cidade Jardim | São Paulo | Brazil | p. 334
> Escape Pub | São Paulo | Brazil | p. 160, 260
> Estação da Luz | São Paulo | Brazil | p. 261
> Ibirapuera Auditorium | São Paulo | Brazil | p. 032, 264
> Luzombra | Showroom La Lampe | São Paulo | Brazil | p. 054, 258, 259

China
> Main Canal | Hangzhou | China | p. 339
> Suzhou Museum | Suzhou | China | p. 323

France
> Renault Trucks façade | Bourg en Bresse | France | p. 072, 285
> 'Théâtre-Temps', Opera | Lyon | France | p. 062
> Fabre museum | Montpellier | France | p. 329, 330
> Porte de Montreuil Subway Station | Montreuil | France | p. 346
> Nestlé headquarters | Noisiel | France | p. 122, 345
> Congress Hall | Paris | France | p. 346
> Lighting in all its States | Paris | France | p. 337
> 'L'Ô' | Quai Branly Museum | Paris | France | p. 086, 291, 292
> Saint-Joseph | Reunion Island | p. 284
> Emaplot districk | Toulouse | France | p. 337
> Garonne river embankment | Toulouse | France | p. 338
> Grand Boulevard | Valence | France | p. 166, 283
> Design Center PSA Peugeot Citroën | Velizy | France | p. 138, 338
> Ploubazlanec Water Tower | France | p. 082, 329

Greece
> 'Rion Antirion Bridge | Greece | p. 096

Germany
> Berlin Medical Society | Berlin | Germany | p. 162, 353
> Galeria Kaufhof Alexanderplatz | Berlin | Germany | p. 016, 360
> Former Coal Washer Zollverein | Essen | Germany | p. 074, 362
> Town Hall | Hamburg | Germany | p. 044, 227
> Pier Bar | Hamburg airport | Germany | p. 150, 204
> Mannheimer-2, corporate headquarters | Mannheim | Germany | p. 090
> World of Jewellery | Pforzheim | Germany | p. 106, 353
> Pfalzgrafenstein Kaub castle | Rhine river | Germany | p. 204
> Phaeno Science Centre Museum | Wolfsburg | Germany | p. 140, 203

India
> Swami Narayan Temple | Gandhinagar | India | p. 383
> 'Anthem' residential Township | Hyderabad | India | p. 239
> Amber Palace | Jaipur | India | p. 098, 218
> Asian Paints Colour Store | Mumbai | India | p. 381
> Mumbai International Airport | Mumbai | India | p. 118
> Bahai Lotus Temple | New Delhi | India | p. 030, 380
> Adlabs Multiplex | Pune | India | p. 070
> Udaipur City Palace | Udaipur | India | p. 042, 219

Italy
> Hortus Conclusus | Benevento | Italy | p. 040, 236
> Tales of Light | Loggia dei Mercanti | Milan | Italy | p. 052, 355
> Bernini | Rome | Italy | p. 374
> Jubilee Church | Rome | Italy | p. 134, 321
> Necropoli Vaticane | Rome | Italy | p. 024, 255
> Piazza del Campidoglio | Rome | Italy | p. 068, 373
> 'Arnolfo di Cambio | San Giovanni Valdarno | Italy | p. 094, 374
> City doors | Treviglio | Italy | p. 080, 208
> San Martino and Assunta church | Treviglio | Italy | p. 084, 207
> Palazzo Grassi | Venise | Italy | p. 034, 256
> Piazza Conti Guidi | Vinci | Italy | p. 128, 235

Japan
> Houses | Ehime | Japan | p. 378
> Tower of Wind | Kanagawa | Japan | p. 325
> Byodoin Temple | Kyoto | Japan | p.142, 378
> The Kinkakuji Temple | Kyoto | Japan | p. 377
> Matsumoto Performing Arts Centre | Nagano | Japan | p. 124, 369
> National Peace Memorial Hall | Nagasaki | Japan | p. 064, 326
> NTT Docomo Tower | Osaka | Japan | p. 370
> Beautiful Fukushima Future Expo | Sukagawa | Japan | p. 060, 378

Malaysia
> Petronas Towers | Kuala Lumpur | Malaysia | p. 232

Mexico
> Plazoleta de San Francisco | Campeche | Mexico | p. 022, 252
> La Luz de los Itzaes | Edzna | Mexico | p. 108, 252
> Eucaliptos | Mexico City | Mexico | p. 146
> San Josemaría Escrivá Iglesia | Santa Fe | Mexico City | México | p. 313
> Casa Fifield, Casa Helfet | Punta Mita | Nayarit | México | p. 148, 311, 312
> Lighting Master Plan | San Luis Potosi | Mexico | p. 056, 211

The Netherlands
> Moniek Toebosch' light installation | Amsterdam Central station |
  The Netherlands | p. 227

Russia
> Wellness park Else Club | Moscow | Russia | p. 228

Singapore
> Lighting Masterplan for Singapore's City Centre | Singapore | p. 326

South Korea
> Haevichi Golf Course | Jeju Island | South Korea | p. 300
> Club Nine Bridge' golf resort | Jeju Island | South Korea | p. 158, 295
> Kyoung-Bok Palace, FIFA VIP reception | Seoul | South Korea | p. 190, 289
> Konkuk University Business Area | Seoul | South Korea | p. 286
> National Museum of Korea | Seoul | South Korea | p. 296
> Seoul Museum of Art | Seoul | South Korea | p. 100, 300
> Seoul Tower | Seoul | South Korea | p. 112, 289
> Sung-Nye-Mun | Seoul | South Korea | p. 288

Sweden
> Apple Tree Garden, PLDA Workshop | Alingsås | Sweden | p. 172, 315

Switzerland
> Novartis campus, WJS-2099 Parking | Basel | Switzerland | p. 126, 361

Taiwan
> Villa 32 | Beitou | Taiwan | p. 144, 243, 244
> Zuo-Ying Station of High Speed Rail | Kaohsiung | Taiwan | p. 136, 244
> Chung Tai Chan Monastery | Nantou | Taiwan | p. 028, 303, 304
> Bei Gan Pedestrian Bridge | Bei Gan | Yunlin | Taiwan | p. 180, 304

Thailand
> Museum Siam | Bangkok | Thailand | p. 350
> Sathira-Dhammasathan Temple | Bangkok | Thailand | p. 178, 246
> Sirocco restaurant | Bangkok | Thailand | p. 164, 223
> Traimit Temple in China town | Bangkok | Thailand | p. 188, 247, 248
> The Barai | Hua Hin | Thailand | p. 194, 224
> Mantra Restaurant | Pattaya | Thailand | p. 050, 349

United Kingdom
> Eastside Viaduct | Birmingham | UK | p. 317
> Princess Hay | Exeter | UK | p. 316
> Saint Mungo's Church | Glasgow | UK | p. 186, 366
> Centre for Health Science | Inverness | UK | p. 130, 366
> 55 Baker Street Facade, Public Artwork | London | UK | p. 274
> Broadgate | London | UK | p. 018, 357
> Finsbury Square | London | UK | p. 358
> 'Recall', Broadwick House | London | UK | p. 076, 276
> 'Switch on your Bluetooth', Tower Bridge | London | UK | p. 277
> Westminster Academy | London | UK | p. 154, 318
> 'Wind to Light', South Bank Centre, Architecture Week | London | UK | p. 176, 276
> Broadgate | London | UK | p. 018, 357
> Riverside Park | Staines | UK | p. 048, 357

USA
> United States Air Force Memorial | Arlington | USA | p.182, 340
> Mall at Millennia | Florida | USA | p. 268
> Lake of Dreams, Wynn hotel | Las Vegas | USA | p. 114
> Social House | Las Vegas | USA | p. 174, 269
> New Orleans Museum of Art Sculpture Garden | New Orleans | USA | p. 046, 216
> 7 World Trade Center | New York | USA | p. 170, 215
> LED Streetlight for the City of New York | USA | p. 343
> Postcards – The Staten Island September 11th Memorial | New York | USA | p. 184, 322
> Statue of Liberty | New York | USA | p. 156, 231
> The New York Times Building | New York | USA | p. 020, 021, 341, 342
> Marcus Center | Milwaukee | USA | p. 088, 267
> Burton Barr Central Library | Phoenix | USA | p. 110, 279
> National World War II Memorial | Washington | USA | p. 132, 278

Copyrights

Nissar Allana | India
> La Candida Erendira… by Gabriel Garcia Marquez | Cartagena
   © **Kaushik Ramaswamy** _ p. 102, 199
> 'Sonata' _ © **Nissar Allana** _ p. 199

Peter Andres | Germany
> Phaeno Science Centre Museum | Wolfsburg | Germany
   © **Beratende Ingenieure für Lichtplanung** _ p. 140, 203
> Pier Bar | Hamburg airport | Germany
   © **Beratende Ingenieure für Lichtplanung** _ p. 150, 204
> Pfalzgrafenstein Kaub castle | Rhine river | Germany
   © **Beratende Ingenieure für Lichtplanung** _ p. 204

Susanna Antico | Italy
> City doors | Treviglio | Italy _ © **Giacomo Artale** _ p. 080, 208
> San Martino and Assunta church | Treviglio | Italy _ © **Giacomo Artale** _ p. 084, 207

Gustavo Avilés | Mexico
> Lighting Master Plan | San Luis Potosi | Mexico _ © **Lighteam** _ p. 056, 211
> Eucaliptos | Mexico City | Mexico _ © **Nicola Larusso** _ p. 146

Francesca Bettridge & Stephen Bernstein | USA
> New Orleans Museum of Art Sculpture Garden | New Orleans | USA _
   © **Richard Sexton** _ p. 046, 216
> 7 World Trade Center | New York | USA _ © **David Sundberg – Esto** _ p. 170, 215

Manav Bhargava | India
> Udaipur City Palace | Udaipur | India _ © **Shriji Arvind Singh Mewar, Maharana of Mewar
   Charitable Trust (MMCF)** _ p. 042, 219
> Amber Palace | Jaipur | India _ © **Manav Bhargava, Mandala** _ p. 098, 218

La-Orchai Boonpiti | Thailand
> Sirocco restaurant | Bangkok | Thailand _ © **Vision Design** _ p. 164, 223
> The Barai | Hua Hin | Thailand _ © **Hyatt Regency Hua Hin and The Barai** _ p. 194, 224

Ulrike Brandi | Germany
> Town Hall, Hamburg | Germany _ © **Jörn Hustedt for Ulrike Brandi Licht** _ p. 044, 227
> Moniek Toebosch' light installation | Amsterdam Central station | The Netherlands
   © **Ulrike Brandi Licht** _ p. 227
> Wellness park Else Club | Moscow | Russia _ © **Ulrike Brandi Licht** _ p. 228

Howard Brandston | USA
> Statue of Liberty | New York | USA _ © **Peter B. Kaplan** _ p. 156, 231
> Petronas Towers | Kuala Lumpur | Malaysia _ © **Jeff Goldberg – Esto** _ p. 232

Filippo Cannata | Italy
> Hortus Conclusus | Benevento | Italy _ © **Pasquale Palmieri** _ p. 040, 236
> Piazza Conti Guidi | Vinci, Florence | Italy _ © **Pasquale Palmieri** _ p. 128, 235

Jaspreet Chandhok & Vilas Prabhu | India
> Adlabs Multiplex | Pune | India _ © **Puneet Chandhok** _ p. 070
> Mumbai International Airport | Mumbai | India _ © **Puneet Chandhok** _ p. 118
> 'Anthem' residential Township | Hyderabad | India _ © **Ambience Properties ltd.** _ p. 239
> Portrait Jaspreet Chandhok _ © **Puneet Chandhok** _ p. 241
> Portrait Vilas Prabhu _ © **Manisha Ingle Mishra** _ p. 241

Ray Chen | Taiwan
> Zuo-Ying Station of High Speed Rail | Kaohsiung | Taiwan _ © **Jeffrey Cheng, Oldc Inc** _ p. 136, 244
> Villa 32 | Beitou | Taiwan _ © **Villa 32** _ p. 144, 243, 244

Acharawan Chutarat | Thailand
> Sathira-Dhammasathan Temple | Bangkok | Thailand _ © **Christian Phongphit** _ p. 178, 246
> Traimit Temple in China town | Bangkok | Thailand _ © **Acharawan Chutarat** _ p. 188, 247, 248
> Portrait Acharawan Chutarat _ © **Christian Phongphit** _ p. 249

Elias Cisneros Avila | Mexico
> Plazoleta de San Francisco | Campeche | Mexico _ © **Elias Cisneros Avila
  and Jorge Luis Borroto** _ p. 022, 252
> La Luz de los Itzaes | Edzna | Mexico _ © **Leobardo Espinoza, Roberto Cárdenas Cabello**
  _ p. 108, 252

Cinzia Ferrara | Italy
> Palazzo Grassi | Venise | Italy _ © **Graziano Arici / Palazzo Grassi** _ p. 034, 256
> Necropoli Vaticane | Rome | Italy _ © **Fabbrica di San Pietro in Vaticano** _ p. 024, 255

Carlos Fortes | Brazil
> Luzombra | showroom La Lampe | São Paulo | Brazil _ © **Andrés Otero, Franco + Fortes**
  _ p. 054, 258, 259
> Escape Pub | São Paulo | Brazil _ © **Arthur Casas, Tuca Reinés** _ p. 160, 260
> Estação da Luz | São Paulo | Brazil _ © **Andrés Otero, Franco + Fortes** _ p. 261

Peter Gasper | Brazil
> Ibirapuera Auditorium | São Paulo | Brazil _ © **Peter Gasper Associados** _ p.032, 264
> Palácio do Planalto | Brasília | Brazil _ © **Peter Gasper Associados** _ p.032
> Museu do Paraná , NovoMuseu | Curitiba | Brazil _ © **Peter Gasper Associados** _ p.192, 263

Paul Gregory | USA
> Marcus Center | Milwaukee | USA _ © **JR Krauza** _ p. 088, 267
> Mall at Millennia | Florida | USA _ © **Tom Hurst** _ p. 268
> Social House | Las Vegas | USA _ © **Michael Weber** _ p. 174, 269

Jürgen Hassler | Germany
> Stadion Center shopping Mall | Vienna | Austria _ © **Make It Real** _ p. 116, 271, 272
> German Movie Award | ZDF | Germany _ © **Make It Real** _ p. 168, 270
> Final Draw for the 2006 FIFA World Cup, ARD | Germany _ © **Make It Real** _ p. 273

Jonathon Hodges | UK
> 'Recall', Broadwick House | London | UK _ © **Julian Abrams (for time lapse combined
  comp.jpg), Jason Bruges Studio** _ p. 076, 276
> 'Wind to Light', South Bank Centre, Architecture Week | London | UK _ © **Jason Bruges Studio**
  p. 176, 276
> 55 Baker Street Facade, Public Artwork | London | UK _ © **Julian Abrams** _ p. 274
> 'Switch on your Bluetooth', Tower Bridge | London | UK _ © **Jason Bruges Studio** _ p. 277

Barbara Horton | USA
> Burton Barr Central Library | Phoenix | USA _ © **Bill Timmerman** _ p. 110, 279
> National World War II Memorial | Washington | USA
  © **Brett Drury, www.architectural-photography.com** _ p. 132, 278

Philippe Hutinet | France
> Renault Trucks façade | Bourg en Bresse | France _ © **Thierry Kuntz** _ p. 072, 285
> Grand Boulevard | Valence | France _ © **Sylvie Hutinet, Agence Hutinet** _ p. 166, 283
> Saint-Joseph | Reunion Island _ © **Agence Hutinet** _ p. 284

Mee Jeong | South Korea
> Seoul Tower | Seoul | South Korea _ © **Chung, Kangwa, Eon Sld.co,. ltd** _ p. 112, 289
> Kyoung-Bok Palace, FIFA VIP reception | Seoul | South Korea _ © **Chung, Kangwa, Eon Sld.co,. ltd.** p. 190, 289
> Konkuk University Business Area | Seoul | South Korea _ © **Chung, Kangwa, Eon Sld.co,. ltd.** _ p. 286
> Sung-Nye-Mun | Seoul | South Korea _ © **Chung, Kangwa, Eon Sld.co,. ltd.** _ p. 288

Yann Kersalé | France
> 'Théâtre-Temps', Opera | Lyon | France _ ©**Yann Kersalé** _ p. 062
> 'L'Ô' | Quai Branly Museum | Paris | France _ ©**Yann Kersalé** _ p. 086, 291, 292
> Portrait Yann Kersalé _ ©**Anne de Vandière** _ p. 293

Kiyoung Ko | South Korea
> Club Nine Bridge' golf resort | Jeju Island | South Korea _ © **Bitzro** _ p. 158, 295
> National Museum of Korea | Seoul | South Korea _ © **Kim Yong-Kwan** _ p. 296

Heayun Lee | South Korea
> Seoul Museum of Art | Seoul | South Korea _ © **Mavericks** _ p. 100, 300
> Haevichi Golf Course | Jeju Island _ © **Mavericks** _ p. 300

Ta-Wei Lin | Taiwan
> Chung Tai Chan Monastery | Nantou | Taiwan _ © **Wei-Ming Yuan** _ p. 028, 303, 304
> Bei Gan Pedestrian Bridge | Bei Gan | Yunlin | Taiwan _ © **Si-Seng Wang** _ p. 180, 304

Mônica Lobo | Brazil
> Lapa dos Mercadores | Rio de Janeiro | Brazil _ © **LD Studio** _ p. 026, 306
> São Francisco de Assis Church | Pampulha | Brazil _ © **LD Studio** _ p. 036, 308
> Hotel Fasano | Rio de Janeiro | Brazil _ © **LD Studio** _ p. 308

Luis Lozoya | Mexico
> Casa Fifield, Casa Helfet | Punta Mita | Nayarit | México _ © **Luz + Form** _ p. 148, 311, 312
> San Josemaría Escrivá Iglesia | Santa Fe | Mexico City | México _ © **Luz + Form** _ p. 313

Martin Lupton | UK
> Westminster Academy | London | UK _ © **Sanna Fisher-Payne / BDP** _ p. 154, 318
> Apple Tree Garden, PLDA Workshop | Alingsås | Sweden © **Robert Persson** _ p. 172, 315
> Princess Hay | Exeter | UK _ © **David Barbour, Insite Arts** _ p. 316
> Eastside Viaduct | Birmingham | UK _ © **BDP Lighting** _ p. 317

Paul Marantz | USA
> Jubilee Church | Rome | Italy _ © **Scott Frances/ESTO** _ p. 134, 321
> Postcards – The Staten Island September 11th Memorial | New York | USA © **Ed Massery** _ p. 184, 322
> Suzhou Museum | Suzhou | China _ © **Pei Partnership** _ p. 323

Kaoru Mende | Japan
> National Peace Memorial Hall | Nagasaki | Japan _ © **Toshio Kaneko** _ p. 064, 326
> Tower of Wind | Kanagawa | Japan _ © **Lighting Planners Associates Inc.** _ p. 325
> Lighting Masterplan for Singapore's City Centre | Singapore © **Lighting Planners Associates Inc** _ p. 326

Francois Migeon | France
> Ploubazlanec Water Tower | France _ © **Yvonning** _ p. 082, 329
> Daniel Buren's new entrance, Fabre museum | Montpellier | France _ © **David Huguenin** _ p. 329
> Pierre Soulages' new building, Fabre Museum | Montpellier | France _ © **Hervé Abbadie** _ p. 330

Antonio Mingrone | Brazil
> Alto do Ipiranga Station | São Paulo | Brazil _ © **Migliore & Melegatti** _ p. 078, 333, 334
> Carlos Miele – Cidade Jardim | São Paulo | Brazil _ © **Migliore & Melegatti** _ p. 334

Roger Narboni | France
> 'Rion Antirion Bridge | Greece _ © **Concepto** _ p. 096
> Design Center PSA Peugeot Citroën | Velizy | France _ © **Concepto** _ p. 138, 338
> Lighting in all its States | Paris | France _ © **Concepto** _ p. 337
> Emaplot district | Toulouse | France _ © **Concepto** _ p. 337
> Garonne river embankment | Toulouse _ © **Concepto** _ p. 338
> Main Canal | Hangzhou | China _ © **Zhongtai & Concepto** _ p. 339

Enrique Peiniger & Jean Sundin | USA
> The New York Times Building | New York | USA _ © **Michel Dénancé** _ p. 020, 342
> The New York Times Building | New York | USA _ © **Frieder Blickle | laif** _ p. 021, 341
> United States Air Force Memorial | Arlington | USA _ © **Thomas Mayer** _ p. 182, 340
> LED Streetlight for the City of New York | USA _ © **Office for Visual Interaction, Inc.** _ p. 343
> Portrait Enrique Peiniger _ © **Frieder Blickle** _ p. 343
> Portrait Jean Sundin _ © **Frieder Blickle** _ p. 343

Michel Pieroni | France
> Nestlé headquarters | Noisiel | France _ © **Guy Roges** _ p. 122, 345
> Congress Hall | Paris | France _ © **Aartill** _ p. 346
> Porte de Montreuil Subway Station | Montreuil | France _ © **Jean Loup Dabadie** _ p. 346

Vannapa Pimviriyakul | Thailand
> Mantra Restaurant | Pattaya | Thailand _ © **Vannapa Pimviriyakul** _ p. 050, 349
> Museum Siam | Bangkok | Thailand _ © **Pruk Dejkamheang** _ p. 350

Michael F. Rohde | Germany
> Tales of Light | Loggia dei Mercanti | Milan | Italy _ © **Herbert Cybulska** _ p. 052, 355
> Mannheimer-2, corporate headquarters | Mannheim | Germany _ © **Dirk Altenkirch** _ p. 090
> World of Jewellery | Pforzheim | Germany _ © **Dirk Altenkirch** _ p. 106, 353
> Berlin Medical Society | Berlin | Germany _ © **Heinrich Hermes** _ p. 162, 353

Tapio Rosenius | UK
> Broadgate | London | UK _ © **Maurice Brill Lighting Design** _ p. 018, 357
> Riverside Park | Staines | UK _ © **Maurice Brill Lighting Design** _ p. 048, 357
> Finsbury Square | London | UK _ © **Maurice Brill Lighting Design** _ p. 358

Andreas Schulz | Germany
> Galeria Kaufhof Alexanderplatz | Berlin | Germany _ © **Luc Bernard** _ p. 016, 360
> Former Coal Washer Zollverein | Essen | Germany _ © **Thomas Mayer** _ p. 074, 362
> Novartis campus, WJS-2099 Parking | Basel | Switzerland _ © **Lukas Roth** _ p. 126, 361

Kevan Shaw | UK
> Centre for Health Science | Inverness | UK _ © **Ewen Weatherspoon** _ p. 130, 366
> Saint Mungo's Church | Glasgow | UK _ © **Ron Scaglione** _ p. 186, 366

Hiroyasu Shoji | Japan
> Matsumoto Performing Arts Centre | Nagano | Japan _ © **Toshio Kaneko** _ p. 124, 369
> NTT Docomo Tower | Osaka | Japan _ © **Toshio Kaneko** _ p. 370

Francesca Storaro | Italy
> Piazza del Campidoglio | Rome | Italy _ © **Vittorio Storaro** _ p. 068, 373
> 'Arnolfo di Cambio | San Giovanni Valdarno | Italy _ © **Francesca Storaro** _ p. 094, 374
> Bernini | Rome | Italy _ © **Luigi Filetici** _ p. 374
> Portrait of Francesca Storaro _ © **Rino Malgrande** _ p. 375

Satoshi Uchihara | Japan
> Beautiful Fukushima Future Expo | Sukagawa | Japan _ © **Kanji Nakayama** _ p. 060, 378
> Byodoin Temple | Kyoto | Japan _ © **Kozo Koyama** _ p.142, 378
> The Kinkakuji Temple | Kyoto | Japan _ © **Kanji Nakayama** _ p. 377
> Houses | Ehime | Japan _ © **Uchihara Creative Lighting Design** _ p. 378

Dolly & Anil Valia | India
> Bahai Lotus Temple | New Delhi | India _ © **Shutterstock** _ p. 030, 380
> Asian Paints Colour Store, Mumbai | India _ © **Api** _ p. 381
> Swami Narayan Temple | Gandhinagar | India _ © **Baps** _ p. 383

Patrick Woodroffe | UK
> Lake of Dreams, Wynn hotel | Las Vegas | USA _ © **Patrick Dierson** _ p. 114
> Genesis Live 2007 | Europe _ © **Adam Bassett** _ p. 386, 387
> The Rolling Stones 2005/2006 | World Tour _ © **Mark Fisher** _ p. 388

Credits

Project manager
Augustina del Bao, Philips Lighting

Art direction and design
Friederike Lambers

Production
ter|Borg Graphic Vision

Editors in chief
Vincent Laganier, Jasmine van der Pol

Copywriters
Jonathan Ellis, Kenneth Gilbert

Qualitative research executive
Roos Molendijk, Synovate

Leading moderators
Daniel Atic, Mônica Bellegarde, Anita Colby, William Landell Mills, Ji Yeon Lee,
Beatriz Lobo, Jan Lorentzson, Cecile Hillairet, Jennifer Hsu, Prashant Singh,
Saisuda Suebsuan, Makiko Yoshida, Edwin Zijderveld, Anna Zinola

Lighting application moderators
Jannette Ballestas, Matthew Cobham, Gladys Gatti, Indranil Goswami,
Vincent Laganier, Jasmine van der Pol, Clara Powell

Special thanks
Indranil Goswami, Haldun Demirdes, Fernand Pereira, Afke Bokma, Marijn Damen,
Anissa Abbou, Laurence Vitale, Peter Roodnat, Eric M.J.B. van Rheden

Published by
Birkhäuser GmbH
P.O. Box, CH-4002 Basel
www.birkhauser.com

Powered by
Philips Lighting B.V.
Professional Lighting Solutions EMEA
Mathildelaan 1, NL-5611 BD Eindhoven
www.philips.com

Printed on Hello Silk (115g), Offset On (90g)
Printed in Spain

A CIP catalog record for this book is available from the Library of Congress,
Washington D.C., USA.

Bibliographic information published by the German National Library
The German National Library lists this publication in
the Deutsche Nationalbibliografie; detailed bibliographic data
are available on the Internet at http://dnb.d-nb.de.

ISBN 978-3-0346-0690-5

© 2011 Koninklijke Philips Electronics N.V., Eindhoven
Published by Birkhäuser GmbH, Basel